175 best
Jams, Jellies, Marmalades
& Other
Soft Spreads

Linda J. Amendt

Robert
ROSE

For complete cataloguing information, see page 297.

Disclaimer

The recipes in this book have been carefully tested by our kitchen and our tasters. To the best of our knowledge, they are safe and nutritious for ordinary use and users. For those people with food or other allergies, or who have special food requirements or health issues, please read the suggested contents of each recipe carefully and determine whether or not they may create a problem for you. All recipes are used at the risk of the consumer.

We cannot be responsible for any hazards, loss or damage that may occur as a result of any recipe use.

For those with special needs, allergies, requirements or health problems, in the event of any doubt, please contact your medical adviser prior to the use of any recipe.

Design and Production: Daniella Zanchetta/PageWave Graphics Inc.
Editor: Sue Sumeraj
Recipe Tester: Jennifer MacKenzie
Proofreader: Sheila Wawanash
Indexer: Gillian Watts
Photography: Colin Erricson
Food Styling: Kathryn Robertson
Prop Styling: Charlene Erricson

Cover image: Sweet Orange Marmalade (page 175), Lemon Marmalade (page 159) and Sunrise Jam (page 99)

We acknowledge the financial support of the Government of Canada through the Book Publishing Industry Development Program (BPIDP) for our publishing activities.

Published by Robert Rose Inc.
120 Eglinton Avenue East, Suite 800, Toronto, Ontario, Canada M4P 1E2
Tel: (416) 322-6552 Fax: (416) 322-6936

Printed and bound in Canada

1 2 3 4 5 6 7 8 9 CPL 16 15 14 13 12 11 10 09 08

Contents

✳

Introduction

✳

WELCOME TO THE wonderful world of soft spreads! We are about to embark on a magical journey.

What is a soft spread, you ask? "Soft spread" is the generic home canning term used to describe all manner of marvelous things you can make to spread on your morning toast, peanut butter sandwich, late-night biscuit and lots of things in between. Jams, jellies, marmalades, preserves, conserves, butters and curds are all soft spreads. Most are gelled, and all are soft and spreadable.

Home canning is a fun and exciting hobby for people of all ages. Home canners take great pride in their flavorful creations, often sharing their homemade treasures with friends and family. At the end of this book, you will find a section with ideas on creatively packaging your spreads for gift-giving.

I have been canning jams and other soft spreads for a good many years, more than I care to count! For many years, I entered my spreads, along with other preserved foods and baked goods, in state and county fairs across the United States, winning over 900 awards, including over 600 blue ribbons and special awards. With the publication of my first cookbook, *Blue Ribbon Preserves: Secrets to Award-Winning Jams, Jellies, Marmalades & More*, I was classified as a food professional and was no longer eligible to enter competitions at fairs.

But my connection to fairs did not stop there. Many of the fairs at which I used to compete asked me to jump to the other side of the table and become a judge in the preserved foods and baked foods divisions. This has proved to be an incredibly rewarding experience, and I enjoy sharing my canning knowledge and expertise with other home canners. My favorite fair to judge is the California State Fair in Sacramento. The fair conducts an open judging, where the entries are judged during the fair in front of an audience that includes many of the competitors. After judging each entry, the judges explain to the audience what is wonderful about the entry, where improvements can be made and what award the entry received. We also answer questions about home canning.

In this book, you will find lots of delicious recipes for sweet spreads, savory spreads and even some tasty concoctions containing liqueurs. There are some classic recipes and a bunch of new recipes I created just for this book. One canning trend that has been growing by leaps and bounds in recent years is the blending of fruit flavors in soft spreads. I wholeheartedly approve of this flavorful trend, and many of my new recipes are combination jams, pairing two or more fruit flavors into delightful and delicious spreads.

I am a big fan of using commercial pectins when making jams and jellies, as they produce exceptional spreads with intense fruit flavor, tantalizing aromas, silky texture and beautiful color. They are also a great time-saver and make canning soft spreads easy and accessible to anyone. All of the jam, jelly, marmalade, preserves and conserve recipes in this book use commercial pectin to create wonderful spreads with excellent character. If you are used to making spreads by the long-boil method, I invite you to have fun, expand your horizons and try the exciting pectin recipes in this book. You just might find some new recipes to add to your repertoire.

The superior quality, flavor, texture and appearance of a well-made homemade spread outshine a store-bought spread every time. The difference between the two is truly amazing. A store-bought spread cannot hold a candle to a jam or jelly you make at home, where you hand-select the fruit and other ingredients and add a little love to every jar.

Anyone with an interest in making homemade soft spreads, whether an experienced canner or a novice making their first few batches of jam, can create incredible jams, jellies, marmalades, preserves, conserves, butters and curds by following the straightforward recipes in this book and using a few special techniques I will share with you along the way. So pull up a water bath canner, explore these pages and travel with me through the flavorful world of soft spreads!

Acknowledgments

I WOULD LIKE TO EXPRESS my thanks to some of the many people who helped make this book possible. To my dad, Lee Amendt, for all your support, help and encouragement. My brothers, Bruce and Brion Amendt, and their families for your advice and understanding and for happily tasting my soft spread creations. Earl and Jeanie Lee for your love and support. My friend Iris Dimond for sharing your food science expertise over many years. My friend Michael Marks, "Your Produce Man," for sharing your remarkable knowledge of fruit. Willie Garrett and everyone at the California State Fair for making judging such a pleasure. Special thanks to all my recipe tasters!

To Lisa Ekus-Saffer, my literary agent, Jane Falla and everyone at the Lisa Ekus Group for your friendship and confidence in my abilities. Bob Dees for believing in me and this book, Marian Jarkovich, Sue Sumeraj and everyone at Robert Rose. Daniella Zanchetta and PageWave Graphics for your wonderful book design. And Colin Erricson, Kathryn Robertson and Charlene Erricson for your beautiful photographs and styling.

Soft Spread Basics

IF YOU ENVISION your mother or grandmother standing over pots of boiling fruit and sugar for hours when you think about making jams and jellies, think again. With the advent of commercial pectins and new and improved canning methods, those long tedious hours are a thing of the past. Now, by following a few simple rules and using the correct equipment and quality ingredients, anyone can enjoy the flavorful rewards of canning soft spreads at home in their own kitchen. Welcome to the world of modern jam- and jelly-making!

Soft Spread Definitions and Characteristics

Soft spreads are a special class of preserved foods with many different flavors, textures and colors. Soft spreads are just what the name implies: they are delicious fruit spreads that hold their shape, yet are soft enough to be easily spread on bread or biscuits. They are preserved with sugar and are either jellied or thickened. These creative spreads vary in flavor and texture, how the fruit is prepared, the ingredient proportions and the cooking method used to make each type.

There are seven distinct types of soft spreads: jams, jellies, marmalades, preserves, conserves, butters and curds. Each type has its own unique characteristics.

- **Jams:** Jams are thick, sweet spreads with intense flavor. They are made from one or more types of fruit that has been crushed or finely chopped. Jams should contain small pieces of fruit, be thick enough to mound up in a spoon and hold their shape, and spread easily.

- **Jellies:** Jellies are translucent spreads made from clear fruit juice. They are very tender, yet firm enough to hold their shape when cut. A good jelly will be crystal clear and have a fresh, fruity flavor.

- **Marmalades:** Marmalades are soft fruit jellies with small pieces of fruit and citrus peel evenly suspended in the transparent jelly. They are traditionally made from citrus fruits, but can also be made with a variety of other fruits blended with the citrus.

- **Preserves:** Preserves are made with small whole fruits or with uniform-size pieces of fruit evenly suspended in a transparent jelly or very thick syrup. The fruit pieces should be tender, plump and flavorful, and should retain their size and shape.

- **Conserves:** Conserves are similar to jams in texture and are made from a combination of two or more kinds of fruit. Conserves traditionally contain nuts, raisins or other dried fruits, or coconut.

- **Butters:** Fruit butters are made by cooking fruit pulp with sugar until the mixture reaches a smooth, thick, spreadable consistency. Spices are often added to butters to complement the flavor of the fruit.

- **Curds:** Curds are thick, rich, silky-smooth spreads made with eggs, butter and citrus juice. Curds have a texture similar to soft cooked custard, will mound up in a spoon, and spread easily.

Canning Equipment

Using the appropriate type and size of home canning equipment — including jars and lids, a water bath canner, pots and pans, and utensils — will help ensure that you produce fantastic soft spreads. Much of the equipment you will need can already be found in your own kitchen. With the addition of home canning jars and a few specialty tools, you will be all set to start canning soft spreads.

Home Canning Jars and Lids

The modern canning jars and two-piece lids available today make home canning safe and easy. Canning jars are sold in boxes of a dozen jars that come with lids and screw bands. They come in a variety of sizes and shapes, with both standard and wide-mouth jar openings.

Old-fashioned canning jars sealed with screw-on lids and rubber-like gaskets are no longer considered safe for home canning, and the United States Department of Agriculture (USDA) does not endorse their continued use. This also applies to jars with wire-bail-attached glass lids and rubber seals. These types of jars should not be used for home canning.

Canning Jars

Home canning jars are made of molded heat-tempered glass. Modern glass canning jars are the only containers recommended for safe home canning. These jars have a wide rim and screw threads that are designed to work with the two-piece metal vacuum lids and screw bands.

✳

New canning jars, packed 12 to a box, can be purchased at grocery stores, hardware stores and some department stores. Used canning jars and screw bands may be reused, but new lids must be purchased. Always check used jars to make sure that the rims do not have any chips, nicks or uneven surfaces that will prevent the lids from sealing tightly. Also check for hairline cracks, bubbles in the glass or other flaws that could cause the jars to break. Jars that show any sign of damage should not be used. With use, jars can weaken and crack during water bath processing. If you have problems with used jars cracking or breaking, it is definitely time to buy new jars.

Do not use any jars that are not specifically designed for home canning. This includes mayonnaise jars, commercial jam and jelly jars, fruit jars, condiment jars, peanut butter jars and baby food jars. Even if home canning lids and rings appear to fit these jars, do not use them. Commercial jars are neither heat-tempered like home canning jars nor sturdy enough to stand up to water bath processing. The rim surface on these types of jars is narrower than the rim of a home canning jar. There is a high probability that the seals will fail during storage, and the jars can shatter during processing.

For canning soft spreads, 8-ounce (250 mL) jars, also called "half-pint" jars, are the best size. They come in a variety of interesting shapes, with either standard openings ($2\frac{3}{8}$ inches/5.7 cm in diameter) or wide-mouth openings (3 inches/7.5 cm in diameter). I also love the newer 4-ounce (125 mL) jars. They are the perfect size for impromptu gifts, or for when you are giving a collection of several different varieties of spreads, and they are ideal when you want to have a few open jars of different-flavored spreads in the refrigerator at the same time.

Some home canners like to use the tall 12-ounce (375 mL) jelly jars. I do not find them very practical, as it can be a challenge to get the last of the spread out of the bottom of the jar, but they do have an elegant look. Other canners like to can their soft spreads in 1-pint (500 mL) jars. This may make sense if you have a large family or eat spreads in great quantity, but it is a lot of spread to finish off in three weeks, the average refrigerator shelf life of a spread after it has been opened.

Soft spreads should never be canned in 1-quart (1 L) jars. These jars are too large and hold too much spread for safe water bath processing. The time that would be required in the water bath to heat the contents in the center of the jar to a safe processing temperature could cause the spread to break down and prevent it from setting when it cools.

Jars specifically designed for freezer canning should not be used for spreads that will be processed in a water bath. Freezer jars are not tempered to withstand the high heat of a water bath and may shatter during processing.

Canning Lids and Screw Bands

Closures for canning jars consist of two pieces: a flat metal lid and a metal screw band. After the jars are filled, the lid is applied and the band is screwed on to hold the lid in place during water bath processing.

The underside of the metal lid has been protected with a food-safe coating that will not react with the acids in the canned food inside the jar. There is a raised channel around the underside of the outer edge of the lid that is filled with a sealing compound. This compound is specially formulated for use in home canning, to adhere the lid to the jar and form a seal during water bath processing.

The screw band is designed to hold the lid firmly in place during processing, and then while the jar cools, until the lid has formed a tight seal with the jar. After the jars are completely cooled, the screw bands should be removed for storage. The screw bands are designed to match the screw threads on the canning jars. To insure a proper fit and a tight seal, it is important to use lids and screw bands made by the same manufacturer as the canning jars you are using.

The flat metal lids are designed for one-time use only and cannot be reused. A new lid must be used each time you seal a jar. While the compound on unused lids has a projected shelf life of up to five years, it is best to purchase new lids each canning season to ensure the effectiveness of the sealing compound.

Screw bands can be reused if they are not rusty. Bent or dented screw bands should not be used, as the band may not hold the lid firmly in place during processing, which could result in a weak seal. Boxes of new lids and bands are available wherever canning jars are sold. Lids may be purchased separately, in packages of 12, or lids and screw bands can be purchased together in boxes that contain 12 of each.

✳ Never Use Paraffin Wax Seals

It used to be considered a safe practice to cover jams and jellies with a thick layer of melted paraffin to seal the jar for storage. Research has shown that this is not safe. Wax seals have a high failure rate, which invites and encourages the growth of mold and other contaminates inside soft spreads. People also believed that if you scraped mold off the surface of a spread, the part underneath was still safe to eat. It has since been discovered that molds have long tendrils that go well below the surface of the spread, carrying toxins deep into the jar. Never attempt to seal a jar of preserved foods with paraffin. And most important, never ever eat any food that has been covered and supposedly preserved with a paraffin seal.

—————————— ✳ ——————————

Water Bath Canner

A water bath canner, also called a boiling water canner, is an essential piece of equipment for making soft spreads. The water bath canner is used to process and seal jars after they have been filled. Water bath processing is no longer considered optional for soft spreads. It is now a requirement for safe canning.

To make their contents safe for storage, jars of soft spreads are heated in boiling water for a specified amount of time until the contents reach an internal temperature high enough to kill bacteria that can contaminate the spreads. The high temperature also deactivates enzymes, molds and yeasts that can cause the spreads to deteriorate over time.

Essentially, a water bath canner is a large stockpot with a rack inside. Jars are placed on the rack so that water can circulate between and under the jars to heat the contents evenly. You can purchase a water bath canner that is specially made for the job (available at cooking supply stores, department stores, hardware stores and some grocery stores) or you can put one together yourself. Commercial canners have racks designed to hold a certain number of jars. I find the racks cumbersome and difficult to lift in and out of the canner, but some home canners rave about them. It is very much a personal choice.

To assemble a water bath canner, you will need a large stockpot, preferably stainless steel, with a tight-fitting lid. The pot should be deep enough to allow for a rack in the bottom, plus the height of the jars, 1 to 2 inches (2.5 cm to 5 cm) of water above the top of the jars and another 1½ to 2 inches (4 cm to 5 cm) of height to keep the water from boiling over. For standard 8-ounce (250 mL) jars, you will need a pot that is at least 8 inches (20 cm) tall, and preferably 10 inches (25 cm) or more. If you plan to use the canner to process spreads in 12-ounce (375 mL) or 1-pint (500 mL) jars — or other types of preserves in 1-quart (1 L) jars — you will need a taller pot to accommodate the height of the taller jars.

The pot also needs to be wide enough to hold a rack. Round metal cake-cooling racks are frequently available in 11-inch (27.5 cm) and 13-inch (32.5 cm) diameter sizes. If you cannot find a rack to fit your pot, a folded kitchen towel placed on the bottom of the pot will work. You can also tie or wire seven screw bands together, with one band in the center and six around it, and use that as a rack to support the jars. When the bands start to rust, replace them with new bands.

For my water bath canner, I use a 20-quart (20 L) stainless steel stockpot with a round metal cake-cooling rack in the bottom. The rack holds the jars level and allows water to circulate under them during processing. The pot is tall, so there is plenty of room above the jars for the water to cover them by 2 inches (5 cm) and still have plenty of room to boil without boiling over.

Pots and Pans

A large stockpot, preferably with an 8-quart (8 L) capacity, is needed to cook soft spreads. The capacity of the pot needs to be of this size to allow room for the spreads to bubble up when boiling without boiling over, and to provide a surface area large enough to permit the proper evaporation of liquid during cooking. The pot should be made of heavy-gauge stainless steel and should have a thick bottom and a tight-fitting lid. Stainless steel is strongly recommended because it is a nonreactive material. Some metals, such as aluminum, can have a chemical reaction with the acid in the spreads. A heavy pot will distribute heat better, heat the spreads evenly and prevent hot spots, which can cause spreads to burn during cooking. Nonstick pots should not be used for preparing soft spreads. Nonstick coatings are not designed to tolerate the high temperatures needed to boil the spread mixture.

You will also need a small saucepan to heat the canning jar lids and keep them hot until you are ready to use them.

A double boiler is the perfect pan for preparing curds. If you do not have a double boiler, you can easily make one by using a metal or tempered glass bowl that fits snugly in the top of a large saucepan. Just make sure the bottom of the bowl does not touch the boiling water.

Measuring Cups and Spoons

Using the correct types of measuring cups to measure the different ingredients in soft spread recipes is crucial to successful canning of these wonderful spreads. The measurements of ingredients must be accurate in order for the spreads to set.

You will need these measuring essentials to make soft spreads:

Liquid Measuring Cups

Use standard glass liquid measuring cups with pour spouts to measure fruit, juice and other liquid ingredients. Glass is recommended over plastic, as plastic can absorb strong flavors when used to measure ingredients such as chile peppers, herbs or liqueurs.

Dry Measuring Cups

Use plastic or metal dry measuring cups with flat rims to measure sugar and other dry ingredients. These come in sets of graduated sizes. When measuring sugar, it is very important to use measuring cups that are designed specifically for dry ingredients. The top of these measuring cups is flat so that you can use a straight utensil or scraper with a straight edge to level sugar even with the top edge for an exact measure. Dry measuring cups should also be used to measure nuts, dried fruits and coconut.

Measuring Spoons and Glasses

Use a set of measuring spoons in graduated sizes to measure small quantities of ingredients. Small measuring glasses are now readily available in many stores and are quite handy for measuring small quantities of liquid ingredients.

Special Utensils for Preserving

While most of the essentials needed to prepare and process soft spreads are standard kitchen tools, there are a few items specific to canning that will make the job a lot easier and faster.

Canning Funnel

A canning funnel is a specially designed wide-mouth metal or plastic funnel that sits securely in the top of a canning jar and makes filling the jars a breeze.

Lid Wand

A lid wand is a nifty tool that has a magnet at one end and is used to pick up lids from the bottom of the pan of hot water. If you do not have a lid wand, a set of kitchen tongs may be used instead. Silicone-coated tongs are recommended to prevent scratching the coating on the underside of the lid.

Jar Lifter

A jar lifter is a specially shaped set of tongs designed to easily and safely lift jars into and out of the water bath canner. The metal jaws that grip the jars are covered with soft, heatproof plastic to prevent damage to the jars and to help lift and hold them securely while transporting the jars between the counter and the canner.

Kitchen Timer

An accurate kitchen timer is an absolute must for home canning. Jams, jellies and other soft spreads require specific cooking times to yield great results.

Zester

A zester is a wonderful little kitchen tool with four to six holes that quickly and easily removes the colored zest from citrus fruits in thin, uniform strips. A zester is a big help for making excellent marmalades.

Microplane Grater

A Microplane grater is a very sharp grater that is perfect for finely grating citrus zest.

Food Mill

In home canning, a food mill is used to remove seeds from berries for seedless spreads and to purée fruit for butters. A fine-mesh strainer will also work well.

Cheesecloth or Jelly Bag

Cheesecloth is used to line a sieve to strain the juice from the fruit pulp when making jellies. A cloth jelly bag can also be used. Jelly bags with metal stands are frequently sold in stores that carry home canning supplies.

 Standard Kitchen Equipment Used in Making Soft Spreads

- Colander for draining rinsed fruit
- Paring knife and chef's knife for peeling and chopping fruit
- Cutting boards for preparing fruit
- Potato or vegetable masher for crushing chopped fruit
- Flat-bottomed pan or bowl for crushing fruit
- Large mixing bowls for holding measured sugar
- Long-handled large metal or wooden spoon for stirring spreads
- Ladle for spooning hot spreads into jars
- Large slotted spoon for transferring blanched fruit
- Fine-mesh sieve for straining ingredients and curds
- Paper towels for wiping jar rims after filling
- Cooling racks or towels for cooling hot jars after processing
- Pot holders or oven mitts to protect your hands when moving hot pans
- Hot pads or trivets for hot pans

Plastic Knife

A small-bladed plastic knife works well to coax trapped bubbles out of jars before processing. Commercial bubble freers come with some canning utensil sets, and can also be purchased separately, but they are rather large and bulky for use with soft spreads. A plastic chopstick is another option, but it is also a little thick for working with soft spreads. A metal knife or spoon should not be used, as the metal can scratch the inside of the jar, which could cause the jar to crack or break during water bath processing or cooling.

Ingredients

The ingredients that go into making a soft spread directly affect the outcome of the finished product. Each ingredient plays a crucial role in determining the intensity and freshness of flavor the spread will have, and also influences the smoothness of texture and the vibrancy of color that are the hallmarks of a great homemade soft spread.

Quality Makes a Difference

Quality applies to all of the ingredients used to make soft spreads, everything from the fruit to the sugar, pectin, acid and any other added ingredients and flavorings. The quality, texture and flavor of the finished spread are determined by the quality of the ingredients used to make it. Always use the best and freshest ingredients available for making soft spreads. This is not the time to skimp on quality.

Balancing Ingredients for Success

Balancing ingredients to achieve both superior texture and outstanding flavor is essential to creating a great soft spread. If the proportion of the ingredients is out of balance, the spread may be too thick or too thin and may lack flavor, or be excessively sweet, or have a harsh taste.

Fruit, sugar, pectin and acid are the building blocks of soft spreads, and each plays a specific role in determining whether a finished jam, jelly or other spread will have the right consistency and texture or will be too thin or too stiff. If the proportion of ingredients is incorrect, the spread may not set up at all or, at the other extreme, the spread may set up so firm that it becomes rubbery and difficult to spoon out of the jar.

These same four ingredients — fruit, sugar, pectin and acid — also determine whether the spread will have a great, intense fruit flavor or will be rather mild and bland. If the ingredient proportions are not properly balanced, the end result could be a spread that is overly sweet, too tart or sour, bitter or even tasteless.

Let's take a closer look at each of these four important ingredients.

Fruit

Fruit is the primary ingredient in any soft spread. It is the main source of flavor, provides the spread with its vibrant color and helps determine the texture of the finished product. The fruit also furnishes a portion of the pectin and acid that are needed for the soft spread to gel.

To make an excellent soft spread, the fruit used must be of the best quality available. The flavor of a finished spread is only as good as the flavor of the fruit you put into it. For an intensely flavored spread with vivid natural color, start with beautiful fruit that has a full flavor and is at the peak of ripeness and freshness. Avoid using fruit that is either underripe or overripe. Underripe fruit lacks the strong flavor essential to a magnificent jam, jelly or other spread. Overripe fruit can have an "off" flavor, resulting in a spread with an unpleasant taste, and may keep the spread from setting.

Quality fruit is also important to achieving a smooth and tender texture. The best texture comes from fruit that is fully ripe, not underripe or overripe. When cooked, pieces of underripe fruit often remain firm and can be tough and chewy. They also do not absorb sugar well. Overripe fruit can become mushy and not provide much texture at all. The natural pectin found in fruit that is underripe or overripe does not gel well when cooked and can hinder the ability of the spread to set. Fruit that is particularly juicy can affect the balance of liquid in the recipe and yield a spread that is either very soft or does not set. Old or shriveled fruit can affect both the flavor and the set of the spread and should not be used.

The fruit used to make soft spreads should be free of bruises and blemishes. Fruit that has fallen from the tree is not a good choice, as bruised or damaged fruit may contain harmful bacteria that could contaminate the spread. Soft fruit can also affect the texture of the spread and may prevent it from setting.

 To Ripen Fruit

Place fruit such as peaches, nectarines, apricots, pears or plums in a single layer in a paper bag. Fold down the top of the bag to close it and let the fruit ripen in the bag at room temperature for two to three days, or more as needed. Adding an apple to the bag will speed up the process because apples emit ethylene gas, which will cause the fruit to ripen faster. Check the fruit each day and use it as soon as the fruit reaches full ripeness.

Use ripe fruit as soon as possible after harvest or purchase. If larger fruits are not fully ripe, allow them to ripen for a couple of days before making the spread. Fruits such as peaches, pears, apricots and plums that are nearly ripe will continue to ripen and improve in flavor after they have been harvested. Berries and other delicate fruits can deteriorate rapidly after harvest and should be canned as quickly as possible to retain the best flavor and texture.

Frozen berries make excellent jams, jellies and other soft spreads. Most berries can be harvested at their prime and then frozen for later use. This is a good option if you have berries available but do not have time to can right away. Store-bought frozen unsweetened berries also work well in home-canned soft spreads. Strawberries are the exception. Commercially frozen strawberries are usually underripe, lack good flavor and do not make good jams and jellies.

 To Freeze Fresh Berries for Later Use

Spread berries such as blackberries, boysenberries, raspberries and blueberries in a single layer on a foil-lined baking sheet. Freeze for several hours or overnight. Pack the frozen berries into labeled zippered freezer bags and store in the freezer until ready to use.

When making jellies, unsweetened bottled or canned fruit juices can be used. If you use commercial products, make sure to select juices that contain no added sugar. The added sugar in a sweetened juice will throw off the balance of ingredients in the recipe and prevent the jelly from setting.

Do not alter the amount or type of fruit called for in a recipe. Most fruits, even those that appear similar to another kind of fruit, are not interchangeable in soft spread recipes. Each type of fruit has its own specific setting requirements. The proportion of fruit has to be balanced with the correct amount of sugar, pectin and acid to attain a good set. Changing the ratio of fruit in relation to the other ingredients may prevent the spread from setting properly and can significantly alter the taste of the spread.

Sugar

The use of cane sugar to make fruit preserves can be traced back to the arrival of the Spanish in the West Indies in the 16th century. Sugar is an essential component in the preservation of the fruit in a soft spread. When present in the proper proportion with fruit, pectin and acid, it aids in the gel formation that allows a spread to set. Sugar also plays several other roles: it adds sweetness to a spread, helps enhance the flavor of the fruit, helps the fruit maintain both shape and texture, and acts as a preservative by inhibiting the growth of microorganisms in the jars during storage.

Granulated sugar made from sugar cane or sugar beets is the primary source of sugar in jams, jellies and other soft spreads. Some recipes call for a small amount of brown sugar where its molasses flavor will enhance the finished flavor of a particular spread. However, brown sugar is not recommended for making most spreads, as its strong flavor will overpower the flavor of the fruit. Corn syrup and honey may be used to replace part of the sugar in some spread recipes, but too much will mask the fruit flavor and alter the gel structure, resulting in a runny spread. If you wish to use honey or corn syrup in your spreads, be sure to use a tested recipe designed for replacing sugar with honey or corn syrup.

The amount of sugar in a recipe should not be altered or reduced. Never cut down on the amount of sugar a recipe calls for unless syrup is the desired end result. Too little sugar will prevent the spread from setting and can allow yeasts and molds to grow in sealed jars.

Artificial sweeteners cannot be substituted for sugar in soft spread recipes. Sugar is essential for gel formation and developing both the flavor and texture of the spread. Artificial sweeteners do none of these. If you are looking for spreads with reduced sugar, try making them with purchased pectins sold specifically for preparing reduced-sugar or no-sugar-added jams and jellies.

Pectin

Pectin is a natural, water-soluble carbohydrate that develops in fruit as the fruit ripens. It is the substance that makes fruit mixtures gel when the fruit is cooked. The highest levels of pectin are found in fruit that is slightly underripe. The pectin in fruit that is significantly underripe or fruit that is overripe will not form a gel.

All fruits contain some amount of pectin. Fruits such as apples, crabapples, currants and cranberries have a naturally high pectin content and may set on their own when cooked. Other fruits, such as strawberries, blackberries, blueberries, boysenberries, raspberries, cherries, peaches, pears, apricots, pomegranates, guavas and grapefruit, contain small amounts of pectin. These fruits usually require the addition of commercial pectin in order to gel properly.

Commercial pectins are made from tart apples or the peels of citrus fruit, both of which are very high in pectin. They are available in both powdered and liquid forms, which have different formulations and require different proportions of fruit, sugar and acid to set. Powdered and liquid pectins are not interchangeable in recipes. Always use the specific type of pectin called for in the recipe.

There are several advantages to using commercial pectins in making soft spreads. They may be used with any type of fruit and are great for making soft spreads that contain combinations of fruit with different pectin levels. Instead of having to use a significant amount of underripe fruit, commercial pectins allow you to use fully ripe fruit, which results in a spread with intense flavor. The cooking time is significantly reduced, so the fruit retains more of its wonderful fresh flavor and you don't have to stand over a boiling pot for a long time. The same amount of fruit will produce a higher yield because the fruit does not have to be cooked down to activate the pectin. The shorter cooking time also produces a spread with a better texture.

Using commercial pectin also eliminates the intimidation and uncertainty of testing fruit to determine its natural pectin content. The pectin content of fruit varies from year to year and from crop to crop. This presents a challenge when cooking spreads without the addition of pectin, because fruit that set on its own last year may not set this year. Spreads made without added pectin also require testing to determine if the cooked spread is done or requires more boiling before it will gel. With commercial pectin, you boil the mixture for a short, set period, thus eliminating the risk of overcooking the fruit in an attempt to get it to set.

When buying pectin, look for packages with a use-by date that is at least a year in the future. This will help ensure that the pectin is fresh and will reduce the chance that the package has been stored over the winter in a warm location. Packages of powdered fruit pectin should be stored in a cool, dry place so it will not deteriorate and will maintain its gel strength. Pouches of liquid pectin are best stored in the refrigerator, as heat will cause the pectin to break down. Always use pectin by the date indicated on the package and use it the same year it was purchased. Old pectin may result in a poor gel.

Special pectins are available for making spreads with no added sugar or with less sugar than regular recipes. Specific recipes for these spreads can be found on the package inserts, and the manufacturer's directions should be followed precisely. The proportions of acid and fruit should not be altered, as these ratios are needed to prevent spoilage. Because sugar acts as a natural preservative, spreads made with reduced sugar should be handled and stored with care. While all soft spreads need to be processed in a water bath to ensure safe self storage, for reduced-sugar and no-sugar-added spreads it is an absolute must to prevent spoilage. Spreads made with little or no sugar have a much shorter shelf life in terms of quality. While these products will keep reasonably well without spoilage, their flavor and color will deteriorate at a much faster rate.

Acid

Acid plays a key role in home canning soft spreads. A sufficient amount of acid, in the correct ratio to the fruit, sugar and pectin, must be present for a soft spread to set. In spreads made with fruits that have very little natural acid, like strawberries, the acid is provided by adding lemon juice, citrus fruit or another acid ingredient, such as vinegar. In many soft spread recipes, the addition of lemon juice provides the acidity level needed to make the spread gel.

The proper level of acidity is critical to gel formation. If there is too little acid, the soft spread will remain thin and runny and will never set. If there is too much acid, the spread will set up firm and will ooze liquid during storage, a process known as "weeping." Weeping is evident by a thin puddle of liquid on the top surface of the spread in the jar or a thin layer of liquid between the inside of the jar and the spread.

In addition to helping a spread set, acid plays two other important roles: ensuring safety in home-canned products and adding flavor. The correct acidity of a soft spread or other canning product is essential to safe canning. If the acid level is too low, bacteria can grow in the jar during storage. A small amount of lemon juice is also added to some spread recipes to enhance the flavor of the fruit.

All products that are high in acid, such as the soft spreads in this book, should be processed in a boiling water bath to seal the jars and make them safe for shelf storage. Foods that have low acid levels, such as vegetables, must be processed in a pressure canner to make them safe for shelf storage.

Never reduce the amount of the lemon juice or other acid that is specified in a recipe. Reducing the acid level can cause the spread to fail to set, alter the flavor and texture of the product and make it unsafe for storage after canning.

Other Ingredients

In addition to the primary ingredients of fruit, sugar, pectin and acid, there are a few other common ingredients used in making soft spreads.

Tomatoes

Tomatoes are an important ingredient in savory soft spreads and have been a staple of home canners for many generations. When cooked with sugar in soft spreads, tomatoes take on a translucent appearance and a delightful texture.

Roma or other plum tomatoes are the best type to use for soft spreads. Plum tomatoes are significantly less juicy and have firmer flesh than salad or slicing tomatoes. They yield a jam that has a strong flavor and smooth texture with a good set. Regular tomatoes make soft, runny jams with a mild flavor.

The tomatoes used for jams should be fresh, fully ripe and firm to the touch, with only a slight give when pressed. The skin should have a deep red color. Underripe tomatoes will lack flavor and be chewier when cooked, while overripe or soft tomatoes will fall apart when cooked. Soft tomatoes also contain too much juice, so the jam may not set. Tomatoes with flesh that is a nice dark color will create a lovely red jam with intense flavor.

Tomatoes have less acid than other fruits. To raise the acidity level for safe water bath canning, lemon juice, lime juice or vinegar is added to tomato recipes. Never reduce the amount of acid in a tomato recipe, as this may encourage bacteria growth. Under no circumstances should spreads containing tomatoes be stored at room temperature without being processed in a water bath.

Hot and Sweet Peppers

Many people think of soft spreads as being strictly sweet preserves, so hot chile peppers and sweet bell peppers may seem like unusual ingredients. In recent years, however, peppers have become a common ingredient for home canners who are looking to add a little heat to their jams and jellies. In addition to combining peppers with tomatoes and herbs, you can also add them to a variety of fruit spreads. The flavors of some fruits, such as apricots, raspberries and cranberries, work very well with hot peppers.

When working with chile peppers, handle them with care. Chile peppers contain strong oils that can cause painful chemical burns on your skin, in your mouth and in your eyes. Always wear latex, plastic or rubber gloves when seeding and chopping hot peppers to avoid direct contact between your skin and the peppers. Do not wipe your hands across your face or rub your eyes while working with hot peppers. The oils from the peppers can transfer to your eyes and cause serious chemical burns.

The ribs that attach the seeds to the inside of the pepper contain a high concentration of these fierce oils and are the hottest part of a chile pepper. When making jams and jellies, it is best to remove the seeds and ribs from the peppers, as the extra heat can overpower the flavor of the fruit or other ingredients in the spread. Pepper seeds can also turn tough when boiled.

The white or light-colored ribs inside bell peppers are very fibrous and can become quite tough when cooked, affecting both the flavor and the texture of a spread. They should be removed from the peppers after seeding and before chopping.

Herbs

Gourmet herb jellies, made with fresh herbs, are quite popular with home canners. Fresh herbs also add a wonderful aromatic flavor to other types of savory soft spreads.

It is always best to use fresh rather than dried herbs in spreads. Fresh herbs have a flavor that cannot be matched by dried herbs. It is essential to use high-quality fresh herbs to extract a strong herb flavor into the herb infusions used to make jellies. Choose young, tender fresh herbs that have a dark green color and undamaged leaves. Do not use wilted herbs, as these will not impart a strong flavor. To preserve the color and fresh flavor of the herbs, prepare them just before you are ready to use them.

Butter

Butter is added to many types of soft spreads to reduce the amount of foaming that develops when the fruit is cooked. When a fruit mixture boils, air becomes trapped in the top layer of fruit in the pan, causing a layer of foam that can be difficult to collapse by stirring. The addition of a small amount of butter helps reduce the amount of foam that forms and helps the foam to break up when the pan is removed from the heat.

Some fruits, such as apricots and plums, create a lot of foam during cooking. Adding butter to these recipes is particularly helpful and can significantly reduce the amount of skimming needed after removing the pan from the heat and before ladling the spread into jars.

Butter should never be added to the juice used to make jellies because it will cause a cloudiness in the finished jelly that detracts from the jelly's appearance.

Always use unsalted butter, also called "sweet" butter, in soft spreads. Never use salted butter. It can add an unpleasant flavor to spreads, and can develop a rancid flavor during storage. Taste the butter before using it to make sure it has a fresh flavor. This is important to the flavor of all spreads, but is absolutely crucial when making curds, where butter adds so much to the flavor and texture.

Except for curds, where butter is an important component of the actual spread, the addition of a small quantity of butter to soft spreads is completely optional. Just be sure to skim off any foam that develops before ladling the spread into the jars.

Nuts and Dried Fruits

A variety of nuts and some dried fruits, such as raisins, currants, cranberries and apricots, may be used to add flavor and texture to spreads, primarily conserves. Coconut is a popular addition to spreads with a tropical flair.

Nuts used in spreads need to be very fresh. Stale or rancid nuts will give the spread an unpleasant flavor. Always taste nuts before using them to make sure they are fresh. Nuts may be lightly toasted to bring out their flavor and accentuate their crunchy texture (see box, below).

 To Lightly Toast Nuts

Preheat oven to 350°F (180°C). Line a baking sheet with foil and spread chopped nuts evenly over the foil in a single layer. Bake for 5 minutes, stirring halfway through so the nuts will toast evenly and to prevent browning. Remove nuts from the pan and let cool on paper towels. Cool completely before using in soft spreads.

Wine and Liqueurs

The popularity of spreads made with wine and flavored liqueurs has grown immensely. Adding liqueurs to jams, jellies and marmalades enhances the flavor of the fruit while giving the spreads a warm, full-bodied flavor. When liqueurs are added to fruit spreads, the flavor of the liqueur should be subtle, not overpowering. Many home canners make the mistake of adding too much liqueur to a spread, to the point where the fresh flavor of the fruit is lost. Adding more liqueur than called for in a recipe can also keep a spread from setting properly.

Use caution when adding wine or liqueur to the pan, as they are flammable and alcohol vapors can be ignited by open flames. Make sure the pan is off the heat and away from any open flames before adding the alcohol.

Ingredients to Avoid

Pumpkin and chocolate, two popular home canning ingredients, are no longer recommended by the USDA for use in soft spreads and other preserves because they are so dense that they cannot be processed safely. During water bath processing, the spread in the center of the jar cannot reach a temperature high enough to kill potentially harmful bacteria. This means that any spreads containing these ingredients cannot be safely stored at room temperature. If you choose to make soft spreads or other preserves that contain pumpkin or chocolate, the jars must be stored in the refrigerator and used within a month of preparation.

Canning Made Easy

IT IS ESTIMATED that at least 25% of all households in the United States do some amount of home canning each year. A recent study by the National Center for Home Food Preservation revealed some startling results about the methods used by home canners. Only 19% of the respondents followed canning instructions from cookbooks or county Cooperative Extension Service canning bulletins, and some of these were badly outdated. Forty-eight percent stated that they obtained canning instructions from friends and relatives. Only 58% of the home canners polled used the water bath method to process their canned goods. Sixteen percent said they used a pressure canner to process filled jars.

The scary numbers, however, are the 21% of people who said they used the unsafe open-kettle method to seal jars. An additional 4% used the hazardous method of processing filled jars in the oven. These numbers are alarming and indicate that there is a lot of unsafe — even downright dangerous — home-canned food being produced every year.

In this chapter, we will discuss the importance of using proper canning techniques and why it is so crucial that all jars of homemade preserves, including all soft spreads, be heat processed by the correct and approved methods to ensure safety.

Making Great Soft Spreads

While some people are intimidated by the thought of home canning, making your own wonderful jams, jellies and other soft spreads is actually fairly easy and straightforward. By following a few simple rules and using some special techniques, anyone can create tender soft spreads that are packed with flavor and have colors that shimmer in the light.

If making soft spreads is a new venture for you, give home canning a try. When that first batch of jewel-like jars stands cooling on your countertop, you will be thrilled that you did.

Use a Tested Recipe

As home canning is both an art and a science, it is essential to start with a balanced, tested recipe. If the recipe is flawed, the resulting soft spread will not live up to expectations. Many factors can affect the quality of a spread: the ingredients used, the way the fruit is prepared, the measuring techniques used, the cooking time and even the weather and humidity. But nothing can ruin a spread faster than a flawed recipe.

The Short-Boil Method vs. the Long-Boil Method

There are two basic ways to make soft spreads: the short-boil method and the long-boil method. Many busy cooks prefer the short-boil method; some traditionalists prefer the long-boil method. The two methods yield spreads with significantly different characteristics, including flavor and texture. The short-boil method produces spreads with a softer texture and a flavor closer to that of fresh fruit. Spreads made using the long-boil method are firmer and have a cooked fruit flavor.

I personally prefer the fresher fruit flavor, tender texture and vibrant color of spreads made using the short-boil method, and all of the recipes in this book use this method.

The Short-Boil Method

In the short-boil method, commercial packaged pectin is added to create spreads with a bright, tantalizing flavor and wonderful texture. This method requires only a few minutes of cooking and dramatically decreases the amount of time it takes to make soft spreads.

Soft spread recipes that use the short-boil method are designed for the specific types of fruit used in the recipe and are formulated to work with the natural pectin of fully ripe fruit. Using fully ripe fruit means the finished spread will have a strong flavor that is closer to the natural flavor of fresh fruit. Because the fruit is cooked for a shorter period of time, the fruit retains more of its intense natural color. The reduced cooking time also yields a spread with a smooth, tender texture.

The two types of commercial packaged pectin — powdered pectin and liquid pectin —both work to gel the fruit mixture. The only real difference is the order in which the ingredients are combined and cooked. With powdered pectin, the pectin and fruit are combined and brought to a boil, then the sugar is added. With liquid pectin, the fruit and sugar are combined and brought to a boil, then the pectin is added. In both cases, the spread is then boiled for one minute and removed from the heat. It is that quick and easy, and the results are fantastic.

The Long-Boil Method

In the long-boil method, the fruit is combined with the sugar and boiled for several minutes until a cooled and tested sample of the spread will hold its shape. It can take many minutes or even up to an hour of cooking for a spread to reach the set point, the stage at which a spread will gel.

There are a number of challenges associated with the long-boil method. The first is determining which fruits contain enough natural pectin to allow them to set on their own if they are boiled long enough. Some fruits are high in natural pectin, while others contain very little. Fruits with a low pectin content must be combined with fruits that are high in pectin. Because apples are high in pectin, they are often added to other fruits that have a low pectin content to help the gelling process. Adding apples increases the pectin content of the mixture, but also decreases the flavor intensity of the primary fruit in the spread.

The pectin content of fruit varies from year to year, so even fruits that are traditionally high in pectin can sometimes be hit and miss. Testing the pectin content of fruit to determine its setting properties is a time-consuming process. It is frequently necessary to use a fairly high percentage of underripe fruit, which contains more pectin than ripe fruit, to get the spread to set. The resulting spread lacks the intense flavor found in fully ripe fruit.

The long-boil method requires constant attention and stirring during the long cooking process. Because the spread must cook over moderately high heat for a long time, the fruit in the bottom of the pan may scorch if it's not watched closely. Even the slightest scorching will give the entire batch an unpleasant flavor. In addition, an extended cooking time can cause the sugar to caramelize and the spread to take on a molasses-like flavor. The constant stirring and extended cooking can also cause the fruit to break down and lose flavor and the spread to develop a tougher texture.

For the long-boil method, a candy thermometer is essential to check the temperature of the boiling spread. To test the set, a small quantity of spread is cooled to room temperature and then checked for consistency and separation of the fruit and juice. If the spread is not thick enough, it is returned to a boil and cooked a few minutes longer, then tested again. Another way to test the doneness of long-boiled spreads, particularly jellies, is the sheeting test, in which hot spread is slowly poured over the edge of a spoon to determine its viscosity and sheeting properties. For the inexperienced home canner, it is difficult to know whether the texture of the sheeting spread is sufficient to ensure a good set once the spread is cooled.

Because long-boil-method spreads set through a combination of evaporation of liquid and activation of pectin to create a gel, there is a tendency to overcook the spread, which can cause it to set up like rubber. As a state and county fair preserved foods judge, I have seen many jars of long-boiled jams and jellies cross my judging table where it was a challenge even to get a spoon into the jar, and spreads that were so firm, tough and rubbery that they would bounce if dropped.

Canning Techniques

Great soft spreads do not happen by accident. Skilled home canners use special techniques to create their outstanding products. Fortunately, these procedures are easily mastered by home canners of any skill level.

Reviewing the Recipe and Assembling Ingredients and Equipment

The first step in creating a great soft spread is reviewing the recipe to make sure you understand the procedures and have all of the necessary ingredients and equipment on hand and ready to use.

Recipes are designed to create one batch of spread at a time. If you want to make more than one batch of the same type of spread, do not double the recipe. Instead, make two separate batches. It is always risky to double soft spread recipes. The quantity of fruit and sugar in the pan determines both the size and surface area of the pan needed to make the spread and the length of cooking time required to achieve a good set. If the pan is too full, insufficient liquid will boil off during cooking and the spread will be very soft and won't set properly.

Before you start, gather all the ingredients — fruit, sugar, pectin, acid and flavorings — you will need for the recipe. Also assemble all the equipment — jars, lids and screw bands, pots and pans, water bath canner, measuring cups and spoons, knives, and canning and kitchen utensils — you will need to prepare and cook the fruit and can the finished spread.

Preparing Jars, Lids and Screw Bands

Canning jars, lids and screw bands need some basic preparation before they are used. Preparing these items correctly will ensure that a good seal forms between the lid and the jar rim.

Inspecting Jars, Lids and Screw Bands

Check jars for scratches, cracks, bubbles in the glass or other flaws that may weaken them and cause them to break during processing. Run your finger around the rims and feel for any nicks, chips, rough spots or unevenness, which can prevent the lids from sealing properly. Discard any damaged jars.

Always use new flat lids specifically designed for canning. To ensure a good seal, use lids made by the same manufacturer as the jars you're using. Never reuse lids, as the compound will be hardened and will not form a tight seal with the jars. Examine the lids to make sure that they are not scratched or warped and that the food-safe coating on the underside is not damaged. Scratches can rust during storage, and warped lids will not seal properly. Check that the sealing compound around the edge of the lid is applied evenly, with no gaps or thin spots. Any gap in the sealing compound will prevent a tight seal and can cause the seal to fail during storage. Discard any damaged lids.

Screw bands can be reused if they are in good condition. Bands that show any signs of rust or corrosion should be discarded. Warped or dented bands will not hold lids securely on the jars during processing and cooling and should not be used.

Washing and Heating Jars

Canning jars that will be processed for 10 minutes or more in a water bath canner after filling do not need to be sterilized. It is important to keep jars hot between washing and filling to reduce the chance that they may break when the hot spread is ladled into the jars.

My preferred method for washing jars is in a dishwasher. It is not only effective and convenient, but it also saves a lot of time and effort. The dishwasher does the washing, rinsing, drying and heating for you, leaving you free to get the ingredients ready. Keep the door shut and locked until you are ready to use the jars, then remove only the jars you need for that batch and shut the door to keep any remaining jars hot. With the door closed, the dishwasher will keep the clean jars hot for a long time. If your dishwasher has a plate-warming feature, you can use it to keep jars hot while you're making several batches of spreads. When removed from the dishwasher, the jars are already dry, so you won't have to worry about residual water in the jars forming a thin layer between the edge of the jar and the spread.

If you don't have a dishwasher, you can wash jars by hand in hot, soapy water. Rinse them well under hot running water to remove all the soap. To keep hand-washed jars hot until you're ready to use them, fill a large stockpot half-full of water. Add the jars to the pot one at a time, filling them with water from the pot. Add enough water to just cover the tops of the jars and place the lid on the pot. Bring the water to a simmer over medium-high heat. Reduce the heat to low and keep the jars hot until ready to use. When ready to use the jars, use a jar lifter to remove the jars from the hot water, tipping the jars to pour the water back into the pot. Turn the jars upside down on a towel for a minute or two to drain out the remaining water. Turn the jars upright and fill.

Home canning jars are not designed to be used with dry heat. Never use the oven to keep jars hot; the dry heat of the oven can weaken the jars and increase the chances that they will break during heat processing in the water bath. For the same reason, the microwave should never be used to quickly heat jars before filling. Both of these methods can be very dangerous.

Washing and Heating Lids

Wash the flat lids in hot, soapy water, rinse well and drain. Fill a small saucepan half-full of water, cover and bring to a simmer over medium heat. Reduce heat to low and keep the water hot while you prepare the fruit for the recipe. When you are ready to prepare the spread, remove the pan from the heat and add the flat lids. Cover the pan and keep the lids hot until you're ready to use them. The lids do not need to be sterilized, so do not boil them. Boiling the lids will damage the sealing compound and cause the seals to fail.

The lids should heat in the hot water for at least 10 minutes to soften the sealing compound. When softened, the sealing compound will mold itself to the rim of the jar, forming a tight seal. Do not heat the lids for longer than 30 minutes, as extended heating can damage the sealing compound.

Washing Screw Bands

Wash the screw bands in hot, soapy water, rinse well and dry thoroughly to prevent rusting. Set aside until needed. Never heat or boil the screw bands, as this will promote rust.

Preparing Fruit

The techniques used to prepare fruit and other ingredients for soft spreads have a direct relationship to the quality of the finished spread. To create a great spread, pay attention to detail when preparing the fruit. The individual recipe chapters provide information on specific techniques for preparing the fruit for each type of soft spread, but here are some general points to keep in mind:

- Make spreads when the fruit is in season and at the peak of ripeness. For the freshest flavor, use the fruit as soon after harvest as possible.

- Bring refrigerated fruit to room temperature before preparing the recipe. Cold fruit may alter the cooking time and the finished texture of the spread. This is particularly true with denser fruits such as apples, which can take significantly longer to cook when cold.

- Wash fruit just before you are ready to use it. Fruit with a soft peel will start to deteriorate after contact with water. Gently rinse fruit under cool running water and drain well. Do not allow fruit to sit in water, as fruit can absorb water and wet fruit will quickly deteriorate. Spread the fruit on paper towels and gently blot dry. Apples and citrus fruits should be lightly scrubbed under running water with a fruit or vegetable brush, then rinsed and dried.

- Prepare and measure fruit as instructed by the individual recipe. To maintain freshness of flavor and color, prepare it just before making the spread and prepare only enough for one batch at a time. Fruit can deteriorate and darken quickly after it is peeled and crushed or chopped.

Peeling Fruit

Peeling the fruit gives the spread a smooth, silky, luxurious texture. Cooked peels can create a grainy or gritty texture, with tough little bits of peel distributed through the spread. Cooked peels have little flavor and add nothing to the quality or enjoyment of the spread. Peels should always be removed from apples, peaches, nectarines and pears.

Most soft spread recipes in other canning books instruct you to leave the skins on plums and apricots. I strongly advise peeling both plums and apricots for all soft spread recipes. The skin on plums can turn bitter, tough and chewy when cooked, giving the spread an unpleasant bitter flavor and coarse texture. Apricot peels darken, turn mushy and develop a musty flavor when cooked, detracting from the bright fresh flavor of the apricots and giving the finished spread an uneven texture.

Handling Berries

Fresh berries are very fragile and need to be handled gently to prevent bruising. To rinse berries, place them in a colander and rinse under cool running water. Gently shake the colander to remove excess water. Spread the berries on layers of paper towels and gently blot dry. Crush berries, one layer at a time, in a large flat-bottomed pan or bowl using a vegetable masher or the back of a large spoon.

If using frozen berries to make spreads, thaw before crushing. Place packages of frozen berries in a bowl or a zippered storage bag to catch any drips. Thaw berries in their packages in the refrigerator or at room temperature. Do not place packages of berries in water to speed up the thawing process; the water can seep into the packages and dilute the flavor of the berries. A microwave should not be used, as it can partially cook the thawing berries.

Peeling and Juicing Citrus Fruits

When peeling citrus fruits, remove all of the outer white pith from the fruit. The white pith is very bitter and will cause the spread to taste quite bitter and unpleasant as well. Using a sharp knife, cut a slice off the top and bottom of the citrus and place it cut side down on a cutting board. Carefully slice off the peel in thick strips, removing all of the white pith from the outside of the fruit.

When juicing citrus fruits, be careful not to squeeze or ream the fruit so much that you press into the outer white pith, as this can turn the juice bitter. Freshly squeezed citrus juices should be strained to remove any seeds. Some citrus seeds can be very bitter, and tiny seeds in the spread affect the smoothness of its texture.

✳ How to Peel Peaches, Apricots and Tomatoes

To make short work of peeling ripe peaches, apricots and tomatoes, gently drop a few pieces of fruit at a time into a pan of boiling water. Let them soak for 30 to 60 seconds, or until the peels on the peaches or apricots start to release or the skins on the tomatoes just start to split. Using a slotted spoon, quickly remove the fruit from the boiling water and plunge it into a large bowl or pan of ice water. Let the fruit sit in the ice water for 1 to 2 minutes to stop the cooking process. Remove the fruit from the water and drain well. Use a small, sharp paring knife to remove the peel from the peaches or apricots or the skin from the tomatoes.

Measuring Accurately

Accurate measurement of the fruit, sugar and other ingredients plays a key role in the outcome of the finished spread, ensuring that it will have a balanced flavor and will set correctly. It is very important to use the correct measuring cups for the different types of ingredients. For the best results, measure all ingredients in a recipe using either all imperial measures or all metric measures.

To measure fruit and juice, use glass measuring cups that are made for measuring liquid ingredients. Level off the top of the fruit and read the markings at eye level to get an accurate measurement. Too much fruit can keep the spread from setting, and too little fruit can cause the spread to set up too firm.

For dry ingredients such as sugar, use measuring cups with flat rims that are specifically designed for measuring dry ingredients. These measuring cups allow you to spoon or pour the sugar into the cup and use a knife or other utensil with a straight edge to scrape the excess off the top of the cup to get an accurate measurement. Dry measuring cups come in graduated sizes of ¼ cup (50 mL), ⅓ cup (75 mL), ½ cup (125 mL), ⅔ cup (150 mL), ¾ cup (175 mL) and 1 cup (250 mL). If you do not have dry measuring cups, I strongly advise you to buy a set and use it. In addition to their use in making soft spreads, dry measuring cups are essential when you're measuring ingredients for baking.

Measure the amount of sugar called for in the recipe into a bowl and set aside before preparing the fruit. The sugar will be ready to use when needed and can be added to the pot all at once rather than a cup at a time.

Use graduated measuring spoons to measure small portions of both liquid and dry ingredients. Small glass measuring glasses may be used to measure small quantities of liquid ingredients.

Cooking Soft Spreads

There are a few special techniques for cooking soft spreads that can really improve the overall quality, flavor and texture of the finished product. The individual recipe chapters cover the specific techniques that apply to each type of spread. Here we will look at important techniques that apply to nearly all soft spreads. Paying close attention to these details can make the difference between producing just an average soft spread and creating a spread that is truly special, with dazzling color, tender texture and outstanding fruit flavor.

Combining Ingredients

The order in which ingredients are combined depends on the type of pectin being used. Powdered pectin is designed to be added to the fruit at the beginning of the cooking process because it is activated by double-boiling, first with just the fruit, and then again after the sugar is added. Liquid pectin is added to the spread mixture after the fruit and sugar have been combined and brought to a boil. It needs to boil only once to gel the spread. If liquid pectin has been stored in the refrigerator, always bring it to room temperature before using it in soft spread recipes.

Powdered pectin and liquid pectin have different formulations and are not interchangeable. Always use the specific type and amount called for in the recipe to get a good set.

Reducing Foam

Foam is created on the surface of soft spreads when the fruit mixture boils and tiny air bubbles become trapped in the boiling fruit juice. Some fruits, such as apricots and plums, create a lot of foam when boiled. Others, such as most berries, generate far less.

To reduce the amount of foam, add ½ teaspoon (2 mL) unsalted butter to the fruit. Be sure to use unsalted butter, as salted butter can alter the flavor of the spread and give it an "off" flavor. Do not add butter to jellies, as it can cause them to turn cloudy.

Cooking the Spread Mixture

To cook outstanding soft spreads, quickly bring the fruit and sugar mixture to a boil, making sure the sugar is completely dissolved. Heating the fruit quickly will produce a product with an intense fruit flavor, a smooth spreadable texture and a bright jewel-tone color.

It is important to bring the spread ingredients to a full rolling boil as instructed in the recipes. A full rolling boil is a hard boil that cannot be stirred down. This means the mixture will continue to boil rapidly when stirred. When making spreads with pectin, the ingredients need to be this hot for the mixture to set properly.

As the spread boils, it must be stirred constantly. Stirring helps combine the fruit and sugar and ensures that the fruit cooks uniformly. It also prevents the fruit from scorching and evenly distributes the pectin throughout the spread to create a uniform gel.

Successful preparation of short-boil spreads depends on accurate timing. Once you have added all of the primary ingredients — fruit, sugar, pectin and acid — to the pot, the mixture must be returned to a full rolling boil and boiled for 1 minute, stirring constantly. This applies to both powdered and liquid pectin recipes. This final boil ensures that the sugar is completely dissolved, the fruit is fully cooked and the pectin is evenly distributed throughout the spread. It also causes some of the liquid in the mixture to evaporate, improving the set.

You'll need an accurate timer to keep track of this crucial 1-minute boiling time. Start the timer when the spread mixture reaches a full rolling boil. When the timer goes off, immediately turn off the heat and remove the pan from the burner. A few extra seconds of cooking will not cause a problem, but if the spread is allowed to boil for 2 minutes or more, the pectin will start to break down and the spread will fail to set.

∗

Skimming Foam

It is important to skim off any foam that has formed on the top of a spread during cooking before ladling the spread into the jars. Failing to skim the foam not only detracts from the appearance of the spread in the jar, but also affects the texture and flavor. Cooled and set foam has an unpleasant, spongy texture, and because it is mostly trapped air, foam has very little flavor.

As a state fair judge, I often see spreads with an inch (2.5 cm) or more of set foam in the top of the jar. Some jars are nearly all foam. It is not an appealing sight, nor a pleasant experience to judge such entries.

It will be easier to skim the foam if, after removing the pan from the heat, you let the spread stand for a minute, allowing the foam to set slightly. Be sure to skim it off before stirring the spread again; otherwise, you will distribute the foam into the spread and trap it there.

When you're making jelly, however, the foam should be quickly skimmed off as soon as the pan is removed from the heat so that the jelly can be immediately ladled into jars before a skin starts to develop on the surface of the jelly.

Preventing Floating Fruit

"Floating fruit" in jams, marmalades, preserves and conserves is a common problem for some home canners. Floating fruit occurs when the pieces of fruit in a soft spread separate from the juice and rise to the top of the jar, creating a thick layer of fruit in the upper part of the jar and a layer of cloudy jelly in the bottom. Once a spread has separated, the only way to get it back together is to stir it after opening the jar and before serving.

The primary cause of floating fruit is using chopped fruit rather than crushed fruit when making spreads. Chopped pieces of fruit often do not cook enough to release the air trapped inside the fruit cells. Another reason chopped fruit floats is that it frequently does not absorb enough sugar to keep the pieces from separating from the juice. As the spread cools, the pieces of fruit rise to the top of the jar.

The best way to prevent floating fruit in jams and conserves is to cut the fruit into small pieces, then gently crush the pieces with a potato or vegetable masher. This process releases the air trapped inside the cells of the fruit and allows it to absorb more sugar during cooking and become heavier. Jams and conserves made with crushed fruit have a smooth texture and great flavor.

When making marmalades, cut the citrus fruit into small pieces and the peel into thin strips that will absorb the sugar. When making preserves, combine the chopped or whole fruit with part of the sugar and let the

---

mixture sit in the pan for the amount of time indicated in the recipe before cooking. This will allow the fruit to release some of its juice and absorb part of the sugar into its cells.

Floating fruit can also be caused by a high proportion of juice or liquid in the spread in relation to the fruit pieces. This can be caused by using very juicy fruit, adding too much liquid in the form of liqueurs or other flavorings, or puréeing the fruit instead of crushing it. Puréeing releases too much juice from the fruit. Excess juice or liquid impedes the gelling process and affects the viscosity of the hot spread, allowing the fruit to rise to the top of the jar rather than remaining evenly suspended.

One technique to prevent floating fruit is to let the spread stand in the pot for 5 minutes after removing it from the heat and before filling the jars. Gently stir it every minute or so to distribute the fruit evenly through the spread. While it's standing, the fruit will continue cooking off the heat, releasing any remaining trapped air, and the fruit will absorb more sugar. The standing period also increases the viscosity of the spread, which will help suspend the fruit as the spread sets in the jars.

If your spread separates and the fruit floats to the top of the jar, resist the urge to invert or shake the jar to try to blend the fruit back into the spread before it sets. Inverting or shaking jars before processing can push the spread between the lid and the jar rim, which can cause a weak seal. Inverting or shaking the jars after processing can cause the seal to fail.

Filling the Jars

Hot canning jars should always be placed on a towel or a heatproof surface such as a wooden cutting board to insulate them from temperature shock. If jars are placed directly on a cold countertop, such as tile or granite, they can break from the sudden change in temperature at the bottom of the jar. Also, when the jars are filled, the contrast between the heat of the spread and the cold of the countertop can cause them to break.

The jar yield given in the recipes is an approximation and should be used as a guide when filling jars. The actual number of jars you will get from a batch of a soft spread may vary up or down by a jar. Jar yields can even vary from batch to batch of the same spread, depending on how dense and juicy the fruit is and how much liquid boils off during cooking. Yields can also vary depending on the shape of the jars you use to can the spread.

✳

Ladling the Spread into Jars

A wide-mouth funnel made specifically for canning is an indispensable tool for filling canning jars with soft spreads. Set the funnel in the top of a jar and use a ladle to dip the spread from the pan and pour it into the jar. Soft spreads should never be poured directly from the pan into the jars because they can pick up undissolved sugar from the side of the pan, which can give the spread a grainy, gritty texture. Undissolved sugar can also cause crystals to form in jellies. Always use a ladle to transfer spreads from the pan to the jars.

Hold the ladle close to the funnel and fill the jars quickly to prevent air bubbles from forming as you pour. Ladling slowly can cause these air bubbles to become trapped in the spread inside the jar. Small air bubbles in spreads are a cosmetic issue attributed to poor ladling technique. Large air bubbles, however, are a cause for concern because they can create an air pocket in the spread where bacteria could grow if the jar is not properly sealed.

Should you end up with air bubbles trapped in your spread, slide a thin-bladed plastic knife down into the jar to create a path for the bubbles to rise to the surface. Be careful not to trap additional air in the jar when you remove the knife. Also take care not to stir the spread, as stirring will create more bubbles.

If air bubbles become trapped in a jelly, it means the jelly started to set up as it was ladled into the jar. Trying to remove air bubbles from jelly is not advised, because the jelly will already be partially set, which will prevent the bubbles from rising to the surface and cause the plastic knife to leave wispy trails through the setting jelly. While small air bubbles detract from the overall appearance of a jelly, the spread is still safe to eat.

Leaving Headspace

Headspace is the amount of space left in the jar between the top of the spread and the top edge of the jar. Using the correct headspace allowance is one of the most important elements in canning soft spreads. It is essential that headspace instructions for home canning be followed closely.

Extensive testing has been done to determine the appropriate amount of headspace to leave inside home canning jars to produce the best seal. For all soft spreads, the USDA strongly advises the use of ¼ inch (0.5 cm) headspace. This standard is to be used for all 4-ounce (125 mL), 8-ounce (250 mL), 12-ounce (375 mL) and 1-pint (500 mL) jars. This means that when you are filling jars with soft spreads, you should leave ¼ inch (0.5 cm) of space between the top of the spread and the top of the jar. No more, no less.

If there is too much headspace, there will be too much air in the jar. During water bath processing, air is vented from the jar to create a vacuum. If there is too much air in the jar, all of the air will not be vented out, a strong vacuum will not be able to form in the jar, and the lid will not be pulled tightly against the jar rim to create a solid seal. Because of the weak vacuum, the seal will be more likely to fail during storage, allowing contaminants to enter the jar. Too much headspace in the jar can also cause the top of the spread to darken and discolor during storage.

If there is not enough headspace, some of the spread may be forced out between the lid and the rim of the jar during processing. Food particles trapped between the lid compound and the jar rim will result in a weak seal. The trapped food particles will create a pathway that can allow bacteria to enter the jar, and the weakened seal will likely fail during storage.

When you fill jars with soft spreads, always use the correct headspace, even if the batch does not fill as many jars as you expected it to. Never leave more headspace in an attempt to make the number of filled jars match the yield given in the recipe. The yield is an approximation. Always use ¼ inch (0.5 cm) headspace for soft spreads. This is a matter of safety.

If you end up with a partially filled jar of spread, let it cool, then cover the jar with a lid or plastic wrap, refrigerate and use the contents within 3 weeks. Instead of a canning jar, extra spread may also be spooned into a small heatproof bowl or container, cooled, covered and stored in the refrigerator.

Wiping Jar Rims

After filling the jars, use a clean, damp paper towel to remove any spilled jam or jelly from the rim of the jar and the jar threads. Always wipe the rim of the jar before applying the lid, even if you do not see any drips or drops on the rim. This step is crucial to creating a good seal and should not be skipped. Any food residue left on the rim of the jars may prevent the lid from making a good bond with the jar rim and can cause a weak seal. Drips of spread left on the screw threads can keep the screw band from pulling the lid down tight against the jar rim.

While a cloth towel can be used to wipe the rims, a paper towel is the best choice for this job. Wiping rims can be a sticky job, and towels quickly become soiled. A paper towel that becomes sticky can be tossed away and replaced with a clean paper towel so that drips of spread are not transferred from one jar to another. To dissolve any sugar residue on the jar, dip the paper towel in hot water before wiping the jar rim and screw threads. If you prefer to use a cloth towel for this job, keep several clean towels at hand and change towels frequently as they start to become soiled and sticky.

Never use a kitchen sponge to wipe down jar rims. Sponges can harbor a host of bacteria that can easily be transferred to the jars, contaminating the soft spread inside.

Applying Lids and Screw Bands

Use a magnetic lid wand or kitchen tongs to carefully remove the heated lids, one at a time, from the pan of hot water. Center the lids on the jars, with the sealing compound centered on the jar rims. Place a screw band on each jar and screw the band down onto the jar threads. Using your fingers, screw the band down until resistance is met, then increase the pressure until the band is fingertip-tight. Do not use a tool or excessive force to tighten the screw band. Over-tightening the screw bands can prevent the jars from venting air during processing, which can lead to seal failure and can cause the jars to break during heat processing because of the excessive pressure trapped inside the jar.

During heat processing, the compound on the flat lid will soften and form a partial seal with the rim of the canning jar. The softened compound will allow air to escape from the jar but will prevent water from entering. After the jar is removed from the water bath, as it starts to cool, a vacuum will form inside the jar, pulling the lid down tight against the jar rim. As the jar continues to cool, the compound will harden and form a permanent seal, holding the lid firmly in place. After 24 hours, when the compound has hardened and the seal is complete, the screw band should be removed from the jar.

During water bath processing, the screw bands may loosen slightly. Never retighten them after the processing is complete. When the jars come out of the water bath, the compound on the lids is hot and very soft. If you retighten the screw bands, you could force all of the compound out from between the lid and the jar rim. This would result in a very weak seal that would likely fail during storage.

Water Bath Processing

Even though sugar and acid act as preservatives in jams, jellies and other soft spreads, molds and bacteria can still grow inside the jars and cause these products to spoil if they are not properly processed. It used to be thought that filling sterilized jars with hot spreads and turning them upside down for a few minutes was sufficient to seal the jars and prevent mold growth. We now know that this is not the case. To prevent mold and bacteria growth, the USDA and the Cooperative Extension Service strongly advise that all soft spreads be processed in a boiling water canner.

Heat processing of spreads is necessary to destroy any microorganisms that could cause the product to spoil during storage. When you process filled jars in a boiling water bath, the jars are submerged in boiling water long enough for the food in the jar to reach a temperature high enough to kill any harmful bacteria, mold spores or yeasts that may be present. Processing also vents air from the jars, creating a vacuum that allows a tight seal to form between the lid and the jar that prevents bacteria from entering the processed jar.

The water bath method is used to process foods that are high in acid. In addition to soft spreads, this includes fruit, fruit juices, tomato products to which lemon juice or vinegar has been added, and pickles. Low-acid foods, such as vegetables, must be processed in a pressure canner. As soft spreads are high in acid, we will be dealing only with water bath processing in this book.

Processing filled jars for the correct length of time, following approved guidelines, will ensure that the product is safe to store at room temperature and will maintain maximum flavor, color and texture. If you are going to take the time to make quality soft spreads for your family and friends, do not pass over this important step. It takes only a few minutes, and you will have peace of mind, knowing that your homemade creations are safe to eat.

Altitude Adjustments

Water boils at 212°F (100°C) at sea level. As altitude increases, water boils at a lower temperature, which means it is less effective at killing bacteria. To compensate for the lower boiling point, processing times need to be increased as altitude increases.

All of the processing times for water bath canning listed in the recipes are based on an altitude of 1,000 feet (305 m) or less. If you live at an altitude above 1,000 feet (305 m), you will need to adjust your processing time as indicated below.

✳ *Altitude Adjustments for Water Bath Processing*

Altitude	Increase Processing Time By
1,001 to 3,000 feet (306 to 915 m)	5 minutes
3,001 to 6,000 feet (916 to 1,830 m)	10 minutes
6,001 to 8,000 feet (1,831 to 2,440 m)	15 minutes
8,001 to 10,000 feet (2,441 to 3,050 m)	20 minutes

Step-by-Step Canning Guide for Soft Spreads

The instructions below guide you step by step through the process of water bath canning so you will be able to can and process soft spreads with ease and confidence.

1. Review the recipe and make sure you have all needed ingredients and equipment on hand. Assemble the equipment and check all items to make sure they are in good working condition.

2. Wash canning jars in the dishwasher and keep hot until ready to use. Or hand-wash jars in hot, soapy water, rinse well and place upright in a large pot. Cover with hot water, cover the pot and keep hot until needed. (Sterilizing jars is required only if filled jars will be processed in a water bath for less than 10 minutes.)

3. Wash lids and screw bands in hot, soapy water, rinse well, dry and set aside.

4. Fill the water bath canner two-thirds full of water. Place on the stovetop, cover and start heating over medium-high heat.

5. Fill a small saucepan half-full of water, cover and bring to a simmer over medium heat. Reduce the heat and keep water hot.

6. Prepare and measure the ingredients according to the recipe.

7. Remove the saucepan from the heat and add the flat lids. Cover and keep lids hot until ready to use. Do not boil the lids.

8. Cook the soft spread according to the recipe. Remove the pan from the heat and skim off any foam.

9. Remove the number of jars you need from the dishwasher or hot water, draining the water back into the pot, and place on a towel or a heatproof cutting board.

10. Use a ladle and wide-mouth canning funnel to quickly fill jars with the spread, leaving ¼ inch (0.5 cm) headspace. Remove any air bubbles.

11. Wipe jar rims and threads with a clean, damp paper towel.

12. Use a lid wand or tongs to remove the lids, one at a time, from the pan of hot water. Center the lids on the jars, with the sealing compound centered on the jar rims. Apply the screw bands and screw them down on the jar threads until fingertip-tight. Do not over-tighten.

13. Position the rack in the water bath canner.

14. Using a jar lifter, carefully load the jars into the water bath, keeping them upright. Make sure the jars are spaced so that they do not touch each other. Check the water level to make sure it is at least 1 to 2 inches (2.5 cm to 5 cm) above the tops of the jars. Adjust to correct height by adding or removing water, if necessary.

15. Place the lid on the canner and bring the water to a boil over high heat. Reduce the heat to maintain a gentle boil during processing.

16. Start the timer after the water reaches a boil. Check the canner periodically to make sure the water is still boiling. If the boiling stops, stop the timer and return the water to a boil. Once it is boiling again, restart the timer, adding back any time that was missed when the water was not boiling. Adjust the processing time for altitudes above 1,000 feet (305 m) (see chart, page 38).

17. When the processing time is complete, turn off the heat and remove the lid from the canner. Using a jar lifter, remove the jars from the canner, keeping them upright. Set the jars on a cooling rack or a cloth towel, spacing them at least 1 inch (2.5 cm) apart. Do not retighten screw bands, as this can damage the seal. Let jars cool, undisturbed, for 24 hours to allow a vacuum to form inside the jars (listen for the friendly popping or pinging sound as the jars cool) and the seals to set.

18. Remove the rack from the water bath canner to prevent it from rusting.

19. After 24 hours, check the seals on the cooled jars. Press down in the center of each jar. If the jar lid is depressed and does not move when pressed, the jar is sealed. If the lid flexes up and down, the jar has failed to seal. Unsealed jars should be reprocessed immediately (see box, page 41) or stored in the refrigerator and the contents used within a few days.

20. Remove the screw bands from the jars. Keeping the jars upright, gently wash them with warm, soapy water. Rinse well under running water and dry thoroughly. Label the jars with the contents and the date of preparation.

21. Pack jars into boxes and store in a cool, dry, dark location. Use spreads within 1 year for the best flavor and texture.

> ## ✳ How to Reprocess Unsealed Jars
>
> To reprocess a jar of soft spread that did not seal, empty the contents into a small saucepan and bring to a boil over medium-high heat, stirring frequently. Ladle the spread into a clean hot jar. Wipe the jar rim, cover with a new hot lid and apply a screw band. Process in a water bath for 10 minutes. Remove from the water bath, let cool for 24 hours, then check the seal.

Unsafe Canning Methods

There are several old-fashioned, outdated home canning methods that used to be considered acceptable practice but have now been proven unsafe. Unfortunately, these methods are still being used today by some home canners. Any home-canned food processed using these outdated methods should be considered unsafe to eat.

The Open-Kettle Method

Open-kettle canning, also known as the inversion method, used to be very common and was considered an acceptable way to seal jars, particularly jars of soft spreads. However, products canned using this method have a high rate of food spoilage, and open-kettle canning is no longer considered a safe or effective way to seal jars. It should not be used under any circumstances.

The theory behind open-kettle canning was that any bacteria or organisms in the spread were killed when the mixture was boiled. The spread was poured into sterilized jars, the rims wiped down, and a lid and screw band applied. The jars were then turned upside down, or inverted, for 5 to 10 minutes. When the jars were turned back upright, the lid would pull down as a vacuum was created inside the jar. Because the spread was considered sterile, it was thought that contaminants would not grow inside the jar.

In reality, open-kettle canning carries many serious health risks. Bacteria and mold spores can easily enter the jar or contaminate the spread before the jar is closed. All it takes is a touch to the jar rim or lid by a hand, or a funnel or ladle that has picked up an unseen contaminant from the countertop. Even the towel used to wipe the rim or the plastic knife used to remove air bubbles can introduce contaminants into the jar.

The seals created by the inversion method tend to be weak and often fail during storage. The temperature of the food inside the jar is rarely hot enough to kill any contaminants that may have entered the jar while it was being filled and closed. In addition, air has not been exhausted from inside the jars to create a strong vacuum, and the headspace in the jar may retain enough oxygen to allow the growth of mold or other contaminants.

Unseen bacteria and mold can run rampant in jars of spreads canned using the open-kettle method. Do not use this method to seal jars, and do not eat foods prepared using this method. Endangering your health, and that of your family and friends, is not worth the risk.

Inverting Jars after Water Bath Processing

Some home canners cannot let go of the notion that jars need to be inverted, even after they have been processed in a water bath. This is a dangerous, old-fashioned practice. Inverting jars after processing can weaken the seal and allow the spread to seep between the jar and lid. Bacteria and mold can then enter and grow inside the jar, contaminating the contents. Jars should never be inverted, either before or after water bath processing.

Other Outdated Canning Methods

Other unsafe and outdated canning methods include attempting to process and seal filled jars in the oven, microwave or dishwasher. There is no way to control the temperature of the jars and their contents with these methods. There is also a high risk of the jars shattering. None of these methods will properly seal jars, and all are considered very dangerous.

Storing Soft Spreads

Once the jars are sealed and the contents have cooled, the screw bands should be removed. The purpose of the screw bands is to hold the lids securely in place during processing and cooling. Screw bands are not needed while the jars are being stored and have a tendency to rust during storage.

After removing the screw bands, wash the jars to remove any residual spread or mineral deposits from the water bath. Keeping the jars upright and level, carefully wash them in warm, soapy water. Rinse under clean running water and dry thoroughly, including around the edge of the lid.

When the jars are completely dry, attach labels to them. The labels should identify the contents of the jars and include the date on which the spread was made. Do not reapply the screw bands.

To keep the jars safe during storage, it is best to pack them in a sturdy box. The box the jars came in is a good choice, as it will securely hold a dozen jars. Store jars of soft spreads in a cool, dark, dry location to preserve the color, flavor and texture of the spread. If a spread is exposed to heat, it can separate, become runny and lose its intense fruit flavor. Exposure to light for an extended period of time speeds up oxidation and can cause the color and flavor to fade. Moist locations can cause the lids to rust. Locations that are both warm and moist can damage the seal and encourage the growth of mold.

The ideal temperature range at which to store jars of home-canned foods, and the one recommended by the USDA, is between 50°F (10°C) and 70°F (21°C). Jars stored at higher temperatures may deteriorate faster. A dry basement or cellar is the perfect place to store home-canned preserves. Other good locations include the back of a pantry, the floor or lower shelves of an interior closet, or under a bed.

Length of Storage

For the best overall quality, all home-canned foods should be used within a year. While a well-canned soft spread should remain safe to eat as long as the jar seal remains intact and the product shows no visible signs of spoilage, the appearance and flavor of the spread will deteriorate over time.

In terms of quality, some jams and jellies have a shorter shelf life than others. For example, those made with lighter-colored fruits may start to darken noticeably faster than those made with darker fruits. Though this is not a safety concern, the spread will definitely have less visual appeal and less flavor. Over extended periods of time, all spreads undergo significant changes in color, flavor and texture.

Shelf Life of Open Jars

When you open a jar, examine the contents carefully to make sure there are no signs of spoilage. If there is any trace of mold in the jar, or any other indication of other spoilage, discard the contents. If you find a jar that is unsealed or has a very weak seal, do not eat the spread. It is better to be safe than sorry.

Open jars of soft spreads need to be stored in the refrigerator and usually have a shelf life of 3 to 4 weeks. After that, they may begin to darken in color, lose flavor and start to weep. Spreads also become more susceptible to mold growth the longer the jar is open. Leaving open jars at room temperature for an extended period of time will shorten the storage life of the spread. Immediately discard any product that shows any sign of spoilage.

Keep a few screw bands on hand to use when you open a jar of spread and store it in the refrigerator. Plastic refrigerator storage lids specifically designed for canning jars can be purchased at many locations where canning jars are sold.

A Final Word on Food Safety

Bacteria and other microorganisms can be found in all foods and live on surfaces in your kitchen. It is important to eliminate as many of these contaminants as possible when preparing home-canned foods. Store-bought and home-grown fruit should be washed in cool, clear water before canning. Always wash your hands before handling food, and make sure your cooking utensils and work surfaces are clean and sanitized.

The key to safely canning soft spreads lies in processing the jars at a high enough temperature for a long enough time to inhibit the growth of bacteria and other microorganisms. Even though sugar and acid help to preserve the fruit in soft spreads, molds can grow in these products if they are not properly processed. Heat processing creates a vacuum inside the jar and seals the jar so that destructive organisms cannot enter during storage.

To ensure that home-canned spreads are safe to eat, filled jars must be heat processed in a boiling water bath. This step is not optional, as some home canners still believe. Water bath processing takes only 10 minutes, and skipping this crucial step is not worth the health risks to you, your family and your friends.

Single-Fruit Jams

✳

About Single-Fruit Jams

HOMEMADE JAMS HAVE A VIBRANT color and intense flavor that cannot be matched by any store-bought jam. The enticing aromas of homemade jams delight the senses, and the flavors practically leap out of the jars.

The most popular of all soft spreads, and the easiest to prepare, jams are made from crushed or finely chopped fruit. The fruit is cooked with sugar until it becomes softened and translucent and the cooled jam will mound up in a spoon. Adding pectin speeds up the cooking process, allowing the jam to retain more of the natural flavor and color of the fresh fruit.

Jams are thicker than preserves, but not as firm as jellies. You should be able to effortlessly spoon jam out of the jar, and it should mound up in the spoon and hold its shape, yet it should spread easily. There should be no separation of fruit and juice in the spread, and the jam should not be runny.

The recipes in this chapter focus on jams made with one fruit. Many of these are classics, while some are new flavors. In the Mixed-Fruit Jams chapter, you will discover an exciting array of jams that combine two or more fruit flavors to create exciting new taste sensations.

Preventing Floating Fruit

Separation of the fruit pulp and the juice in a jam is a common problem for some home canners. This separation is known as "floating fruit," and is easy to spot. If the top part of a jar of jam contains a dense layer with lots of fruit pieces in it and the bottom part contains a cloudy jelly with no fruit pieces, you have floating fruit.

Floating fruit is usually the result of an imbalance in the ratio of liquid or juice to the amount of fruit pulp in the jam. This can occur if the fruit is particularly juicy or can be caused by added liquid in the recipe. It can also occur if the fruit is cut into pieces that are too large. Large pieces of fruit often do not release the air trapped inside the fruit cells and do not absorb enough sugar to keep the fruit from separating from the juice. As the jam cools, the fruit floats to the top of the jar.

To prevent floating fruit in jams, it is best to cut the fruit into small pieces and then gently crush the pieces with a potato or vegetable masher. This releases the air from the fruit cells so that the fruit will not be filled with air and lighter than the juice, and also allows the fruit to absorb more of the sugar. Absorption of the sugar will turn the fruit translucent and make it shimmer, and will unify the jam in taste and texture. Apples and pears release air and absorb sugar well during cooking and should not be crushed. Cut apples into small pieces about ⅜ inch (0.75 cm) in diameter and pears into pieces about ¼ inch (0.5 cm) in diameter.

Another technique that helps prevent floating fruit is to let the jam sit in the pot for 5 minutes after removing the pot from the heat and before filling the jars. Gently stir the jam every minute or so to help distribute the fruit evenly through the jam.

Preparing Fruit for Jams

Gently rinse fruit under cool running water to remove any dirt or dust. Spread fruit on paper towels in a single layer and gently blot dry. Wash berries just before using and handle them carefully, as they bruise easily. Peel and pit stone fruits, peel and core apples and pears, and hull or stem berries.

To quickly and easily peel peaches and apricots, gently drop the fruit, a few at a time, into a pot of boiling water for 30 seconds. Using a slotted spoon, remove the fruit from the boiling water and immediately plunge them into a bowl or pan of ice water for 1 to 2 minutes to stop the cooking process. Drain the fruit and use a small, sharp paring knife to remove the peels.

Cut peeled fruit into small pieces. Using a potato or vegetable masher, gently crush the fruit, one layer at a time, in a flat-bottomed pan or bowl. Transfer crushed fruit to a measuring cup before adding more fruit and crushing the next layer. Don't get carried away with the masher — you don't want to mash out all the lumps or purée the fruit. Jams should contain lots of small crushed pieces of fruit. (The exception is a seedless berry jam, where the process of removing the seeds creates a puréed berry pulp.) Apples and pears should not be crushed, as they will break down too much during cooking, resulting in a jam with a texture more like a butter.

A food processor should not be used to chop or crush fruit for jams because it is too easy to purée the fruit. Just a couple of seconds can make the difference between fruit that is finely chopped and fruit that is puréed. Puréeing releases too much juice from the fruit and will result in a spread with a texture closer to a butter than a jam. Jams made with puréed fruit tend to either set up quite firm or fail to set. Puréed jams also do not have the same intense flavor or wonderful texture as jams made with crushed fruit. It may take longer to prepare the fruit by hand, but the superior quality of the finished product is well worth the extra time.

Cherries are the exception to the food processor rule. Because of their firm texture, they chop well without easily puréeing. Use the pulse button, a second or two at a time, until the cherry pieces are about ¼ inch (0.5 cm) in diameter.

Adding Pectin

Be sure to use the specific type of pectin called for in the jam recipes. Liquid and powdered pectins have different formulations and different setting properties, and are not interchangeable. Using a different type of pectin than the one called for will result in a jam that does not set. If liquid pectin has been stored in the refrigerator, let it come to room temperature before using. Be sure to squeeze out the entire contents of the liquid pectin pouch into the pan.

Apple Pie Jam

**Makes about
six 8-ounce
(250 mL) jars**

*This wonderful jam
will delight any apple
pie fan. The spice
amounts can be
adjusted to suit your
taste. The amounts
given in the recipe
yield a moderately
spicy jam.*

Tips: When making
jams, choose cooking
apples that have good
flavor, such as Granny
Smith, Jonathan, Rome
Beauty, Winesap,
Northern Spy or
Braeburn.

For 6 cups (1.5 L)
finely chopped apples,
you'll need about
2½ lbs (1.25 kg) or
about 7 medium apples.

6 cups	finely chopped cored peeled Granny Smith apples	1.5 L
1½ cups	unsweetened apple juice	375 mL
1 tbsp	freshly squeezed lemon juice	15 mL
½ tsp	unsalted butter (optional)	2 mL
5 cups	granulated sugar	1.25 L
1¾ tsp	ground cinnamon	8 mL
½ tsp	ground nutmeg	2 mL
1	pouch (3 oz/85 mL) liquid pectin	1

1. Prepare canning jars and lids and bring water in water bath canner to a boil.

2. In an 8-quart (8 L) stainless steel stockpot, combine apples, apple juice, lemon juice and butter, if using. Bring to a boil over medium heat. Reduce heat, cover and simmer for 5 minutes, stirring occasionally.

3. Uncover and gradually add sugar, stirring constantly until sugar is completely dissolved. Stir in cinnamon and nutmeg.

4. Increase heat to medium-high and bring to a full rolling boil, stirring constantly. Stir in pectin. Return to a full rolling boil, stirring constantly, and boil for 1 minute.

5. Remove pot from heat and skim off any foam. Let jam cool in the pot for 5 minutes, stirring occasionally.

6. Ladle hot jam into hot jars, leaving ¼ inch (0.5 cm) headspace. Remove any air bubbles. Wipe jar rims and threads with a clean, damp paper towel. Center hot lids on jars and screw on bands until fingertip-tight.

7. Place jars in canner, making sure they are covered by at least 1 inch (2.5 cm) of water. Cover and bring to a gentle boil. Process 4-ounce (125 mL) jars and 8-ounce (250 mL) jars for 10 minutes; process 1-pint (500 mL) jars for 15 minutes.

8. Remove jars from canner and place on a wire rack or cloth towel. Let cool for 24 hours, then check seals. Wash and dry jars and store in a cool, dry, dark location.

Caramel Apple Jam

✳

**Makes about
six 8-ounce
(250 mL) jars**

*This marvelous jam
is delicious spread on
pancakes or used as a
filling for flaky pastries.*

Tips: Apples should be
at room temperature
before they are prepared.
Cold apples will alter
the cooking time and
the finished texture
of the jam.

For 6 cups (1.5 L) finely
chopped apples, you'll
need about 2½ lbs
(1.25 kg) or about
7 medium apples.

6 cups	finely chopped cored peeled Granny Smith apples	1.5 L
1½ cups	unsweetened apple juice	375 mL
1 tbsp	freshly squeezed lemon juice	15 mL
½ tsp	unsalted butter (optional)	2 mL
3 cups	firmly packed light brown sugar	750 mL
2 cups	granulated sugar	500 mL
1	pouch (3 oz/85 mL) liquid pectin	1

1. Prepare canning jars and lids and bring water in water bath canner to a boil.

2. In an 8-quart (8 L) stainless steel stockpot, combine apples, apple juice, lemon juice and butter, if using. Bring to a boil over medium heat. Reduce heat, cover and simmer for 5 minutes, stirring occasionally.

3. Uncover and gradually add brown sugar and granulated sugar, stirring constantly until sugars are completely dissolved.

4. Increase heat to medium-high and bring to a full rolling boil, stirring constantly. Stir in pectin. Return to a full rolling boil, stirring constantly, and boil for 1 minute.

5. Remove pot from heat and skim off any foam. Let jam cool in the pot for 5 minutes, stirring occasionally.

6. Ladle hot jam into hot jars, leaving ¼ inch (0.5 cm) headspace. Remove any air bubbles. Wipe jar rims and threads with a clean, damp paper towel. Center hot lids on jars and screw on bands until fingertip-tight.

7. Place jars in canner, making sure they are covered by at least 1 inch (2.5 cm) of water. Cover and bring to a gentle boil. Process 4-ounce (125 mL) jars and 8-ounce (250 mL) jars for 10 minutes; process 1-pint (500 mL) jars for 15 minutes.

8. Remove jars from canner and place on a wire rack or cloth towel. Let cool for 24 hours, then check seals. Wash and dry jars and store in a cool, dry, dark location.

Apricot Jam

**Makes eight or
nine 8-ounce
(250 mL) jars**

*Packed with fresh
apricot flavor, this jam
is a real winner.*

Tips: Peeling the
apricots gives this jam
a smoother texture
and a stronger flavor.

For 4½ cups (1.125 L)
crushed apricots, you'll
need about 4 lbs (2 kg)
medium apricots.

4½ cups	crushed pitted peeled apricots	1.125 L
¼ cup	freshly squeezed lemon juice	50 mL
1	box (1.75 oz/49 to 57 g) regular powdered fruit pectin	1
6⅓ cups	granulated sugar, divided	1.575 L
½ tsp	unsalted butter (optional)	2 ml

1. Prepare canning jars and lids and bring water in water bath canner to a boil.

2. In an 8-quart (8 L) stainless steel stockpot, combine apricots and lemon juice.

3. In a small bowl, combine pectin and ¼ cup (50 mL) of the sugar. Gradually stir into the fruit. Add butter, if using.

4. Bring fruit mixture to a full rolling boil over medium-high heat, stirring constantly. Gradually stir in the remaining sugar. Return to a full rolling boil, stirring constantly, and boil for 1 minute.

5. Remove pot from heat and skim off any foam. Let jam cool in the pot for 5 minutes, stirring occasionally.

6. Ladle hot jam into hot jars, leaving ¼ inch (0.5 cm) headspace. Remove any air bubbles. Wipe jar rims and threads with a clean, damp paper towel. Center hot lids on jars and screw on bands until fingertip-tight.

7. Place jars in canner, making sure they are covered by at least 1 inch (2.5 cm) of water. Cover and bring to a gentle boil. Process 4-ounce (125 mL) jars and 8-ounce (250 mL) jars for 10 minutes; process 1-pint (500 mL) jars for 15 minutes.

8. Remove jars from canner and place on a wire rack or cloth towel. Let cool for 24 hours, then check seals. Wash and dry jars and store in a cool, dry, dark location.

Almond Apricot Jam

*The touch of almond
flavor enhances the
apricot flavor in this
delightful jam.*

Tips: Choose
unblemished apricots
with good color. Avoid
apricots that are pale
yellow, very firm or very
soft, as these will not
produce a spread with a
strong apricot flavor.

For 4 cups (1 L) crushed
apricots, you'll need
about 4 lbs (2 kg)
medium apricots.

4 cups	crushed pitted peeled apricots	1 L
6 tbsp	freshly squeezed lemon juice	90 mL
6 cups	granulated sugar	1.5 L
½ tsp	unsalted butter (optional)	2 mL
1	pouch (3 oz/85 mL) liquid pectin	1
1 tsp	pure almond extract	5 mL

1. Prepare canning jars and lids and bring water in water bath canner to a boil.

2. In an 8-quart (8 L) stainless steel stockpot, combine apricots and lemon juice. Gradually stir in sugar and butter, if using. Bring to a boil over medium heat, stirring constantly until sugar is completely dissolved.

3. Increase heat to medium-high and bring to a full rolling boil, stirring constantly. Stir in pectin. Return to a full rolling boil, stirring constantly, and boil for 1 minute.

4. Remove pot from heat and skim off any foam. Stir in almond extract. Let jam cool in the pot for 5 minutes, stirring occasionally.

5. Ladle hot jam into hot jars, leaving ¼ inch (0.5 cm) headspace. Remove any air bubbles. Wipe jar rims and threads with a clean, damp paper towel. Center hot lids on jars and screw on bands until fingertip-tight.

6. Place jars in canner, making sure they are covered by at least 1 inch (2.5 cm) of water. Cover and bring to a gentle boil. Process 4-ounce (125 mL) jars and 8-ounce (250 mL) jars for 10 minutes; process 1-pint (500 mL) jars for 15 minutes.

7. Remove jars from canner and place on a wire rack or cloth towel. Let cool for 24 hours, then check seals. Wash and dry jars and store in a cool, dry, dark location.

Blackberry Jam

✳

*For a special treat, use
this amazing jam as a
filling for thumbprint
jam cookies.*

Tips: To reduce the
amount of seeds in the
finished jam, press
about one-quarter of the
crushed berries through
a fine-mesh sieve
before measuring.

Each 16-oz (454 g) bag
of frozen unsweetened
blackberries will yield
about 1¾ cups (425 mL)
crushed blackberries.

For 5 cups (1.25 L)
crushed blackberries,
you'll need about 3 lbs
(1.5 kg) or 8 cups (2 L)
blackberries.

5 cups	crushed blackberries	1.25 L
1	box (1.75 oz/49 to 57 g) regular powdered fruit pectin	1
6⅓ cups	granulated sugar, divided	1.575 L
½ tsp	unsalted butter (optional)	2 mL

1. Prepare canning jars and lids and bring water in water bath canner to a boil.
2. Pour blackberries into an 8-quart (8 L) stainless steel stockpot.
3. In a small bowl, combine pectin and ¼ cup (50 mL) of the sugar. Gradually stir into the fruit. Add butter, if using.
4. Bring fruit mixture to a full rolling boil over medium-high heat, stirring constantly. Gradually stir in the remaining sugar. Return to a full rolling boil, stirring constantly, and boil for 1 minute.
5. Remove pot from heat and skim off any foam. Let jam cool in the pot for 5 minutes, stirring occasionally.
6. Ladle hot jam into hot jars, leaving ¼ inch (0.5 cm) headspace. Remove any air bubbles. Wipe jar rims and threads with a clean, damp paper towel. Center hot lids on jars and screw on bands until fingertip-tight.
7. Place jars in canner, making sure they are covered by at least 1 inch (2.5 cm) of water. Cover and bring to a gentle boil. Process 4-ounce (125 mL) jars and 8-ounce (250 mL) jars for 10 minutes; process 1-pint (500 mL) jars for 15 minutes.
8. Remove jars from canner and place on a wire rack or cloth towel. Let cool for 24 hours, then check seals. Wash and dry jars and store in a cool, dry, dark location.

Seedless Blackberry Jam

9 cups	fresh blackberries	2.25 L
6¾ cups	granulated sugar	1.675 L
½ tsp	unsalted butter (optional)	2 mL
1	pouch (3 oz/85 mL) liquid pectin	1

Makes six or seven 8-ounce (250 mL) jars

This is a great jam for people who prefer a berry jam without seeds.

Tips: If you use a food mill to crush and seed the berries, fit it with the finest plate.

Defrosted frozen blackberries also make great seedless jam. Each 16-oz (454 g) bag of frozen unsweetened blackberries will yield about 1⅓ cups (325 mL) seedless blackberry pulp.

Variation

Seedless Boysenberry Jam: Substitute crushed seeded boysenberries for the blackberries.

1. Prepare canning jars and lids and bring water in water bath canner to a boil.

2. In a flat-bottomed pan or bowl, crush blackberries in small batches. Using the back of a spoon, press crushed blackberries through a fine-mesh sieve to remove the seeds. (Or use a food mill to crush the fruit and remove the seeds.) Measure 3¾ cups (925 mL) seedless blackberry pulp.

3. In an 8-quart (8 L) stainless steel stockpot, combine blackberry pulp, sugar and butter, if using. Bring to a boil over medium heat, stirring constantly until sugar is completely dissolved.

4. Increase heat to medium-high and bring to a full rolling boil, stirring constantly. Stir in pectin. Return to a full rolling boil, stirring constantly, and boil for 1 minute.

5. Remove pot from heat and skim off any foam. Let jam cool in the pot for 5 minutes, stirring occasionally.

6. Ladle hot jam into hot jars, leaving ¼ inch (0.5 cm) headspace. Remove any air bubbles. Wipe jar rims and threads with a clean, damp paper towel. Center hot lids on jars and screw on bands until fingertip-tight.

7. Place jars in canner, making sure they are covered by at least 1 inch (2.5 cm) of water. Cover and bring to a gentle boil. Process 4-ounce (125 mL) jars and 8-ounce (250 mL) jars for 10 minutes; process 1-pint (500 mL) jars for 15 minutes.

8. Remove jars from canner and place on a wire rack or cloth towel. Let cool for 24 hours, then check seals. Wash and dry jars and store in a cool, dry, dark location.

Blueberry Jam

※

*Take advantage of
fresh blueberry season
to make a batch or
two of heavenly
Blueberry Jam.*

Tips: Fresh or defrosted
frozen blueberries both
work well in this recipe.

Each 12-oz (340 g) bag
of frozen unsweetened
blueberries will yield
about 1⅓ cups (325 mL)
crushed blueberries.

For 4 cups (1 L) crushed
blueberries, you'll need
about 2½ lbs (1.25 kg)
or 6 cups (1.5 L)
blueberries.

4 cups	crushed blueberries	1 L
1 tbsp	freshly squeezed lemon juice	15 mL
1	box (1.75 oz/49 to 57 g) regular powdered fruit pectin	1
4 cups	granulated sugar, divided	1 L
½ tsp	unsalted butter (optional)	2 mL

1. Prepare canning jars and lids and bring water in water bath canner to a boil.

2. In an 8-quart (8 L) stainless steel stockpot, combine blueberries and lemon juice.

3. In a small bowl, combine pectin and ¼ cup (50 mL) of the sugar. Gradually stir into fruit. Add butter, if using.

4. Bring fruit mixture to a full rolling boil over medium-high heat, stirring constantly. Gradually stir in the remaining sugar. Return to a full rolling boil, stirring constantly, and boil for 1 minute.

5. Remove pot from heat and skim off any foam. Let jam cool in the pot for 5 minutes, stirring occasionally.

6. Ladle hot jam into hot jars, leaving ¼ inch (0.5 cm) headspace. Remove any air bubbles. Wipe jar rims and threads with a clean, damp paper towel. Center hot lids on jars and screw on bands until fingertip-tight.

7. Place jars in canner, making sure they are covered by at least 1 inch (2.5 cm) of water. Cover and bring to a gentle boil. Process 4-ounce (125 mL) jars and 8-ounce (250 mL) jars for 10 minutes; process 1-pint (500 mL) jars for 15 minutes.

8. Remove jars from canner and place on a wire rack or cloth towel. Let cool for 24 hours, then check seals. Wash and dry jars and store in a cool, dry, dark location.

Boysenberry Jam

When my boysenberry vines are overflowing with ripe sweet berries, I head for the kitchen to make batches of this incredible family favorite.

Tips: To reduce the amount of seeds in the finished jam, press about one-quarter of the crushed berries through a fine-mesh sieve before measuring.

Each 16-oz (454 g) bag of frozen unsweetened boysenberries will yield about 1¾ cups (425 mL) crushed boysenberries.

For 5 cups (1.25 L) crushed boysenberries, you'll need about 3 lbs (1.5 kg) or 8 cups (2 L) boysenberries.

5 cups	crushed boysenberries	1.25 L
1	box (1.75 oz/49 to 57 g) regular powdered fruit pectin	1
6⅓ cups	granulated sugar, divided	1.575 L
½ tsp	unsalted butter (optional)	2 mL

1. Prepare canning jars and lids and bring water in water bath canner to a boil.

2. Pour boysenberries into an 8-quart (8 L) stainless steel stockpot.

3. In a small bowl, combine pectin and ¼ cup (50 mL) of the sugar. Gradually stir into fruit. Add butter, if using.

4. Bring fruit mixture to a full rolling boil over medium-high heat, stirring constantly. Gradually stir in the remaining sugar. Return to a full rolling boil, stirring constantly, and boil for 1 minute.

5. Remove pot from heat and skim off any foam. Let jam cool in the pot for 5 minutes, stirring occasionally.

6. Ladle hot jam into hot jars, leaving ¼ inch (0.5 cm) headspace. Remove any air bubbles. Wipe jar rims and threads with a clean, damp paper towel. Center hot lids on jars and screw on bands until fingertip-tight.

7. Place jars in canner, making sure they are covered by at least 1 inch (2.5 cm) of water. Cover and bring to a gentle boil. Process 4-ounce (125 mL) jars and 8-ounce (250 mL) jars for 10 minutes; process 1-pint (500 mL) jars for 15 minutes.

8. Remove jars from canner and place on a wire rack or cloth towel. Let cool for 24 hours, then check seals. Wash and dry jars and store in a cool, dry, dark location.

Cherry Pie Jam

✳

*This jam is like cherry
pie in a jar!*

Tips: A cherry pitter
makes quick work of
removing pits from
cherries. Handheld
cherry pitters are
available in most
kitchen supply stores
and some grocery
stores. Many stores
also carry more
elaborate cherry pitters,
which can really come
in handy when you're
pitting large quantities
of cherries.

For 4 cups (1 L) finely
chopped cherries, you'll
need about 3½ lbs
(1.75 kg) cherries.

4 cups	finely chopped pitted fresh sour cherries	1 L
1 tbsp	freshly squeezed lemon juice	15 mL
1	box (1.75 oz/49 to 57 g) regular powdered fruit pectin	1
4¾ cups	granulated sugar, divided	1.175 l
½ tsp	unsalted butter (optional)	2 mL
1½ tsp	pure almond extract	7 mL

1. Prepare canning jars and lids and bring water in water bath canner to a boil.

2. In an 8-quart (8 L) stainless steel stockpot, combine cherries and lemon juice.

3. In a small bowl, combine pectin and ¼ cup (50 mL) of the sugar. Gradually stir into fruit. Add butter, if using.

4. Bring fruit mixture to a full rolling boil over medium-high heat, stirring constantly. Gradually stir in the remaining sugar. Return to a full rolling boil, stirring constantly, and boil for 1 minute.

5. Remove pot from heat and skim off any foam. Stir in almond extract. Let jam cool in the pot for 5 minutes, stirring occasionally.

6. Ladle hot jam into hot jars, leaving ¼ inch (0.5 cm) headspace. Remove any air bubbles. Wipe jar rims and threads with a clean, damp paper towel. Center hot lids on jars and screw on bands until fingertip-tight.

7. Place jars in canner, making sure they are covered by at least 1 inch (2.5 cm) of water. Cover and bring to a gentle boil. Process 4-ounce (125 mL) jars and 8-ounce (250 mL) jars for 10 minutes; process 1-pint (500 mL) jars for 15 minutes.

8. Remove jars from canner and place on a wire rack or cloth towel. Let cool for 24 hours, then check seals. Wash and dry jars and store in a cool, dry, dark location.

Sweet Cherry Jam

✳

**Makes about
six 8-ounce
(250 mL) jars**

*Intensely flavorful,
this heavenly jam is
a favorite among my
family and friends.
The hint of almond
complements the
cherries and gives the
jam a depth of flavor.
If you cannot find
fresh Bing cherries,
other varieties of sweet
cherries may be used.*

Tips: Pulse cherries in
a food processor for a
few seconds at a time
until pieces are about
¼ inch (0.5 cm) in size.
Be careful not to purée
the cherries.

For 4 cups (1 L) finely
chopped cherries,
you'll need about 3 lbs
(1.5 kg) cherries.

4 cups	finely chopped pitted fresh Bing cherries	1 L
½ cup	freshly squeezed lemon juice	125 mL
1	box (1.75 oz/49 to 57 g) regular powdered fruit pectin	1
4¾ cups	granulated sugar, divided	1.175 L
½ tsp	unsalted butter (optional)	2 mL
1 tsp	pure almond extract	5 mL

1. Prepare canning jars and lids and bring water in water bath canner to a boil.

2. In an 8-quart (8 L) stainless steel stockpot, combine cherries and lemon juice.

3. In a small bowl, combine pectin and ¼ cup (50 mL) of the sugar. Gradually stir into fruit. Add butter, if using.

4. Bring fruit mixture to a full rolling boil over medium-high heat, stirring constantly. Gradually stir in the remaining sugar. Return to a full rolling boil, stirring constantly, and boil for 1 minute.

5. Remove pot from heat and skim off any foam. Stir in almond extract. Let jam cool in the pot for 5 minutes, stirring occasionally.

6. Ladle hot jam into hot jars, leaving ¼ inch (0.5 cm) headspace. Remove any air bubbles. Wipe jar rims and threads with a clean, damp paper towel. Center hot lids on jars and screw on bands until fingertip-tight.

7. Place jars in canner, making sure they are covered by at least 1 inch (2.5 cm) of water. Cover and bring to a gentle boil. Process 4-ounce (125 mL) jars and 8-ounce (250 mL) jars for 10 minutes; process 1-pint (500 mL) jars for 15 minutes.

8. Remove jars from canner and place on a wire rack or cloth towel. Let cool for 24 hours, then check seals. Wash and dry jars and store in a cool, dry, dark location.

Nectarine Jam

Makes about seven 8-ounce (250 mL) jars

Sweet nectarines make an exceptional jam.

Tips: If nectarines reach ripeness before you are ready to use them, they may be stored in the refrigerator for a few days. Let them warm to room temperature before using.

For 4 cups (1 L) crushed nectarines, you'll need about 4 lbs (2 kg) or about 12 medium nectarines.

4 cups	crushed pitted peeled nectarines	1 L
2 tbsp	freshly squeezed lemon juice	30 mL
1	box (1.75 oz/49 to 57 g) regular powdered fruit pectin	1
5½ cups	granulated sugar, divided	1.375 L
½ tsp	unsalted butter (optional)	2 mL

1. Prepare canning jars and lids and bring water in water bath canner to a boil.

2. In an 8-quart (8 L) stainless steel stockpot, combine nectarines and lemon juice.

3. In a small bowl, combine pectin and ¼ cup (50 mL) of the sugar. Gradually stir into fruit. Add butter, if using.

4. Bring fruit mixture to a full rolling boil over medium-high heat, stirring constantly. Gradually stir in the remaining sugar. Return to a full rolling boil, stirring constantly, and boil for 1 minute.

5. Remove pot from heat and skim off any foam. Let jam cool in the pot for 5 minutes, stirring occasionally.

6. Ladle hot jam into hot jars, leaving ¼ inch (0.5 cm) headspace. Remove any air bubbles. Wipe jar rims and threads with a clean, damp paper towel. Center hot lids on jars and screw on bands until fingertip-tight.

7. Place jars in canner, making sure they are covered by at least 1 inch (2.5 cm) of water. Cover and bring to a gentle boil. Process 4-ounce (125 mL) jars and 8-ounce (250 mL) jars for 10 minutes; process 1-pint (500 mL) jars for 15 minutes.

8. Remove jars from canner and place on a wire rack or cloth towel. Let cool for 24 hours, then check seals. Wash and dry jars and store in a cool, dry, dark location.

Olallieberry Jam

Makes about
eight 8-ounce
(250 mL) jars

4 cups	crushed olallieberries	1 L
7 cups	granulated sugar	1.75 L
½ tsp	unsalted butter (optional)	2 mL
1	pouch (3 oz/85 mL) liquid pectin	1

Olallieberries, a flavorful cross between a blackberry and a loganberry, are great for making jam. Loganberries, which are a cross between a blackberry and a boysenberry, also make a jam with intense flavor.

Tips: To reduce the amount of seeds in the finished jam, press about one-quarter of the crushed berries through a fine-mesh sieve before measuring.

For 4 cups (1 L) crushed olallieberries, you'll need about 2½ lbs (1.25 kg) or 7 cups (1.7 L) olallieberries.

Variation

Loganberry Jam: Substitute crushed loganberries for the olallieberries.

1. Prepare canning jars and lids and bring water in water bath canner to a boil.

2. In an 8-quart (8 L) stainless steel stockpot, combine olallieberries, sugar and butter, if using. Bring to a boil over medium heat, stirring constantly until sugar is completely dissolved.

3. Increase heat to medium-high and bring to a full rolling boil, stirring constantly. Stir in pectin. Return to a full rolling boil, stirring constantly, and boil for 1 minute.

4. Remove pot from heat and skim off any foam. Let jam cool in the pot for 5 minutes, stirring occasionally.

5. Ladle hot jam into hot jars, leaving ¼ inch (0.5 cm) headspace. Remove any air bubbles. Wipe jar rims and threads with a clean, damp paper towel. Center hot lids on jars and screw on bands until fingertip-tight.

6. Place jars in canner, making sure they are covered by at least 1 inch (2.5 cm) of water. Cover and bring to a gentle boil. Process 4-ounce (125 mL) jars and 8-ounce (250 mL) jars for 10 minutes; process 1-pint (500 mL) jars for 15 minutes.

7. Remove jars from canner and place on a wire rack or cloth towel. Let cool for 24 hours, then check seals. Wash and dry jars and store in a cool, dry, dark location.

60   SINGLE-FRUIT JAMS

Peach Jam

Makes about seven 8-ounce (250 mL) jars

The flavor of fresh peaches really comes through in this gorgeous jam.

Tips: Yellow-fleshed peaches make the best-tasting jam. White-fleshed peaches make a mild-flavored jam with a softer set.

For 4 cups (1 L) crushed peaches, you'll need about 4 lbs (2 kg) or about 12 medium peaches.

4 cups	crushed pitted peeled peaches	1 L
2 tbsp	freshly squeezed lemon juice	30 mL
1	box (1.75 oz/49 to 57 g) regular powdered fruit pectin	1
5½ cups	granulated sugar, divided	1.375 mL
½ tsp	unsalted butter (optional)	2 mL

1. Prepare canning jars and lids and bring water in water bath canner to a boil.

2. In an 8-quart (8 L) stainless steel stockpot, combine peaches and lemon juice.

3. In a small bowl, combine pectin and ¼ cup (50 mL) of the sugar. Gradually stir into fruit. Add butter, if using.

4. Bring fruit mixture to a full rolling boil over medium-high heat, stirring constantly. Gradually stir in the remaining sugar. Return to a full rolling boil, stirring constantly, and boil for 1 minute.

5. Remove pot from heat and skim off any foam. Let jam cool in the pot for 5 minutes, stirring occasionally.

6. Ladle hot jam into hot jars, leaving ¼ inch (0.5 cm) headspace. Remove any air bubbles. Wipe jar rims and threads with a clean, damp paper towel. Center hot lids on jars and screw on bands until fingertip-tight.

7. Place jars in canner, making sure they are covered by at least 1 inch (2.5 cm) of water. Cover and bring to a gentle boil. Process 4-ounce (125 mL) jars and 8-ounce (250 mL) jars for 10 minutes; process 1-pint (500 mL) jars for 15 minutes.

8. Remove jars from canner and place on a wire rack or cloth towel. Let cool for 24 hours, then check seals. Wash and dry jars and store in a cool, dry, dark location.

Summertime Peach Vanilla Bean Jam

✳

Makes about seven 8-ounce (250 mL) jars

Fragrant vanilla bean sugar enhances the flavor of the peaches, making this jam a tantalizing topping for French toast or ice cream.

Tips: For 4 cups (1 L) crushed peaches, you'll need about 4 lbs (2 kg) or about 12 medium peaches.

To make vanilla bean sugar: Measure 7 cups (1.75 L) granulated sugar into a large bowl or container. Split 2 vanilla beans in half lengthwise. Gently scrape inside of vanilla pods to release some seeds into the sugar. Cut pods into 1-inch (2.5 cm) pieces. Add to sugar and stir until well combined. Cover tightly with lid or plastic wrap. Let stand for 48 hours, stirring once or twice a day. Sift sugar through a sieve to remove pods and break up any lumps of sugar. Save pods for making more vanilla sugar or other uses. Makes 7 cups (1.75 L).

4 cups	crushed pitted peeled peaches	1 L
2 tbsp	freshly squeezed lemon juice	30 mL
7 cups	vanilla bean sugar (see tip, at left)	1.75 L
½ tsp	unsalted butter (optional)	2 mL
1	pouch (3 oz/85 mL) liquid pectin	1

1. Prepare canning jars and lids and bring water in water bath canner to a boil.

2. In an 8-quart (8 L) stainless steel stockpot, combine peaches and lemon juice. Gradually stir in vanilla bean sugar and butter, if using. Bring to a boil over medium heat, stirring constantly until sugar is completely dissolved.

3. Increase heat to medium-high and bring to a full rolling boil, stirring constantly. Stir in pectin. Return to a full rolling boil, stirring constantly, and boil for 1 minute.

4. Remove pot from heat and skim off any foam. Let jam cool in the pot for 5 minutes, stirring occasionally.

5. Ladle hot jam into hot jars, leaving ¼ inch (0.5 cm) headspace. Remove any air bubbles. Wipe jar rims and threads with a clean, damp paper towel. Center hot lids on jars and screw on bands until fingertip-tight.

6. Place jars in canner, making sure they are covered by at least 1 inch (2.5 cm) of water. Cover and bring to a gentle boil. Process 4-ounce (125 mL) jars and 8-ounce (250 mL) jars for 10 minutes; process 1-pint (500 mL) jars for 15 minutes.

7. Remove jars from canner and place on a wire rack or cloth towel. Let cool for 24 hours, then check seals. Wash and dry jars and store in a cool, dry, dark location.

Pear Jam

✳

*Bartlett pears have
excellent flavor and
texture and make
a lovely jam.*

Tips: Use unbruised
pears that are golden-
yellow in color, yield to
gentle pressure and
have a strong pear
aroma. Avoid using
soft, overripe pears,
as they will fall apart
when cooked and the
jam may not set. Firm,
underripe pears lack
flavor and will give the
jam an unpleasant
grainy texture.

To keep pears from
turning brown, peel
and chop them just
before making the jam
and immediately
combine them with
the lemon juice.

For 4 cups (1 L)
finely chopped pears,
you'll need about
4 lbs (2 kg) or about
12 medium pears.

4 cups	finely chopped cored peeled Bartlett pears	1 L
3 tbsp	freshly squeezed lemon juice	45 mL
1	box (1.75 oz/49 to 57 g) regular powdered fruit pectin	1
5 cups	granulated sugar, divided	1.25 L
½ tsp	unsalted butter (optional)	2 mL

1. Prepare canning jars and lids and bring water in water bath canner to a boil.

2. In an 8-quart (8 L) stainless steel stockpot, combine pears and lemon juice.

3. In a small bowl, combine pectin and ¼ cup (50 mL) of the sugar. Gradually stir into fruit. Add butter, if using.

4. Bring fruit mixture to a full rolling boil over medium-high heat, stirring constantly. Gradually stir in the remaining sugar. Return to a full rolling boil, stirring constantly, and boil for 1 minute.

5. Remove pot from heat and skim off any foam. Let jam cool in the pot for 5 minutes, stirring occasionally.

6. Ladle hot jam into hot jars, leaving ¼ inch (0.5 cm) headspace. Remove any air bubbles. Wipe jar rims and threads with a clean, damp paper towel. Center hot lids on jars and screw on bands until fingertip-tight.

7. Place jars in canner, making sure they are covered by at least 1 inch (2.5 cm) of water. Cover and bring to a gentle boil. Process 4-ounce (125 mL) jars and 8-ounce (250 mL) jars for 10 minutes; process 1-pint (500 mL) jars for 15 minutes.

8. Remove jars from canner and place on a wire rack or cloth towel. Let cool for 24 hours, then check seals. Wash and dry jars and store in a cool, dry, dark location.

Pineapple Jam

✳

**Makes about
six 8-ounce
(250 mL) jars**

*Add a tropical treat to
your breakfast table!*

Tips: Fresh pineapples
contain an enzyme
that inhibits jam from
setting. It is always best
to use canned pineapple
in jam recipes.

A 20-oz can (567 mL)
of crushed pineapple
will yield about
1 1/8 cups (280 mL)
drained pineapple. If
using a can size other
than 20 oz (567 mL),
you will need 3 3/8 cups
(840 mL) drained
crushed pineapple for
this recipe.

3	cans (each 20 oz/567 mL) juice-packed crushed pineapple, drained (see tip, at left)	3
1/3 cup	freshly squeezed lemon juice	75 mL
1	box (1.75 oz/49 to 57 g) regular powdered fruit pectin	1
5 cups	granulated sugar, divided	1.25 L
1/2 tsp	unsalted butter (optional)	2 mL

1. Prepare canning jars and lids and bring water in water bath canner to a boil.

2. In an 8-quart (8 L) stainless steel stockpot, combine pineapple and lemon juice.

3. In a small bowl, combine pectin and 1/4 cup (50 mL) of the sugar. Gradually stir into fruit. Add butter, if using.

4. Bring fruit mixture to a full rolling boil over medium-high heat, stirring constantly. Gradually stir in the remaining sugar. Return to a full rolling boil, stirring constantly, and boil for 1 minute.

5. Remove pot from heat and skim off any foam. Let jam cool in the pot for 5 minutes, stirring occasionally.

6. Ladle hot jam into hot jars, leaving 1/4 inch (0.5 cm) headspace. Remove any air bubbles. Wipe jar rims and threads with a clean, damp paper towel. Center hot lids on jars and screw on bands until fingertip-tight.

7. Place jars in canner, making sure they are covered by at least 1 inch (2.5 cm) of water. Cover and bring to a gentle boil. Process 4-ounce (125 mL) jars and 8-ounce (250 mL) jars for 10 minutes; process 1-pint (500 mL) jars for 15 minutes.

8. Remove jars from canner and place on a wire rack or cloth towel. Let cool for 24 hours, then check seals. Wash and dry jars and store in a cool, dry, dark location.

Plum Jam (page 65)

Overleaf: Pineapple Jam (page 64)
and Blueberry Jam (page 55)

Plum Jam

✳

**Makes about
seven 8-ounce
(250 mL) jars**

4 cups	crushed pitted peeled plums	1 L
6⅔ cups	granulated sugar	1.65 L
½ tsp	unsalted butter (optional)	2 mL
1	pouch (3 oz/85 mL) liquid pectin	1

*This jam is dazzling in
both texture and flavor.*

Tips: Plum skins turn
tough and bitter when
cooked. Peeling the
plums produces a jam
with a smooth, silky
texture and an amazing
flavor. The results are
definitely worth the extra
effort. See page 30 for
peeling instructions.

For 4 cups (1 L) crushed
plums, you'll need
about 3½ lbs (1.75 kg)
medium plums.

1. Prepare canning jars and lids and bring water in water bath canner to a boil.

2. In an 8-quart (8 L) stainless steel stockpot, combine plums, sugar and butter, if using. Bring to a boil over medium heat, stirring constantly until sugar is completely dissolved.

3. Increase heat to medium-high and bring to a full rolling boil, stirring constantly. Stir in pectin. Return to a full rolling boil, stirring constantly, and boil for 1 minute.

4. Remove pot from heat and skim off any foam. Let jam cool in the pot for 5 minutes, stirring occasionally.

5. Ladle hot jam into hot jars, leaving ¼ inch (0.5 cm) headspace. Remove any air bubbles. Wipe jar rims and threads with a clean, damp paper towel. Center hot lids on jars and screw on bands until fingertip-tight.

6. Place jars in canner, making sure they are covered by at least 1 inch (2.5 cm) of water. Cover and bring to a gentle boil. Process 4-ounce (125 mL) jars and 8-ounce (250 mL) jars for 10 minutes; process 1-pint (500 mL) jars for 15 minutes.

7. Remove jars from canner and place on a wire rack or cloth towel. Let cool for 24 hours, then check seals. Wash and dry jars and store in a cool, dry, dark location.

Overleaf: Pear Lime Jam
(page 88)

Orange Strawberry Jam
(page 84)

Red Raspberry Jam

5 cups	crushed red raspberries	1.25 L
1 tbsp	freshly squeezed lemon juice	15 mL
1	box (1.75 oz/49 to 57 g) regular powdered fruit pectin	1
7 cups	granulated sugar, divided	1.75 L
½ tsp	unsalted butter (optional)	2 mL

Makes about nine 8-ounce (250 mL) jars

This jam makes a scrumptious filling for tender bar cookies.

Tips: To reduce the amount of seeds in the finished jam, press about one-quarter of the crushed berries through a fine-mesh sieve before measuring.

Each 12-oz (340 g) bag of frozen unsweetened raspberries will yield about 1½ cups (375 mL) crushed raspberries before sieving.

For 5 cups (1.25 L) crushed raspberries, you'll need about 3 lbs (1.5 kg) or 12 cups (3 L) raspberries.

1. Prepare canning jars and lids and bring water in water bath canner to a boil.

2. In an 8-quart (8 L) stainless steel stockpot, combine raspberries and lemon juice.

3. In a small bowl, combine pectin and ¼ cup (50 mL) of the sugar. Gradually stir into fruit. Add butter, if using.

4. Bring fruit mixture to a full rolling boil over medium-high heat, stirring constantly. Gradually stir in the remaining sugar. Return to a full rolling boil, stirring constantly, and boil for 1 minute.

5. Remove pot from heat and skim off any foam. Let jam cool in the pot for 5 minutes, stirring occasionally.

6. Ladle hot jam into hot jars, leaving ¼ inch (0.5 cm) headspace. Remove any air bubbles. Wipe jar rims and threads with a clean, damp paper towel. Center hot lids on jars and screw on bands until fingertip-tight.

7. Place jars in canner, making sure they are covered by at least 1 inch (2.5 cm) of water. Cover and bring to a gentle boil. Process 4-ounce (125 mL) jars and 8-ounce (250 mL) jars for 10 minutes; process 1-pint (500 mL) jars for 15 minutes.

8. Remove jars from canner and place on a wire rack or cloth towel. Let cool for 24 hours, then check seals. Wash and dry jars and store in a cool, dry, dark location.

Seedless Raspberry Jam

✳

Makes about seven 8-ounce (250 mL) jars

All of the intense flavor of raspberry jam, but without the seeds!

Tips: If you use a food mill to crush and seed the berries, fit it with the finest plate.

Defrosted frozen raspberries also make great seedless jam. Each 12-oz (340 g) bag of frozen unsweetened raspberries will yield about 1 cup (250 mL) seedless raspberry pulp.

12 cups	fresh raspberries	3 L
1 tbsp	freshly squeezed lemon juice	15 mL
6½ cups	granulated sugar	1.625 L
½ tsp	unsalted butter (optional)	2 mL
1	pouch (3 oz/85 mL) liquid pectin	1

1. Prepare canning jars and lids and bring water in water bath canner to a boil.

2. In a flat-bottomed pan or bowl, crush raspberries in small batches. Using the back of a spoon, press crushed raspberries through a fine-mesh sieve to remove the seeds. (Or use a food mill to crush the fruit and remove the seeds.) Measure 3¾ cups (925 mL) seedless raspberry pulp.

3. In an 8-quart (8 L) stainless steel stockpot, combine raspberry pulp and lemon juice. Gradually stir in sugar and butter, if using. Bring to a boil over medium heat, stirring constantly until sugar is completely dissolved.

4. Increase heat to medium-high and bring to a full rolling boil, stirring constantly. Stir in pectin. Return to a full rolling boil, stirring constantly, and boil for 1 minute.

5. Remove pot from heat and skim off any foam. Let jam cool in the pot for 5 minutes, stirring occasionally.

6. Ladle hot jam into hot jars, leaving ¼ inch (0.5 cm) headspace. Remove any air bubbles. Wipe jar rims and threads with a clean, damp paper towel. Center hot lids on jars and screw on bands until fingertip-tight.

7. Place jars in canner, making sure they are covered by at least 1 inch (2.5 cm) of water. Cover and bring to a gentle boil. Process 4-ounce (125 mL) jars and 8-ounce (250 mL) jars for 10 minutes; process 1-pint (500 mL) jars for 15 minutes.

8. Remove jars from canner and place on a wire rack or cloth towel. Let cool for 24 hours, then check seals. Wash and dry jars and store in a cool, dry, dark location.

Strawberry Jam

This classic jam has a beautiful color and is bursting with fresh strawberry flavor.

Tips: A tomato huller quickly and easily removes the caps from the strawberries; it works much better than a strawberry huller.

For 5 cups (1.25 L) crushed strawberries, you'll need about 3½ lbs (1.75 kg) or 10 cups (2.5 L) strawberries.

5 cups	crushed hulled strawberries	1.25 L
2 tbsp	freshly squeezed lemon juice	30 mL
1	box (1.75 oz/49 to 57 g) regular powdered fruit pectin	1
7 cups	granulated sugar, divided	1.75 L
½ tsp	unsalted butter (optional)	2 mL

1. Prepare canning jars and lids and bring water in water bath canner to a boil.

2. In an 8-quart (8 L) stainless steel stockpot, combine strawberries and lemon juice.

3. In a small bowl, combine pectin and ¼ cup (50 mL) of the sugar. Gradually stir into fruit. Add butter, if using.

4. Bring fruit mixture to a full rolling boil over medium-high heat, stirring constantly. Gradually stir in the remaining sugar. Return to a full rolling boil, stirring constantly, and boil for 1 minute.

5. Remove pot from heat and skim off any foam. Let jam cool in the pot for 5 minutes, stirring occasionally.

6. Ladle hot jam into hot jars, leaving ¼ inch (0.5 cm) headspace. Remove any air bubbles. Wipe jar rims and threads with a clean, damp paper towel. Center hot lids on jars and screw on bands until fingertip-tight.

7. Place jars in canner, making sure they are covered by at least 1 inch (2.5 cm) of water. Cover and bring to a gentle boil. Process 4-ounce (125 mL) jars and 8-ounce (250 mL) jars for 10 minutes; process 1-pint (500 mL) jars for 15 minutes.

8. Remove jars from canner and place on a wire rack or cloth towel. Let cool for 24 hours, then check seals. Wash and dry jars and store in a cool, dry, dark location.

Mixed-Fruit Jams

✳

About Mixed-Fruit Jams

MIXED-FRUIT JAMS ARE a category of spread that is rapidly gaining in popularity. The tantalizing combinations of fruit produce complex flavors not found in single-fruit jams. The key to a successful mixed-fruit jam is to balance the flavors of the fruit so that the jam has a pleasing blend in which no one fruit overpowers another and the flavor of each fruit shines through. In some of the jam recipes in this chapter, the flavor of one fruit will take the lead, with the other fruit as the finishing flavor. In other jams, both flavors will come through together. There are even recipes that combine three or more fruits into one jam.

All of the techniques that apply to single-fruit jams also apply to mixed-fruit jams. The addition of pectin to the fruit allows for the creation of new and exciting jam flavors that would otherwise be very difficult to achieve.

Each type of fruit has a different level of natural pectin and different requirements in order for the jam to set. The proportions of each type of fruit in these recipes, along with the sugar, pectin and acid, have been balanced to achieve a good set. Changing the quantities of fruit in a recipe is not advised. Altering the proportions of fruit also requires adjusting the amounts of sugar, pectin and lemon juice; otherwise, the jam will fail to set.

Mixed-fruit jams are delicious spreads for toast, biscuits, scones and bread. They also make wonderful fillings for pastries, crêpes, cakes and cookies, and have many other cooking uses.

I had a lot of fun creating these recipes and finding the best flavor combinations. I hope you enjoy these new treats as much as my family and I do!

Apple Pear Jam

✳

3 cups	finely chopped cored peeled apples	750 mL
3 cups	finely chopped cored peeled pears	750 mL
2 tbsp	freshly squeezed lemon juice	30 mL
1	package (1.75 oz/49 to 57 g) regular powdered fruit pectin	1
5 cups	granulated sugar, divided	1.25 L
½ tsp	unsalted butter (optional)	2 mL

1. Prepare canning jars and lids and bring water in water bath canner to a boil.

2. In an 8-quart (8 L) stainless steel stockpot, combine apples, pears and lemon juice.

3. In a small bowl, combine pectin and ¼ cup (50 mL) of the sugar. Gradually stir into fruit. Add butter, if using.

4. Bring fruit mixture to a full rolling boil over medium-high heat, stirring constantly. Gradually stir in the remaining sugar. Return to a full rolling boil, stirring constantly, and boil for 1 minute.

5. Remove pot from heat and skim off any foam. Let jam cool in the pot for 5 minutes, stirring occasionally.

6. Ladle hot jam into hot jars, leaving ¼ inch (0.5 cm) headspace. Remove any air bubbles. Wipe jar rims and threads with a clean, damp paper towel. Center hot lids on jars and screw on bands until fingertip-tight.

7. Place jars in canner, making sure they are covered by at least 1 inch (2.5 cm) of water. Cover and bring to a gentle boil. Process 4-ounce (125 mL) jars and 8-ounce (250 mL) jars for 10 minutes; process 1-pint (500 mL) jars for 15 minutes.

8. Remove jars from canner and place on a wire rack or cloth towel. Let cool for 24 hours, then check seals. Wash and dry jars and store in a cool, dry, dark location.

Apricot Peach Jam

✳

*This jam makes a
wonderful topping to
spread over French
toast or filling for crêpes.*

Tips: White peaches
have a very mild
flavor and are not
recommended for
making jam.

For 1¾ cups (425 mL)
crushed apricots, you'll
need about 2 lbs (1 kg)
medium apricots. For
1¾ cups (425 mL)
crushed peaches, you'll
need about 2 lbs (1 kg)
or about 6 medium
peaches.

1¾ cups	crushed pitted peeled apricots	425 mL
1¾ cups	crushed pitted peeled peaches	425 mL
5 tbsp	freshly squeezed lemon juice	75 mL
6½ cups	granulated sugar	1.625 L
½ tsp	unsalted butter (optional)	2 mL
1	pouch (3 oz/85 mL) liquid pectin	1

1. Prepare canning jars and lids and bring water in water bath canner to a boil.

2. In an 8-quart (8 L) stainless steel stockpot, combine apricots, peaches and lemon juice. Gradually stir in sugar and butter, if using. Bring to a boil over medium heat, stirring constantly until sugar is completely dissolved.

3. Increase heat to medium-high and bring to a full rolling boil, stirring constantly. Stir in pectin. Return to a full rolling boil, stirring constantly, and boil for 1 minute.

4. Remove pot from heat and skim off any foam. Let jam cool in the pot for 5 minutes, stirring occasionally.

5. Ladle hot jam into hot jars, leaving ¼ inch (0.5 cm) headspace. Remove any air bubbles. Wipe jar rims and threads with a clean, damp paper towel. Center hot lids on jars and screw on bands until fingertip-tight.

6. Place jars in canner, making sure they are covered by at least 1 inch (2.5 cm) of water. Cover and bring to a gentle boil. Process 4-ounce (125 mL) jars and 8-ounce (250 mL) jars for 10 minutes; process 1-pint (500 mL) jars for 15 minutes.

7. Remove jars from canner and place on a wire rack or cloth towel. Let cool for 24 hours, then check seals. Wash and dry jars and store in a cool, dry, dark location.

Apricot Pineapple Jam

*

3 cups	crushed pitted peeled apricots	750 mL
1	can (20 oz/567 g) juice-packed crushed pineapple, drained (see tip, at left)	1
1/3 cup	freshly squeezed lemon juice	75 mL
1	package (1.75 oz/49 to 57 g) regular powdered fruit pectin	1
6 1/2 cups	granulated sugar, divided	1.625 L
1/2 tsp	unsalted butter (optional)	2 mL

Makes about seven 8-ounce (250 mL) jars

The classic pairing of apricots and pineapple makes a wonderful jam.

Tips: If using a can size other than 20 oz (567 mL), you will need 1 1/8 cups (280 mL) drained crushed pineapple for this recipe.

Do not reduce the proportions of lemon juice in a recipe. In many recipes, the lemon juice provides the acidity level needed to make the spread gel and achieve the proper set.

For 3 cups (750 mL) crushed apricots, you'll need about 3 lbs (1.5 kg) medium apricots.

1. Prepare canning jars and lids and bring water in water bath canner to a boil.

2. In an 8-quart (8 L) stainless steel stockpot, combine apricots, pineapple and lemon juice.

3. In a small bowl, combine pectin and 1/4 cup (50 mL) of the sugar. Gradually stir into fruit. Add butter, if using.

4. Bring fruit mixture to a full rolling boil over medium-high heat, stirring constantly. Gradually stir in the remaining sugar. Return to a full rolling boil, stirring constantly, and boil for 1 minute.

5. Remove pot from heat and skim off any foam. Let jam cool in the pot for 5 minutes, stirring occasionally.

6. Ladle hot jam into hot jars, leaving 1/4 inch (0.5 cm) headspace. Remove any air bubbles. Wipe jar rims and threads with a clean, damp paper towel. Center hot lids on jars and screw on bands until fingertip-tight.

7. Place jars in canner, making sure they are covered by at least 1 inch (2.5 cm) of water. Cover and bring to a gentle boil. Process 4-ounce (125 mL) jars and 8-ounce (250 mL) jars for 10 minutes; process 1-pint (500 mL) jars for 15 minutes.

8. Remove jars from canner and place on a wire rack or cloth towel. Let cool for 24 hours, then check seals. Wash and dry jars and store in a cool, dry, dark location.

Apricot Plum Jam

A delightful combination of summer flavors, this jam is sure to please.

Tips: It is risky to double jam and jelly recipes. The quantity of fruit in the pan can affect both the size and surface area of the pan needed to make the spread and the cooking time required to achieve a good set.

Santa Rosa plums are particularly good in this jam, but almost any variety of red, purple or yellow plum will work well.

For 2½ cups (625 mL) crushed apricots, you'll need about 2½ lbs (1.25 kg) medium apricots. For 1½ cups (375 mL) crushed plums, you'll need about 1½ lbs (750g) medium plums.

2½ cups	crushed pitted peeled apricots	625 mL
1½ cups	crushed pitted peeled plums	375 mL
2 tbsp	freshly squeezed lemon juice	30 mL
7 cups	granulated sugar	1.75 L
½ tsp	unsalted butter (optional)	2 mL
1	pouch (3 oz/85 mL) liquid pectin	1

1. Prepare canning jars and lids and bring water in water bath canner to a boil.

2. In an 8-quart (8 L) stainless steel stockpot, combine apricots, plums and lemon juice. Gradually stir in sugar and butter, if using. Bring to a boil over medium heat, stirring constantly until sugar is completely dissolved.

3. Increase heat to medium-high and bring to a full rolling boil, stirring constantly. Stir in pectin. Return to a full rolling boil, stirring constantly, and boil for 1 minute.

4. Remove pot from heat and skim off any foam. Let jam cool in the pot for 5 minutes, stirring occasionally.

5. Ladle hot jam into hot jars, leaving ¼ inch (0.5 cm) headspace. Remove any air bubbles. Wipe jar rims and threads with a clean, damp paper towel. Center hot lids on jars and screw on bands until fingertip-tight.

6. Place jars in canner, making sure they are covered by at least 1 inch (2.5 cm) of water. Cover and bring to a gentle boil. Process 4-ounce (125 mL) jars and 8-ounce (250 mL) jars for 10 minutes; process 1-pint (500 mL) jars for 15 minutes.

7. Remove jars from canner and place on a wire rack or cloth towel. Let cool for 24 hours, then check seals. Wash and dry jars and store in a cool, dry, dark location.

Apricot Raspberry Jam

✳

3 cups	fresh red raspberries	750 mL
2¾ cups	crushed pitted peeled apricots	675 mL
⅓ cup	freshly squeezed lemon juice	75 mL
6 cups	granulated sugar	1.5 L
½ tsp	unsalted butter (optional)	2 mL
1	pouch (3 oz/85 mL) liquid pectin	1

Makes six or seven 8-ounce (250 mL) jars

Try spreading this dazzling jam over the top of a cheesecake to create a fabulous and striking dessert for a special occasion.

Tips: If you use a food mill to crush and seed the berries, fit it with the finest plate.

Frozen raspberries also work in this recipe. Each 12-oz (340 g) bag of frozen unsweetened raspberries will yield about 1 cup (250 mL) seedless raspberry pulp. Be sure to use unsweetened raspberries, as sweetened raspberries will change the ratio of sugar in the recipe and may affect the set of the jam.

For 2¾ cups (675 mL) crushed apricots, you'll need about 3 lbs (1.5 kg) medium apricots.

1. Prepare canning jars and lids and bring water in water bath canner to a boil.

2. In a flat-bottomed pan or bowl, crush raspberries in small batches. Using the back of a spoon, press crushed raspberries through a fine-mesh sieve to remove the seeds. (Or use a food mill to crush the fruit and remove the seeds.) Measure 1 cup (250 mL) seedless raspberry pulp.

3. In an 8 quart (8 L) stainless steel stockpot, combine raspberry pulp, apricots and lemon juice. Gradually stir in sugar and butter, if using. Bring to a boil over medium heat, stirring constantly until sugar is completely dissolved.

4. Increase heat to medium-high and bring to a full rolling boil, stirring constantly. Stir in pectin. Return to a full rolling boil, stirring constantly, and boil for 1 minute.

5. Remove pot from heat and skim off any foam. Let jam cool in the pot for 5 minutes, stirring occasionally.

6. Ladle hot jam into hot jars, leaving ¼ inch (0.5 cm) headspace. Remove any air bubbles. Wipe jar rims and threads with a clean, damp paper towel. Center hot lids on jars and screw on bands until fingertip-tight.

7. Place jars in canner, making sure they are covered by at least 1 inch (2.5 cm) of water. Cover and bring to a gentle boil. Process 4-ounce (125 mL) jars and 8-ounce (250 mL) jars for 10 minutes; process 1-pint (500 mL) jars for 15 minutes.

8. Remove jars from canner and place on a wire rack or cloth towel. Let cool for 24 hours, then check seals. Wash and dry jars and store in a cool, dry, dark location.

Berry Medley Jam

✳

*When berries are at
their peak of flavor,
it's time to make this
scrumptious jam.*

Tips: Handle berries
gently to prevent
bruising.

For 2 cups (500 mL)
crushed strawberries,
you'll need about
1½ lbs (750 g) or 4 cups
(1 L) strawberries.
For 1¼ cups (300 mL)
crushed raspberries,
you'll need about
12 oz (375 g) or 3 cups
(750 mL) raspberries.
For ¾ cup (175 mL)
crushed blackberries,
you'll need about 12 oz
(375 g) or 1½ cups
(375 mL) blackberries.

2 cups	crushed hulled strawberries	500 mL
1¼ cups	crushed raspberries	300 mL
¾ cup	crushed blackberries	175 mL
2 tbsp	freshly squeezed lemon juice	30 mL
6¾ cups	granulated sugar	1.675 L
½ tsp	unsalted butter (optional)	2 mL
1	pouch (3 oz/85 mL) liquid pectin	1

1. Prepare canning jars and lids and bring water in water bath canner to a boil.

2. In an 8-quart (8 L) stainless steel stockpot, combine strawberries, raspberries, blackberries and lemon juice. Gradually stir in sugar and butter, if using. Bring to a boil over medium heat, stirring constantly until sugar is completely dissolved.

3. Increase heat to medium-high and bring to a full rolling boil, stirring constantly. Stir in pectin. Return to a full rolling boil, stirring constantly, and boil for 1 minute.

4. Remove pot from heat and skim off any foam. Let jam cool in the pot for 5 minutes, stirring occasionally.

5. Ladle hot jam into hot jars, leaving ¼ inch (0.5 cm) headspace. Remove any air bubbles. Wipe jar rims and threads with a clean, damp paper towel. Center hot lids on jars and screw on bands until fingertip-tight.

6. Place jars in canner, making sure they are covered by at least 1 inch (2.5 cm) of water. Cover and bring to a gentle boil. Process 4-ounce (125 mL) jars and 8-ounce (250 mL) jars for 10 minutes; process 1-pint (500 mL) jars for 15 minutes.

7. Remove jars from canner and place on a wire rack or cloth towel. Let cool for 24 hours, then check seals. Wash and dry jars and store in a cool, dry, dark location.

Black and Blue Jam

2 cups	crushed blackberries	500 mL
1¼ cups	crushed blueberries	300 mL
1 tbsp	freshly squeezed lemon juice	15 mL
5¼ cups	granulated sugar	1.3 L
½ tsp	unsalted butter (optional)	2 mL
1	pouch (3 oz/85 mL) liquid pectin	1

1. Prepare canning jars and lids and bring water in water bath canner to a boil.

2. In an 8-quart (8 L) stainless steel stockpot, combine blackberries, blueberries and lemon juice. Gradually stir in sugar and butter, if using. Bring to a boil over medium heat, stirring constantly until sugar is completely dissolved.

3. Increase heat to medium-high and bring to a full rolling boil, stirring constantly. Stir in pectin. Return to a full rolling boil, stirring constantly, and boil for 1 minute.

4. Remove pot from heat and skim off any foam. Let jam cool in the pot for 5 minutes, stirring occasionally.

5. Ladle hot jam into hot jars, leaving ¼ inch (0.5 cm) headspace. Remove any air bubbles. Wipe jar rims and threads with a clean, damp paper towel. Center hot lids on jars and screw on bands until fingertip-tight.

6. Place jars in canner, making sure they are covered by at least 1 inch (2.5 cm) of water. Cover and bring to a gentle boil. Process 4-ounce (125 mL) jars and 8-ounce (250 mL) jars for 10 minutes; process 1-pint (500 mL) jars for 15 minutes.

7. Remove jars from canner and place on a wire rack or cloth towel. Let cool for 24 hours, then check seals. Wash and dry jars and store in a cool, dry, dark location.

Blackberry Cherry Jam

✳

Makes about seven 8-ounce (250 mL) jars

The fantastic flavor of this mixed-fruit jam lingers in the memory long after the jar is empty.

Tips: Liquid and powdered pectins have different setting properties and are not interchangeable.

For 2 cups (500 mL) crushed blackberries, you'll need about 1½ lbs (750 g) or 3½ cups (875 mL) blackberries. For 2 cups (500 mL) finely chopped cherries, you'll need about 1¾ lbs (875 g) cherries.

2 cups	crushed blackberries	500 mL
2 cups	finely chopped pitted fresh sweet cherries	500 mL
¼ cup	freshly squeezed lemon juice	50 mL
6 cups	granulated sugar	1.5 L
½ tsp	unsalted butter (optional)	2 mL
1	pouch (3 oz/85 mL) liquid pectin	1

1. Prepare canning jars and lids and bring water in water bath canner to a boil.

2. In an 8-quart (8 L) stainless steel stockpot, combine blackberries, cherries and lemon juice. Gradually stir in sugar and butter, if using. Bring to a boil over medium heat, stirring constantly until sugar is completely dissolved.

3. Increase heat to medium-high and bring to a full rolling boil, stirring constantly. Stir in pectin. Return to a full rolling boil, stirring constantly, and boil for 1 minute.

4. Remove pot from heat and skim off any foam. Let jam cool in the pot for 5 minutes, stirring occasionally.

5. Ladle hot jam into hot jars, leaving ¼ inch (0.5 cm) headspace. Remove any air bubbles. Wipe jar rims and threads with a clean, damp paper towel. Center hot lids on jars and screw on bands until fingertip-tight.

6. Place jars in canner, making sure they are covered by at least 1 inch (2.5 cm) of water. Cover and bring to a gentle boil. Process 4-ounce (125 mL) jars and 8-ounce (250 mL) jars for 10 minutes; process 1-pint (500 mL) jars for 15 minutes.

7. Remove jars from canner and place on a wire rack or cloth towel. Let cool for 24 hours, then check seals. Wash and dry jars and store in a cool, dry, dark location.

Blueberry Lemon Jam

✳

*The zesty tang of
lemons complements
the intense flavor of
the blueberries.*

Tips: Fresh blueberries
will keep well in the
refrigerator for several
days after purchase.

Remove all white pith
and membranes from
lemon sections before
chopping to improve
jam texture and
prevent bitterness.

For 2 cups (500 mL)
crushed blueberries,
you'll need about
1¼ lbs (625 g) or 3 cups
(750 mL) blueberries.
For 1 cup (250 mL)
finely chopped lemons,
you'll need about
8 medium lemons.

2 cups	crushed blueberries	500 mL
1 cup	finely chopped sectioned peeled lemons	250 mL
5 cups	granulated sugar	1.25 L
½ tsp	unsalted butter (optional)	2 mL
1	pouch (3 oz/85 mL) liquid pectin	1

1. Prepare canning jars and lids and bring water in water bath canner to a boil.

2. In an 8-quart (8 L) stainless steel stockpot, combine blueberries and lemons. Gradually stir in sugar and butter, if using. Bring to a boil over medium heat, stirring constantly until sugar is completely dissolved.

3. Increase heat to medium-high and bring to a full rolling boil, stirring constantly. Stir in pectin. Return to a full rolling boil, stirring constantly, and boil for 1 minute.

4. Remove pot from heat and skim off any foam. Let jam cool in the pot for 5 minutes, stirring occasionally.

5. Ladle hot jam into hot jars, leaving ¼ inch (0.5 cm) headspace. Remove any air bubbles. Wipe jar rims and threads with a clean, damp paper towel. Center hot lids on jars and screw on bands until fingertip-tight.

6. Place jars in canner, making sure they are covered by at least 1 inch (2.5 cm) of water. Cover and bring to a gentle boil. Process 4-ounce (125 mL) jars and 8-ounce (250 mL) jars for 10 minutes; process 1-pint (500 mL) jars for 15 minutes.

7. Remove jars from canner and place on a wire rack or cloth towel. Let cool for 24 hours, then check seals. Wash and dry jars and store in a cool, dry, dark location.

Cherry Blueberry Jam

※

Makes about six 8-ounce (250 mL) jars

A great jam to spread on English muffins.

Tips: Be careful when working with sweet cherries, as cherry juice can stain clothing.

For 2½ cups (625 mL) finely chopped cherries, you'll need about 2 lbs (1 kg) cherries. For 1 cup (250 mL) crushed blueberries, you'll need about 12 oz (375 g) or 1½ cups (375 mL) blueberries.

2½ cups	finely chopped pitted fresh sweet cherries	625 mL
1 cup	crushed blueberries	250 mL
6 tbsp	freshly squeezed lemon juice	90 mL
5⅔ cups	granulated sugar	1.4 L
½ tsp	unsalted butter (optional)	2 mL
1	pouch (3 oz/85 mL) liquid pectin	1

1. Prepare canning jars and lids and bring water in water bath canner to a boil.

2. In an 8-quart (8 L) stainless steel stockpot, combine cherries, blueberries and lemon juice. Gradually stir in sugar and butter, if using. Bring to a boil over medium heat, stirring constantly until sugar is completely dissolved.

3. Increase heat to medium-high and bring to a full rolling boil, stirring constantly. Stir in pectin. Return to a full rolling boil, stirring constantly, and boil for 1 minute.

4. Remove pot from heat and skim off any foam. Let jam cool in the pot for 5 minutes, stirring occasionally.

5. Ladle hot jam into hot jars, leaving ¼ inch (0.5 cm) headspace. Remove any air bubbles. Wipe jar rims and threads with a clean, damp paper towel. Center hot lids on jars and screw on bands until fingertip-tight.

6. Place jars in canner, making sure they are covered by at least 1 inch (2.5 cm) of water. Cover and bring to a gentle boil. Process 4-ounce (125 mL) jars and 8-ounce (250 mL) jars for 10 minutes; process 1-pint (500 mL) jars for 15 minutes.

7. Remove jars from canner and place on a wire rack or cloth towel. Let cool for 24 hours, then check seals. Wash and dry jars and store in a cool, dry, dark location.

Cherry Raspberry Jam

✳

The flavors of cherry and raspberry complement each other, resulting in a fabulous jam.

Tips: If you use a food mill to crush and seed the berries, fit it with the finest plate.

Defrosted frozen raspberries also make great seedless jam. Each 12-oz (340 g) bag of frozen unsweetened raspberries will yield about 1 cup (250 mL) seedless raspberry pulp. Be sure to use unsweetened raspberries. Raspberries frozen with sugar should not be used, as the extra sugar can upset the balance of ingredients in the recipe, which can prevent the jam from setting.

For 2 cups (500 mL) finely chopped cherries, you'll need about 1¾ lbs (875 g) cherries.

6 cups	fresh raspberries	1.5 L
2 cups	finely chopped pitted fresh sweet cherries	500 mL
3 tbsp	freshly squeezed lemon juice	45 mL
5¾ cups	granulated sugar	1.425 L
½ tsp	unsalted butter (optional)	2 mL
1	pouch (3 oz/85 mL) liquid pectin	1
½ tsp	pure almond extract	2 mL

1. Prepare canning jars and lids and bring water in water bath canner to a boil.

2. In a flat-bottomed pan or bowl, crush raspberries in small batches. Using the back of a spoon, press crushed raspberries through a fine-mesh sieve to remove the seeds. (Or use a food mill to crush the fruit and remove the seeds.) Measure 2 cups (500 mL) seedless raspberry pulp.

3. In an 8-quart (8 L) stainless steel stockpot, combine raspberry pulp, cherries and lemon juice. Gradually stir in sugar and butter, if using. Bring to a boil over medium heat, stirring constantly until sugar is completely dissolved.

4. Increase heat to medium-high and bring to a full rolling boil, stirring constantly. Stir in pectin. Return to a full rolling boil, stirring constantly, and boil for 1 minute.

5. Remove pot from heat and skim off any foam. Stir in almond extract. Let jam cool in the pot for 5 minutes, stirring occasionally.

6. Ladle hot jam into hot jars, leaving ¼ inch (0.5 cm) headspace. Remove any air bubbles. Wipe jar rims and threads with a clean, damp paper towel. Center hot lids on jars and screw on bands until fingertip-tight.

7. Place jars in canner, making sure they are covered by at least 1 inch (2.5 cm) of water. Cover and bring to a gentle boil. Process 4-ounce (125 mL) jars and 8-ounce (250 mL) jars for 10 minutes; process 1-pint (500 mL) jars for 15 minutes.

8. Remove jars from canner and place on a wire rack or cloth towel. Let cool for 24 hours, then check seals. Wash and dry jars and store in a cool, dry, dark location.

Citrus Jam

**Makes about
five 8-ounce
(250 mL) jars**

*A delicious blend of
oranges and lemons,
with a bright fresh
flavor.*

Tips: Do not use navel
oranges for making jam.
Navel oranges become
tough when cooked,
and they contain an
enzyme that will cause
the fruit to turn bitter
during storage.

Remove all white pith
and membranes from
orange and lemon
sections before
chopping to improve
jam texture and
prevent bitterness.

For 2 cups (500 mL)
finely chopped
Valencia oranges,
you'll need about
15 medium oranges.
For 1 cup (250 mL)
finely chopped lemons,
you'll need about
8 medium lemons.

2 cups	finely chopped sectioned peeled Valencia oranges	500 mL
1 cup	finely chopped sectioned peeled lemons	250 mL
5 cups	granulated sugar	1.25 L
½ tsp	unsalted butter (optional)	2 mL
1	pouch (3 oz/85 mL) liquid pectin	1

1. Prepare canning jars and lids and bring water in water bath canner to a boil.

2. In an 8-quart (8 L) stainless steel stockpot, combine oranges and lemons. Gradually stir in sugar and butter, if using. Bring to a boil over medium heat, stirring constantly until sugar is completely dissolved.

3. Increase heat to medium-high and bring to a full rolling boil, stirring constantly. Stir in pectin. Return to a full rolling boil, stirring constantly, and boil for 1 minute.

4. Remove pot from heat and skim off any foam. Let jam cool in the pot for 5 minutes, stirring occasionally.

5. Ladle hot jam into hot jars, leaving ¼ inch (0.5 cm) headspace. Remove any air bubbles. Wipe jar rims and threads with a clean, damp paper towel. Center hot lids on jars and screw on bands until fingertip-tight.

6. Place jars in canner, making sure they are covered by at least 1 inch (2.5 cm) of water. Cover and bring to a gentle boil. Process 4-ounce (125 mL) jars and 8-ounce (250 mL) jars for 10 minutes; process 1-pint (500 mL) jars for 15 minutes.

7. Remove jars from canner and place on a wire rack or cloth towel. Let cool for 24 hours, then check seals. Wash and dry jars and store in a cool, dry, dark location.

Four Berry Jam

✳

*Berries, berries and
more berries! Yum!*

Tips: A berry is defined
as a multi-celled fruit
with many seeds.
In addition to the fruits
we normally think
of as berries, such
as blackberries,
blueberries, raspberries
and strawberries, many
other fruits are also
considered berries,
including grapes and
watermelon.

For 1½ cups (375 mL)
crushed strawberries,
you'll need about 1½ lbs
(750 g) or 3 cups
(750 mL) strawberries.
For 1 cup (250 mL)
crushed raspberries,
you'll need about 12 oz
(375 g) or 2½ cups
(625 mL) raspberries.
For ¾ cup (175 mL)
crushed blackberries,
you'll need about 12 oz
(375 g) or 1½ cups
(375 mL) blackberries.
For ¾ cup (175 mL)
crushed blueberries,
you'll need about 10 oz
(300 g) or 1½ cups
(375 mL) blueberries.

1½ cups	crushed hulled strawberries	375 mL
1 cup	crushed raspberries	250 mL
¾ cup	crushed blackberries	175 mL
¾ cup	crushed blueberries	175 mL
2 tbsp	freshly squeezed lemon juice	30 mL
6½ cups	granulated sugar	1.625 L
½ tsp	unsalted butter (optional)	2 mL
1	pouch (3 oz/85 mL) liquid pectin	1

1. Prepare canning jars and lids and bring water in water bath canner to a boil.

2. In an 8-quart (8 L) stainless steel stockpot, combine strawberries, raspberries, blackberries, blueberries and lemon juice. Gradually stir in sugar and butter, if using. Bring to a boil over medium heat, stirring constantly until sugar is completely dissolved.

3. Increase heat to medium-high and bring to a full rolling boil, stirring constantly. Stir in pectin. Return to a full rolling boil, stirring constantly, and boil for 1 minute.

4. Remove pot from heat and skim off any foam. Let jam cool in the pot for 5 minutes, stirring occasionally.

5. Ladle hot jam into hot jars, leaving ¼ inch (0.5 cm) headspace. Remove any air bubbles. Wipe jar rims and threads with a clean, damp paper towel. Center hot lids on jars and screw on bands until fingertip-tight.

6. Place jars in canner, making sure they are covered by at least 1 inch (2.5 cm) of water. Cover and bring to a gentle boil. Process 4-ounce (125 mL) jars and 8-ounce (250 mL) jars for 10 minutes; process 1-pint (500 mL) jars for 15 minutes.

7. Remove jars from canner and place on a wire rack or cloth towel. Let cool for 24 hours, then check seals. Wash and dry jars and store in a cool, dry, dark location.

Orange Strawberry Jam

✳

Makes about seven 8-ounce (250 mL) jars

An excellent jam! The fresh orange flavor complements the luscious strawberries.

Tips: Remove all white pith and membranes from orange sections before chopping to improve jam's texture and prevent bitterness.

Doubling jam and jelly recipes is not advised. If the pan is too full, not enough liquid will boil off during cooking and the spread likely will not set properly.

For 2 cups (500 mL) crushed strawberries, you'll need about 1½ lbs (750 g) or 4 cups (1 L) strawberries. For 1½ cups (375 mL) finely chopped Valencia oranges, you'll need about 12 medium oranges.

2 cups	crushed hulled strawberries	500 mL
1½ cups	finely chopped sectioned peeled Valencia oranges	375 mL
2 tbsp	freshly squeezed lemon juice	30 mL
6 cups	granulated sugar	1.5 L
½ tsp	unsalted butter (optional)	2 mL
1	pouch (3 oz/85 mL) liquid pectin	1

1. Prepare canning jars and lids and bring water in water bath canner to a boil.

2. In an 8-quart (8 L) stainless steel stockpot, combine strawberries, oranges and lemon juice. Gradually stir in sugar and butter, if using. Bring to a boil over medium heat, stirring constantly until sugar is completely dissolved.

3. Increase heat to medium-high and bring to a full rolling boil, stirring constantly. Stir in pectin. Return to a full rolling boil, stirring constantly, and boil for 1 minute.

4. Remove pot from heat and skim off any foam. Let jam cool in the pot for 5 minutes, stirring occasionally.

5. Ladle hot jam into hot jars, leaving ¼ inch (0.5 cm) headspace. Remove any air bubbles. Wipe jar rims and threads with a clean, damp paper towel. Center hot lids on jars and screw on bands until fingertip-tight.

6. Place jars in canner, making sure they are covered by at least 1 inch (2.5 cm) of water. Cover and bring to a gentle boil. Process 4-ounce (125 mL) jars and 8-ounce (250 mL) jars for 10 minutes; process 1-pint (500 mL) jars for 15 minutes.

7. Remove jars from canner and place on a wire rack or cloth towel. Let cool for 24 hours, then check seals. Wash and dry jars and store in a cool, dry, dark location.

Peach Blackberry Jam

Makes about eight 8-ounce (250 mL) jars

Delicious at breakfast, this exciting jam is a great way to start the day.

Tips: If you prefer a seedless jam, press the crushed blackberries through a fine-mesh sieve to remove the seeds before measuring.

For 2⅔ cups (650 mL) crushed peaches, you'll need about 3 lbs (1.5 kg) or about 8 medium peaches. For 1⅓ cups (325 mL) crushed blackberries, you'll need about 1 lb (500 g) or 2½ cups (625 mL) blackberries.

2⅔ cups	crushed pitted peeled peaches	650 mL
1⅓ cups	crushed blackberries	325 mL
3 tbsp	freshly squeezed lemon juice	45 mL
7⅓ cups	granulated sugar	1.825 L
½ tsp	unsalted butter (optional)	2 mL
1	pouch (3 oz/85 mL) liquid pectin	1

1. Prepare canning jars and lids and bring water in water bath canner to a boil.

2. In an 8-quart (8 L) stainless steel stockpot, combine peaches, blackberries and lemon juice. Gradually stir in sugar and butter, if using. Bring to a boil over medium heat, stirring constantly until sugar is completely dissolved.

3. Increase heat to medium-high and bring to a full rolling boil, stirring constantly. Stir in pectin. Return to a full rolling boil, stirring constantly, and boil for 1 minute.

4. Remove pot from heat and skim off any foam. Let jam cool in the pot for 5 minutes, stirring occasionally.

5. Ladle hot jam into hot jars, leaving ¼ inch (0.5 cm) headspace. Remove any air bubbles. Wipe jar rims and threads with a clean, damp paper towel. Center hot lids on jars and screw on bands until fingertip-tight.

6. Place jars in canner, making sure they are covered by at least 1 inch (2.5 cm) of water. Cover and bring to a gentle boil. Process 4-ounce (125 mL) jars and 8-ounce (250 mL) jars for 10 minutes; process 1-pint (500 mL) jars for 15 minutes.

7. Remove jars from canner and place on a wire rack or cloth towel. Let cool for 24 hours, then check seals. Wash and dry jars and store in a cool, dry, dark location.

Peach Nectarine Jam

Makes about eight 8-ounce (250 mL) jars

Makes about eight 8-ounce (250 mL) jars

This jam is exquisite, in both color and flavor.

Tips: Yellow-fleshed peaches and nectarines are the best choice for this recipe. White nectarines and peaches have a milder flavor and tend to lose their shape when cooked.

For 2 cups (500 mL) crushed peaches, you'll need about 2 lbs (1 kg) or about 6 medium peaches. For 2 cups (500 mL) crushed nectarines, you'll need about 2 lbs (1 kg) or about 6 medium nectarines.

2 cups	crushed pitted peeled peaches	500 mL
2 cups	crushed pitted peeled nectarines	500 mL
1/4 cup	freshly squeezed lemon juice	50 mL
7 1/2 cups	granulated sugar	1.875 L
1/2 tsp	unsalted butter (optional)	2 mL
1	pouch (3 oz/85 mL) liquid pectin	1

1. Prepare canning jars and lids and bring water in water bath canner to a boil.

2. In an 8-quart (8 L) stainless steel stockpot, combine peaches, nectarines and lemon juice. Gradually stir in sugar and butter, if using. Bring to a boil over medium heat, stirring constantly until sugar is completely dissolved.

3. Increase heat to medium-high and bring to a full rolling boil, stirring constantly. Stir in pectin. Return to a full rolling boil, stirring constantly, and boil for 1 minute.

4. Remove pot from heat and skim off any foam. Let jam cool in the pot for 5 minutes, stirring occasionally.

5. Ladle hot jam into hot jars, leaving 1/4 inch (0.5 cm) headspace. Remove any air bubbles. Wipe jar rims and threads with a clean, damp paper towel. Center hot lids on jars and screw on bands until fingertip-tight.

6. Place jars in canner, making sure they are covered by at least 1 inch (2.5 cm) of water. Cover and bring to a gentle boil. Process 4-ounce (125 mL) jars and 8-ounce (250 mL) jars for 10 minutes; process 1-pint (500 mL) jars for 15 minutes.

7. Remove jars from canner and place on a wire rack or cloth towel. Let cool for 24 hours, then check seals. Wash and dry jars and store in a cool, dry, dark location.

Peach Plum Jam

✳

*This lively, aromatic
jam has a charming
rosy color.*

Tips: Make Peach Plum
Jam when fresh local
peaches and plums are
at the peak of their
season and have the
best flavor.

Almost any variety of
red, purple or yellow
plum will work well
in this recipe.

For 2½ cups (625 mL)
crushed peaches, you'll
need about 2½ lbs
(1.25 kg) or about
8 medium peaches.
For 1½ cups (375 mL)
crushed plums, you'll
need about 1½ lbs
(750 g) medium plums.

2½ cups	crushed pitted peeled peaches	625 mL
1½ cups	crushed pitted peeled plums	375 mL
2 tbsp	freshly squeezed lemon juice	30 mL
7¼ cups	granulated sugar	1.8 L
½ tsp	unsalted butter (optional)	2 mL
1	pouch (3 oz/85 mL) liquid pectin	1

1. Prepare canning jars and lids and bring water in water bath canner to a boil.

2. In an 8-quart (8 L) stainless steel stockpot, combine peaches, plums and lemon juice. Gradually stir in sugar and butter, if using. Bring to a boil over medium heat, stirring constantly until sugar is completely dissolved.

3. Increase heat to medium-high and bring to a full rolling boil, stirring constantly. Stir in pectin. Return to a full rolling boil, stirring constantly, and boil for 1 minute.

4. Remove pot from heat and skim off any foam. Let jam cool in the pot for 5 minutes, stirring occasionally.

5. Ladle hot jam into hot jars, leaving ¼ inch (0.5 cm) headspace. Remove any air bubbles. Wipe jar rims and threads with a clean, damp paper towel. Center hot lids on jars and screw on bands until fingertip-tight.

6. Place jars in canner, making sure they are covered by at least 1 inch (2.5 cm) of water. Cover and bring to a gentle boil. Process 4-ounce (125 mL) jars and 8-ounce (250 mL) jars for 10 minutes; process 1-pint (500 mL) jars for 15 minutes.

7. Remove jars from canner and place on a wire rack or cloth towel. Let cool for 24 hours, then check seals. Wash and dry jars and store in a cool, dry, dark location.

Pear Lime Jam

✳

Makes about six 8-ounce (250 mL) jars

Light and refreshing, pear and lime make an enchanting jam.

Tips: Using a Microplane grater to grate lime zest makes the job quick and easy, and only the outer green layer of the peel is removed from the fruit.

I like to use Bartlett pears for this recipe because their flavor blends beautifully with the lime.

For 4½ cups (1.125 L) finely chopped pears, you'll need about 4½ lbs (2.25 kg) or about 14 medium pears.

4½ cups	finely chopped cored peeled pears	1.125 L
1 tbsp	grated lime zest	15 mL
3 tbsp	freshly squeezed lime juice	45 mL
1	package (1.75 oz/49 to 57 g) regular powdered fruit pectin	1
5 cups	granulated sugar, divided	1.25 L
½ tsp	unsalted butter (optional)	2 mL

1. Prepare canning jars and lids and bring water in water bath canner to a boil.

2. In an 8-quart (8 L) stainless steel stockpot, combine pears and lime juice.

3. In a small bowl, combine pectin and ¼ cup (50 mL) of the sugar. Gradually stir into fruit. Add butter, if using.

4. Bring fruit mixture to a full rolling boil over medium-high heat, stirring constantly. Gradually stir in the remaining sugar. Return to a full rolling boil, stirring constantly, and boil for 1 minute.

5. Remove pot from heat and skim off any foam. Stir in lime zest. Let jam cool in the pot for 5 minutes, stirring occasionally.

6. Ladle hot jam into hot jars, leaving ¼ inch (0.5 cm) headspace. Remove any air bubbles. Wipe jar rims and threads with a clean, damp paper towel. Center hot lids on jars and screw on bands until fingertip-tight.

7. Place jars in canner, making sure they are covered by at least 1 inch (2.5 cm) of water. Cover and bring to a gentle boil. Process 4-ounce (125 mL) jars and 8-ounce (250 mL) jars for 10 minutes; process 1-pint (500 mL) jars for 15 minutes.

8. Remove jars from canner and place on a wire rack or cloth towel. Let cool for 24 hours, then check seals. Wash and dry jars and store in a cool, dry, dark location.

Pear Plum Jam

Makes about six 8-ounce (250 mL) jars

The sweet flavor of ripe pears combines well with the refreshing tang of plums.

Tips: Pears darken quickly after being cut. To prevent browning, peel and chop pears just before making the jam.

Bartlett pears are a good choice for any jam because they have a great flavor and hold their shape well when cooked.

Red plums, such as Santa Rosa, or yellow plums are good choices for this jam because their flavor will not overpower the pears.

For 3 cups (750 mL) finely chopped pears, you'll need about 3 lbs (1.5 kg) or about 9 medium pears. For 1 cup (250 mL) crushed plums, you'll need about 1 lb (500 g) medium plums.

3 cups	finely chopped cored peeled pears	750 mL
1 cup	crushed pitted peeled plums	250 mL
2 tbsp	freshly squeezed lemon juice	30 mL
1	package (1.75 oz/49 to 57 g) regular powdered fruit pectin	1
5 cups	granulated sugar, divided	1.25 L
½ tsp	unsalted butter (optional)	2 mL

1. Prepare canning jars and lids and bring water in water bath canner to a boil.

2. In an 8-quart (8 L) stainless steel stockpot, combine pears, plums and lemon juice.

3. In a small bowl, combine pectin and ¼ cup (50 mL) of the sugar. Gradually stir into fruit. Add butter, if using.

4. Bring fruit mixture to a full rolling boil over medium-high heat, stirring constantly. Gradually stir in the remaining sugar. Return to a full rolling boil, stirring constantly, and boil for 1 minute.

5. Remove pot from heat and skim off any foam. Let jam cool in the pot for 5 minutes, stirring occasionally.

6. Ladle hot jam into hot jars, leaving ¼ inch (0.5 cm) headspace. Remove any air bubbles. Wipe jar rims and threads with a clean, damp paper towel. Center hot lids on jars and screw on bands until fingertip-tight.

7. Place jars in canner, making sure they are covered by at least 1 inch (2.5 cm) of water. Cover and bring to a gentle boil. Process 4-ounce (125 mL) jars and 8-ounce (250 mL) jars for 10 minutes; process 1-pint (500 mL) jars for 15 minutes.

8. Remove jars from canner and place on a wire rack or cloth towel. Let cool for 24 hours, then check seals. Wash and dry jars and store in a cool, dry, dark location.

Pineapple Pear Jam

✳

Makes six to seven 8-ounce (250 mL) jars

The blending of pineapple and pears creates a lovely jam with a delightful flavor and a tantalizing fresh aroma.

Tips: Fresh pineapples contain an enzyme that inhibits jam from setting. It is always best to use canned pineapple in jam recipes.

To keep pears from turning brown, peel and chop them just before making the jam and immediately combine them with the pineapple and lemon juice.

For 2 cups (500 mL) finely chopped pears, you'll need about 2 lbs (1 kg) or about 6 medium pears.

2 cups	finely chopped cored peeled Bartlett pears	500 mL
1²/₃ cups	drained canned juice-packed crushed pineapple	400 mL
¼ cup	freshly squeezed lemon juice	50 mL
1	box (1.75 oz/49 to 57 g) regular powdered fruit pectin	1
5 cups	granulated sugar, divided	1.25 L
½ tsp	unsalted butter (optional)	2 mL

1. Prepare canning jars and lids and bring water in water bath canner to a boil.

2. In an 8-quart (8 L) stainless steel stockpot, combine pears, pineapple and lemon juice.

3. In a small bowl, combine pectin and ¼ cup (50 mL) of the sugar. Gradually stir into fruit. Add butter, if using.

4. Bring fruit mixture to a full rolling boil over medium-high heat, stirring constantly. Gradually stir in the remaining sugar. Return to a full rolling boil, stirring constantly, and boil for 1 minute.

5. Remove pot from heat and skim off any foam. Let jam cool in the pot for 5 minutes, stirring occasionally.

6. Ladle hot jam into hot jars, leaving ¼ inch (0.5 cm) headspace. Remove any air bubbles. Wipe jar rims and threads with a clean, damp paper towel. Center hot lids on jars and screw on bands until fingertip-tight.

7. Place jars in canner, making sure they are covered by at least 1 inch (2.5 cm) of water. Cover and bring to a gentle boil. Process 4-ounce (125 mL) jars and 8-ounce (250 mL) jars for 10 minutes; process 1-pint (500 mL) jars for 15 minutes.

8. Remove jars from canner and place on a wire rack or cloth towel. Let cool for 24 hours, then check seals. Wash and dry jars and store in a cool, dry, dark location.

Plum Cherry Jam

✳

Makes about seven 8-ounce (250 mL) jars

A great favorite with my family and friends, this intoxicating jam disappears fast.

Tips: Most recipes for plum jams instruct you to leave the skins on the plums. I strongly advise peeling plums, as the skins can turn quite bitter, tough and chewy when cooked.

The flavor of Santa Rosa plums pairs nicely with cherries, but you may use any variety of red or purple plum in this recipe.

For 2 cups (500 mL) crushed plums, you'll need about 2 lbs (1 kg) medium plums. For 2 cups (500 mL) finely chopped cherries, you'll need about 1¾ lbs (875 g) cherries.

2 cups	crushed pitted peeled plums	500 mL
2 cups	finely chopped pitted fresh sweet cherries	500 mL
¼ cup	freshly squeezed lemon juice	50 mL
5¾ cups	granulated sugar	1.425 L
½ tsp	unsalted butter (optional)	2 mL
1	pouch (3 oz/85 mL) liquid pectin	1

1. Prepare canning jars and lids and bring water in water bath canner to a boil.

2. In an 8-quart (8 L) stainless steel stockpot, combine plums, cherries and lemon juice. Gradually stir in sugar and butter, if using. Bring to a boil over medium heat, stirring constantly until sugar is completely dissolved.

3. Increase heat to medium-high and bring to a full rolling boil, stirring constantly. Stir in pectin. Return to a full rolling boil, stirring constantly, and boil for 1 minute.

4. Remove pot from heat and skim off any foam. Let jam cool in the pot for 5 minutes, stirring occasionally.

5. Ladle hot jam into hot jars, leaving ¼ inch (0.5 cm) headspace. Remove any air bubbles. Wipe jar rims and threads with a clean, damp paper towel. Center hot lids on jars and screw on bands until fingertip-tight.

6. Place jars in canner, making sure they are covered by at least 1 inch (2.5 cm) of water. Cover and bring to a gentle boil. Process 4-ounce (125 mL) jars and 8-ounce (250 mL) jars for 10 minutes; process 1-pint (500 mL) jars for 15 minutes.

7. Remove jars from canner and place on a wire rack or cloth towel. Let cool for 24 hours, then check seals. Wash and dry jars and store in a cool, dry, dark location.

Raspberry Peach Jam

※

Makes about seven 8-ounce (250 mL) jars

This sophisticated jam has a sparkling color and a complex flavor that is sure to delight.

Tips: If you use a food mill to crush and seed the berries, fit it with the finest plate.

Frozen raspberries also work in this recipe. Each 12-oz (340 g) bag of frozen unsweetened raspberries will yield about 1 cup (250 mL) seedless raspberry pulp.

If peaches reach ripeness before you are ready to use them, they may be stored in the refrigerator for a few days.

For 3 cups (750 mL) crushed peaches, you'll need about 3 lbs (1.5 kg) or about 9 medium peaches.

3 cups	fresh red raspberries	750 mL
3 cups	crushed pitted peeled peaches	750 mL
3 tbsp	freshly squeezed lemon juice	45 mL
7¼ cups	granulated sugar	1.8 L
½ tsp	unsalted butter (optional)	2 mL
1	pouch (3 oz/85 mL) liquid pectin	1

1. Prepare canning jars and lids and bring water in water bath canner to a boil.

2. In a flat-bottomed pan or bowl, crush raspberries in small batches. Using the back of a spoon, press crushed raspberries through a fine-mesh sieve to remove the seeds. (Or use a food mill to crush the fruit and remove the seeds.) Measure 1 cup (250 mL) seedless raspberry pulp.

3. In an 8-quart (8 L) stainless steel stockpot, combine raspberry pulp, peaches and lemon juice. Gradually stir in sugar and butter, if using. Bring to a boil over medium heat, stirring constantly until sugar is completely dissolved.

4. Increase heat to medium-high and bring to a full rolling boil, stirring constantly. Stir in pectin. Return to a full rolling boil, stirring constantly, and boil for 1 minute.

5. Remove pot from heat and skim off any foam. Let jam cool in the pot for 5 minutes, stirring occasionally.

6. Ladle hot jam into hot jars, leaving ¼ inch (0.5 cm) headspace. Remove any air bubbles. Wipe jar rims and threads with a clean, damp paper towel. Center hot lids on jars and screw on bands until fingertip-tight.

7. Place jars in canner, making sure they are covered by at least 1 inch (2.5 cm) of water. Cover and bring to a gentle boil. Process 4-ounce (125 mL) jars and 8-ounce (250 mL) jars for 10 minutes; process 1-pint (500 mL) jars for 15 minutes.

8. Remove jars from canner and place on a wire rack or cloth towel. Let cool for 24 hours, then check seals. Wash and dry jars and store in a cool, dry, dark location.

Raspberry Plum Jam

*This elegant jam
is a celebration of
summer fruits.*

Tips: If you prefer
a seedless jam, press
the crushed raspberries
through a fine-mesh
sieve to remove the
seeds before measuring.

The flavor of Santa Rosa
plums pairs nicely with
raspberries, but you
may use any variety of
red or purple plum in
this recipe.

For 2 cups (500 mL)
crushed raspberries,
you'll need about 1½ lbs
(750 g) or 5 cups (1.25 L)
raspberries. For 2 cups
(500 mL) crushed plums,
you'll need about 2 lbs
(1 kg) medium plums.

2 cups	crushed raspberries	500 mL
2 cups	crushed pitted peeled plums	500 mL
7 cups	granulated sugar	1.75 L
½ tsp	unsalted butter (optional)	2 mL
1	pouch (3 oz/85 mL) liquid pectin	1

1. Prepare canning jars and lids and bring water in water bath canner to a boil.

2. In an 8-quart (8 L) stainless steel stockpot, combine raspberries and plums. Gradually stir in sugar and butter, if using. Bring to a boil over medium heat, stirring constantly until sugar is completely dissolved.

3. Increase heat to medium-high and bring to a full rolling boil, stirring constantly. Stir in pectin. Return to a full rolling boil, stirring constantly, and boil for 1 minute.

4. Remove pot from heat and skim off any foam. Let jam cool in the pot for 5 minutes, stirring occasionally.

5. Ladle hot jam into hot jars, leaving ¼ inch (0.5 cm) headspace. Remove any air bubbles. Wipe jar rims and threads with a clean, damp paper towel. Center hot lids on jars and screw on bands until fingertip-tight.

6. Place jars in canner, making sure they are covered by at least 1 inch (2.5 cm) of water. Cover and bring to a gentle boil. Process 4-ounce (125 mL) jars and 8-ounce (250 mL) jars for 10 minutes; process 1-pint (500 mL) jars for 15 minutes.

7. Remove jars from canner and place on a wire rack or cloth towel. Let cool for 24 hours, then check seals. Wash and dry jars and store in a cool, dry, dark location.

Razzleberry Jam

✳

Makes about six 8-ounce (250 mL) jars

A jazzy berry jam with lots of berry flavor.

Tips: Defrosted frozen unsweetened red raspberries and blueberries work very well in this recipe. Each 12-oz (340 g) bag of frozen unsweetened raspberries will yield about 1 1/2 cups (375 mL) crushed raspberries. Each 12-oz (340 g) bag of frozen unsweetened blueberries will yield about 1 1/3 cups (325 mL) crushed blueberries.

For 2 cups (500 mL) crushed raspberries, you'll need about 1 1/2 lbs (750 g) or 5 cups (1.25 L) raspberries. For 1 1/4 cups (300 mL) crushed blueberries, you'll need about 1 lb (500 g) or 2 cups (500 mL) blueberries.

2 cups	crushed raspberries	500 mL
1 1/4 cups	crushed blueberries	300 mL
1 tbsp	freshly squeezed lemon juice	15 mL
5 1/4 cups	granulated sugar	1.3 L
1/2 tsp	unsalted butter (optional)	2 mL
1	pouch (3 oz/85 mL) liquid pectin	1

1. Prepare canning jars and lids and bring water in water bath canner to a boil.

2. In an 8-quart (8 L) stainless steel stockpot, combine raspberries, blueberries and lemon juice. Gradually stir in sugar and butter, if using. Bring to a boil over medium heat, stirring constantly until sugar is completely dissolved.

3. Increase heat to medium-high and bring to a full rolling boil, stirring constantly. Stir in pectin. Return to a full rolling boil, stirring constantly, and boil for 1 minute.

4. Remove pot from heat and skim off any foam. Let jam cool in the pot for 5 minutes, stirring occasionally.

5. Ladle hot jam into hot jars, leaving 1/4 inch (0.5 cm) headspace. Remove any air bubbles. Wipe jar rims and threads with a clean, damp paper towel. Center hot lids on jars and screw on bands until fingertip-tight.

6. Place jars in canner, making sure they are covered by at least 1 inch (2.5 cm) of water. Cover and bring to a gentle boil. Process 4-ounce (125 mL) jars and 8-ounce (250 mL) jars for 10 minutes; process 1-pint (500 mL) jars for 15 minutes.

7. Remove jars from canner and place on a wire rack or cloth towel. Let cool for 24 hours, then check seals. Wash and dry jars and store in a cool, dry, dark location.

Strawberry Kiwi Jam

✳

**Makes about
nine 8-ounce
(250 mL) jars**

*Kiwifruit gives classic
strawberry jam a
tropical twist.*

Tips: Use fully ripe,
moderately firm
strawberries for making
jam. Avoid very firm,
very soft or particularly
juicy berries, as these
can cause the jam to
set up too firm or not
set at all.

For 2¾ cups (675 mL)
crushed strawberries,
you'll need about
2 lbs (1 kg) or 5½ cups
(1.375 L) strawberries.
For 1½ cups (375 mL)
crushed kiwifruit,
you'll need about
10 medium kiwis.

2¾ cups	crushed hulled strawberries	675 mL
1½ cups	crushed seeded kiwifruit	375 mL
2 tbsp	freshly squeezed lemon juice	30 mL
7 cups	granulated sugar	1.75 L
½ tsp	unsalted butter (optional)	2 mL
1	pouch (3 oz/85 mL) liquid pectin	1

1. Prepare canning jars and lids and bring water in water bath canner to a boil.

2. In an 8-quart (8 L) stainless steel stockpot, combine strawberries, kiwis and lemon juice. Gradually stir in sugar and butter, if using. Bring to a boil over medium heat, stirring constantly until sugar is completely dissolved.

3. Increase heat to medium-high and bring to a full rolling boil, stirring constantly. Stir in pectin. Return to a full rolling boil, stirring constantly, and boil for 1 minute.

4. Remove pot from heat and skim off any foam. Let jam cool in the pot for 5 minutes, stirring occasionally.

5. Ladle hot jam into hot jars, leaving ¼ inch (0.5 cm) headspace. Remove any air bubbles. Wipe jar rims and threads with a clean, damp paper towel. Center hot lids on jars and screw on bands until fingertip-tight.

6. Place jars in canner, making sure they are covered by at least 1 inch (2.5 cm) of water. Cover and bring to a gentle boil. Process 4-ounce (125 mL) jars and 8-ounce (250 mL) jars for 10 minutes; process 1-pint (500 mL) jars for 15 minutes.

7. Remove jars from canner and place on a wire rack or cloth towel. Let cool for 24 hours, then check seals. Wash and dry jars and store in a cool, dry, dark location.

Strawberry Peach Jam

✳

Makes about eight 8-ounce (250 mL) jars

The exceptional flavor and fragrant aroma of this enchanting jam makes it a special treat on cold winter days.

Tips: For a uniform texture, cut strawberries and peaches into pieces before gently crushing them with a potato or vegetable masher.

For 2 cups (500 mL) crushed strawberries, you'll need about 1½ lbs (750 g) or 4 cups (1 L) strawberries. For 2 cups (500 mL) crushed peaches, you'll need about 2 lbs (1 kg) or about 6 medium peaches.

2 cups	crushed hulled strawberries	500 mL
2 cups	crushed pitted peeled peaches	500 mL
3 tbsp	freshly squeezed lemon juice	45 mL
7¼ cups	granulated sugar	1.8 L
½ tsp	unsalted butter (optional)	2 mL
1	pouch (3 oz/85 mL) liquid pectin	1

1. Prepare canning jars and lids and bring water in water bath canner to a boil.

2. In an 8-quart (8 L) stainless steel stockpot, combine strawberries, peaches and lemon juice. Gradually stir in sugar and butter, if using. Bring to a boil over medium heat, stirring constantly until sugar is completely dissolved.

3. Increase heat to medium-high and bring to a full rolling boil, stirring constantly. Stir in pectin. Return to a full rolling boil, stirring constantly, and boil for 1 minute.

4. Remove pot from heat and skim off any foam. Let jam cool in the pot for 5 minutes, stirring occasionally.

5. Ladle hot jam into hot jars, leaving ¼ inch (0.5 cm) headspace. Remove any air bubbles. Wipe jar rims and threads with a clean, damp paper towel. Center hot lids on jars and screw on bands until fingertip-tight.

6. Place jars in canner, making sure they are covered by at least 1 inch (2.5 cm) of water. Cover and bring to a gentle boil. Process 4-ounce (125 mL) jars and 8-ounce (250 mL) jars for 10 minutes; process 1-pint (500 mL) jars for 15 minutes.

7. Remove jars from canner and place on a wire rack or cloth towel. Let cool for 24 hours, then check seals. Wash and dry jars and store in a cool, dry, dark location.

Strawberry Pineapple Jam

**Makes about
seven 8-ounce
(250 mL) jars**

*Pretty and delicious —
a fantastic combination!*

Tips: Using canned
crushed pineapple in
jams is a real time-saver,
and jams made with
canned pineapple set
better than those made
with fresh pineapple.

For 3 cups (750 mL)
crushed strawberries,
you'll need about
2½ lbs (1.25 kg)
or 6 cups (1.5 L)
strawberries.

3 cups	crushed hulled strawberries	750 mL
1 cup	drained canned juice-packed crushed pineapple	250 mL
2 tbsp	freshly squeezed lemon juice	30 mL
6½ cups	granulated sugar	1.625 L
½ tsp	unsalted butter (optional)	2 mL
1	pouch (3 oz/85 mL) liquid pectin	1

1. Prepare canning jars and lids and bring water in water bath canner to a boil.

2. In an 8-quart (8 L) stainless steel stockpot, combine strawberries, pineapple and lemon juice. Gradually stir in sugar and butter, if using. Bring to a boil over medium heat, stirring constantly until sugar is completely dissolved.

3. Increase heat to medium-high and bring to a full rolling boil, stirring constantly. Stir in pectin. Return to a full rolling boil, stirring constantly, and boil for 1 minute.

4. Remove pot from heat and skim off any foam. Let jam cool in the pot for 5 minutes, stirring occasionally.

5. Ladle hot jam into hot jars, leaving ¼ inch (0.5 cm) headspace. Remove any air bubbles. Wipe jar rims and threads with a clean, damp paper towel. Center hot lids on jars and screw on bands until fingertip-tight.

6. Place jars in canner, making sure they are covered by at least 1 inch (2.5 cm) of water. Cover and bring to a gentle boil. Process 4-ounce (125 mL) jars and 8-ounce (250 mL) jars for 10 minutes; process 1-pint (500 mL) jars for 15 minutes.

7. Remove jars from canner and place on a wire rack or cloth towel. Let cool for 24 hours, then check seals. Wash and dry jars and store in a cool, dry, dark location.

Strawberry Raspberry Jam

✳

6 cups	fresh raspberries	1.5 L
2 cups	crushed hulled strawberries	500 mL
1 tbsp	freshly squeezed lemon juice	15 mL
6¾ cups	granulated sugar	1.675 L
½ tsp	unsalted butter (optional)	2 mL
1	pouch (3 oz/85 mL) liquid pectin	1

Makes seven or eight 8-ounce (250 mL) jars

The magnificent flavor and stunning appearance of this jam make it an excellent choice to give as a gift.

Tips: If you use a food mill to crush and seed the berries, fit it with the finest plate.

Fresh strawberries are strongly recommended for making jams. Frozen strawberries are frequently underripe and lack flavor, and many are packed in sugar, which can upset the balance of the recipe and prevent the jam from setting.

Defrosted frozen raspberries also make great seedless jam. Each 12-oz (340 g) bag of frozen unsweetened raspberries will yield about 1 cup (250 mL) seedless raspberry pulp.

For 2 cups (500 mL) crushed strawberries, you'll need about 1½ lbs (750 g) or 4 cups (1 L) strawberries.

1. Prepare canning jars and lids and bring water in water bath canner to a boil.

2. In a flat-bottomed pan or bowl, crush raspberries in small batches. Using the back of a spoon, press crushed raspberries through a fine-mesh sieve to remove the seeds. (Or use a food mill to crush the fruit and remove the seeds.) Measure 2 cups (500 mL) seedless raspberry pulp.

3. In an 8-quart (8 L) stainless steel stockpot, combine raspberry pulp, strawberries and lemon juice. Gradually stir in sugar and butter, if using. Bring to a boil over medium heat, stirring constantly until sugar is completely dissolved.

4. Increase heat to medium-high and bring to a full rolling boil, stirring constantly. Stir in pectin. Return to a full rolling boil, stirring constantly, and boil for 1 minute.

5. Remove pot from heat and skim off any foam. Let jam cool in the pot for 5 minutes, stirring occasionally.

6. Ladle hot jam into hot jars, leaving ¼ inch (0.5 cm) headspace. Remove any air bubbles. Wipe jar rims and threads with a clean, damp paper towel. Center hot lids on jars and screw on bands until fingertip-tight.

7. Place jars in canner, making sure they are covered by at least 1 inch (2.5 cm) of water. Cover and bring to a gentle boil. Process 4-ounce (125 mL) jars and 8-ounce (250 mL) jars for 10 minutes; process 1-pint (500 mL) jars for 15 minutes.

8. Remove jars from canner and place on a wire rack or cloth towel. Let cool for 24 hours, then check seals. Wash and dry jars and store in a cool, dry, dark location.

Sunrise Jam

———— ✳ ————

**Makes seven
or eight 8-ounce
(250 mL) jars**

*The warm golden
color and radiant
fruit flavors of this
delightful jam brighten
any morning.*

Tips: Butter is added
to jam recipes to help
reduce the amount of
foam created when the
fruit boils. The butter is
an optional ingredient
and may be eliminated,
if you prefer.

For 1½ cups (375 mL)
crushed strawberries,
you'll need about
1½ lbs (750 g) or 3 cups
(750 mL) strawberries.
For 1½ cups (375 mL)
crushed apricots, you'll
need about 1½ lbs
(750 g) medium
apricots.

1½ cups	crushed hulled strawberries	375 mL
1½ cups	crushed pitted peeled apricots	375 mL
¾ cup	drained canned juice-packed crushed pineapple	175 mL
¼ cup	freshly squeezed lemon juice	50 mL
6 cups	granulated sugar	1.5 L
½ tsp	unsalted butter (optional)	2 mL
1	pouch (3 oz/85 mL) liquid pectin	1

1. Prepare canning jars and lids and bring water in water bath canner to a boil.

2. In an 8-quart (8 L) stainless steel stockpot, combine strawberries, apricots, pineapple and lemon juice. Gradually stir in sugar and butter, if using. Bring to a boil over medium heat, stirring constantly until sugar is completely dissolved.

3. Increase heat to medium-high and bring to a full rolling boil, stirring constantly. Stir in pectin. Return to a full rolling boil, stirring constantly, and boil for 1 minute.

4. Remove pot from heat and skim off any foam. Let jam cool in the pot for 5 minutes, stirring occasionally.

5. Ladle hot jam into hot jars, leaving ¼ inch (0.5 cm) headspace. Remove any air bubbles. Wipe jar rims and threads with a clean, damp paper towel. Center hot lids on jars and screw on bands until fingertip-tight.

6. Place jars in canner, making sure they are covered by at least 1 inch (2.5 cm) of water. Cover and bring to a gentle boil. Process 4-ounce (125 mL) jars and 8-ounce (250 mL) jars for 10 minutes; process 1-pint (500 mL) jars for 15 minutes.

7. Remove jars from canner and place on a wire rack or cloth towel. Let cool for 24 hours, then check seals. Wash and dry jars and store in a cool, dry, dark location.

Triple Berry Jam

✳

The combination of berry flavors is a lovely reminder of warm summer days.

Tips: To wash berries, place them in a colander and rinse under cool running water. Gently shake the colander to remove excess water. Spread berries on top of layers of paper towels and gently blot dry.

For 2 cups (500 mL) crushed strawberries, you'll need about 1½ lbs (750 g) or 4 cups (1 L) strawberries. For 1 cup (250 mL) crushed raspberries, you'll need about 12 oz (375 g) or 2½ cups (625 mL) raspberries. For ¾ cup (175 mL) crushed blueberries, you'll need about 10 oz (300 g) or 1½ cups (375 mL) blueberries.

2 cups	crushed hulled strawberries	500 mL
1 cup	crushed raspberries	250 mL
¾ cup	crushed blueberries	175 mL
2 tbsp	freshly squeezed lemon juice	30 mL
6 cups	granulated sugar	1.5 L
½ tsp	unsalted butter (optional)	2 mL
1	pouch (3 oz/85 mL) liquid pectin	1

1. Prepare canning jars and lids and bring water in water bath canner to a boil.

2. In an 8-quart (8 L) stainless steel stockpot, combine strawberries, raspberries, blueberries and lemon juice. Gradually stir in sugar and butter, if using. Bring to a boil over medium heat, stirring constantly until sugar is completely dissolved.

3. Increase heat to medium-high and bring to a full rolling boil, stirring constantly. Stir in pectin. Return to a full rolling boil, stirring constantly, and boil for 1 minute.

4. Remove pot from heat and skim off any foam. Let jam cool in the pot for 5 minutes, stirring occasionally.

5. Ladle hot jam into hot jars, leaving ¼ inch (0.5 cm) headspace. Remove any air bubbles. Wipe jar rims and threads with a clean, damp paper towel. Center hot lids on jars and screw on bands until fingertip-tight.

6. Place jars in canner, making sure they are covered by at least 1 inch (2.5 cm) of water. Cover and bring to a gentle boil. Process 4-ounce (125 mL) jars and 8-ounce (250 mL) jars for 10 minutes; process 1-pint (500 mL) jars for 15 minutes.

7. Remove jars from canner and place on a wire rack or cloth towel. Let cool for 24 hours, then check seals. Wash and dry jars and store in a cool, dry, dark location.

Jellies

✳

About Jellies

JELLY IS A PRESERVER'S GEM. Jellies are transparent, jewel-like spreads made from the extracted juice of the fruit. A well-made jelly will be crystal clear, will sparkle and shimmer in the light and will have the delightful fresh flavor of the fruit from which it is made. Jellies have a tender texture. They are firm enough to hold their shape when cut or spooned from the jar, but still quiver when moved and spread easily on toast or biscuits.

The process of making jelly is similar to that of making jam, except that jelly-making involves two processes: one to extract the juice from the fruit and the second to transform the juice into jelly. The additional steps of extracting the juice from the fruit and filtering out the fruit pulp from the juice are what differentiate jelly from jam. To separate the fruit pulp from the juice, the juice is strained through several layers of cheesecloth or a cloth jelly bag. While jellies can take longer to make than jams, they are well worth the effort.

Jellies can be made from sweet, savory or even hot ingredients. In addition to fruit juices, wine, Champagne and other liquids, such as herb infusions, make lovely jellies. The recipes in this chapter focus specifically on fruit jellies. Recipes for jellies containing herbs, hot peppers and liqueurs can be found in the Savory Spreads and Drunken Spreads chapters.

Unsweetened bottled juices make excellent jellies and eliminate the time needed to extract the juice from the fruit. If the bottled juice is unfiltered, it will need to be strained before being made into jelly. Filtered juices are a real time-saver and may be used straight from the bottle. Unsweetened fruit juices can be found in grocery stores, specialty food stores and health food stores. Unsweetened apple, cranberry, grape and pomegranate juices are all readily available. Whenever possible, use pure fruit juice rather than juice blends. Avoid juice drinks or juice cocktails, as both contain large amounts of sugar, which will throw off the balance of ingredients in the recipe and prevent the jelly from setting.

Pectin is added to jelly recipes because few fruit juices contain enough natural pectin to create a gel on their own. The addition of pectin also substantially reduces the cooking time, which means the jelly will have a fresher flavor closer to that of the natural flavor of the fruit. Jellies made with added pectin have a tender texture that does not turn rubbery when cooled. Jellies made by the long-boil method, without the addition of pectin, are often very firm and can lose that fresh fruit flavor, acquiring an unpleasant, overcooked, molasses-like flavor from the extensive cooking.

While the soft spread recipes in other chapters in this book include the addition of a small amount of butter to the fruit to reduce the amount of foaming during cooking, butter should not be added to jellies. The addition of butter will make the jelly cloudy.

In the other soft spread recipes, I also advise cooling the spread in the pan for a few minutes before filling the jars to prevent floating fruit. As jellies do not contain fruit pieces and a skin can quickly form on the surface of the jelly as it cools in the pan, jelly should be ladled into jars immediately after it has been removed from the heat and any foam has been quickly skimmed off the top.

Extracting Juice for Jelly

The fruit used to make jellies should be peeled and pitted. The peels can give the extracted juice a bitter or earthy taste, so it is best to remove them before juicing the fruit. The fruit should then be crushed or finely chopped to allow it to cook rapidly and release the juice rapidly. Never purée the fruit when making jellies. Puréeing blends the fruit pulp and juice together, rather than allowing the juice to separate from the pulp. Jellies made from puréed fruits will be very cloudy and will not have the glowing translucence of a quality jelly.

Heat is the best way to extract the juice from most fruits. The fruit is heated and cooked until soft to release the juice from the fruit. The fruit and juice are then spooned into a sieve lined with damp, very fine-knit cheesecloth or into a damp jelly bag, which slowly strains the juice from the fruit pulp. When the dripping has stopped, the juice is chilled to allow any remaining sediment to settle to the bottom of the container before the juice is strained again.

The process of juice extraction should never be rushed by trying to force the juice through the cheesecloth or by squeezing the jelly bag. If you do so, the juice will lose its clarity. Tiny pieces of fruit pulp will be pushed through the cheesecloth or jelly bag and into the strained juice, causing the finished jelly to be cloudy.

If the fibers of the fabric become clogged with pulp, pour the fruit and undrained juice into a container, then rinse the cheesecloth or jelly bag to clean the fabric. Resume the straining process with the clean fabric. Depending on the fruit being strained, it may be necessary to rinse the fabric a few times in order to extract all of the juice from the cooked fruit.

The quantities of fruit listed in each recipe should provide ample juice for making jelly. However, the juiciness of fruit can vary from variety to variety, from year to year, and from one growing region to the next. If the fruit you are using does not produce an adequate amount of juice for the recipe, there are a couple of solutions to increase the juice yield from the fruit.

The best method, resulting in the strongest flavor, is to heat the strained fruit pulp and a small amount of water to produce more juice. In a pan, combine the strained fruit pulp and ½ cup (125 mL) to 1 cup (250 mL) of water, depending on how much more juice you need. Stir gently until the fruit and water are combined. Cover the pan and heat the mixture over medium heat until hot, but do not let it boil. Remove the pan from the heat and let stand, covered, for 20 minutes. This standing period allows the water to absorb the flavor of the fruit and the fruit to release any remaining juice. Strain the fruit and juice as instructed in the recipe. Add the juice to the yield you obtained from the first straining and proceed with making the jelly.

If you are short on time, simply combine the water with the strained fruit pulp, give it a quick stir and strain it again without heating. This method is easier and faster but will produce a very mild-flavored colored water, reducing the intensity of flavor in the finished jelly. Unless you are only short a spoonful or two of juice, I do not recommend adding water to the strained juice to make up the difference. The water will weaken the overall flavor of the jelly, and adding too much water may keep the jelly from setting properly.

If you do not have time to make jelly when fresh fruit is ripe and ready to use, the juice may be extracted from the fruit and strained, then packaged in zippered freezer bags or airtight containers and frozen for later use.

Apple Cider Jelly

*

**Makes about
seven 8-ounce
(250 mL) jars**

*Apple cider creates a
jelly with intense apple
flavor. Use warmed
Apple Cider Jelly as a
glaze for apple tarts.*

Variation

Unsweetened apple
juice may be substituted
for the apple cider;
however, the jelly will
have a milder flavor.

3¾ cups	unsweetened apple cider	925 mL
6½ cups	granulated sugar	1.625 L
2	pouches (each 3 oz/85 mL) liquid pectin	2

1. Prepare canning jars and lids and bring water in water bath canner to a boil.

2. If the cider contains sediment or pulp, strain it before measuring. To strain cider, place a sieve over a pan or bowl and line it with a piece of damp folded fine-knit cheesecloth. Pour cider into the lined sieve, being careful not to disturb any sediment in the bottom of the container.

3. In an 8-quart (8 L) stainless steel stockpot, combine cider and sugar. Bring to a boil over medium heat, stirring constantly until sugar is completely dissolved.

4. Increase heat to medium-high and bring to a full rolling boil, stirring constantly. Stir in pectin. Return to a full rolling boil, stirring constantly, and boil for 1 minute.

5. Remove pot from heat and quickly skim off any foam.

6. Immediately ladle hot jelly into hot jars, leaving ¼ inch (0.5 cm) headspace. Wipe jar rims and threads with a clean, damp paper towel. Center hot lids on jars and screw on bands until fingertip-tight.

7. Place jars in canner, making sure they are covered by at least 1 inch (2.5 cm) of water. Cover and bring to a gentle boil. Process 4-ounce (125 mL) jars and 8-ounce (250 mL) jars for 10 minutes; process 1-pint (500 mL) jars for 15 minutes.

8. Remove jars from canner and place on a wire rack or cloth towel. Let cool for 24 hours, then check seals. Wash and dry jars and store in a cool, dry, dark location.

Apricot Peach Jelly

✳

This lovely golden jelly makes an excellent spread for scones or biscuits.

Tips: For best flavor, use ripe apricots and peaches that yield to gentle pressure.

To quickly and easily peel peaches and apricots, gently drop the fruit, a few at a time, into a pot of boiling water for 30 seconds. Using a slotted spoon, remove the fruit from the boiling water and immediately plunge into a bowl or pan of ice water for 1 to 2 minutes to stop the cooking process. Drain the fruit and use a small, sharp paring knife to remove the peels.

3 lbs	apricots, peeled, pitted and crushed or finely chopped	1.5 kg
3 lbs	peaches, peeled, pitted and crushed or finely chopped	1.5 kg
1½ cups	water	375 mL
⅓ cup	freshly squeezed lemon juice	75 mL
6⅔ cups	granulated sugar	1.65 L
2	pouches (each 3 oz/85 mL) liquid pectin	2

1. In an 8-quart (8 L) stainless steel stockpot, combine apricots, peaches and water. Bring to a boil over medium-high heat. Reduce heat, cover and simmer gently for 5 minutes. Remove from heat and let stand for 20 minutes.

2. Place a fine-mesh sieve over a pan or bowl. Ladle the cooked fruit into the sieve and drain the juice from the fruit pulp. Discard the pulp. Rinse the sieve and line it with a piece of damp folded fine-knit cheesecloth. Strain juice through the cheesecloth twice, rinsing cheesecloth as necessary to remove any sediment that blocks the juice flow. (The juice may be strained through a jelly bag instead, if you prefer.) Cover juice and refrigerate for several hours or overnight to allow any remaining sediment to settle to the bottom of the container.

3. Prepare canning jars and lids and bring water in water bath canner to a boil.

4. Place a sieve over a pan or bowl and line it with a piece of damp folded cheesecloth. Ladle or pour juice into the lined sieve, being careful not to disturb any sediment in the bottom of the container. Measure 3¼ cups (800 mL) juice.

5. In an 8-quart (8 L) stainless steel stockpot, combine fruit juice, lemon juice and sugar. Bring to a boil over medium heat, stirring constantly until sugar is completely dissolved.

6. Increase heat to medium-high and bring to a full rolling boil, stirring constantly. Stir in pectin. Return to a full rolling boil, stirring constantly, and boil for 1 minute.

7. Remove pot from heat and quickly skim off any foam.

8. Immediately ladle hot jelly into hot jars, leaving ¼ inch (0.5 cm) headspace. Wipe jar rims and threads with a clean, damp paper towel. Center hot lids on jars and screw on bands until fingertip-tight.

9. Place jars in canner, making sure they are covered by at least 1 inch (2.5 cm) of water. Cover and bring to a gentle boil. Process 4-ounce (125 mL) jars and 8-ounce (250 mL) jars for 10 minutes; process 1-pint (500 mL) jars for 15 minutes.

10. Remove jars from canner and place on a wire rack or cloth towel. Let cool for 24 hours, then check seals. Wash and dry jars and store in a cool, dry, dark location.

Apricot Plum Jelly

Makes about six 8-ounce (250 mL) jars

The jewel-like color of this exquisite jelly dances in the light.

Tips: While a small amount of butter is frequently added to jams to reduce the amount of foaming, butter should not be added to jellies, as it will make the finished jelly cloudy.

Choose unblemished apricots with good color. Avoid apricots that are pale yellow, very firm or very soft, as these will not produce spreads with a strong apricot flavor.

4 lbs	apricots, peeled, pitted and crushed or finely chopped	2 kg
2 lbs	plums, peeled, pitted and crushed or finely chopped	1 kg
1½ cups	water	375 mL
¼ cup	freshly squeezed lemon juice	50 mL
6 cups	granulated sugar	1.5 L
2	pouches (each 3 oz/85 mL) liquid pectin	2

1. In an 8-quart (8 L) stainless steel stockpot, combine apricots, plums and water. Bring to a boil over medium-high heat. Reduce heat, cover and simmer gently for 10 minutes. Remove from heat and let stand for 20 minutes.

2. Place a fine-mesh sieve over a pan or bowl. Ladle the cooked fruit into the sieve and drain the juice from the fruit pulp. Discard the pulp. Rinse the sieve and line it with a piece of damp folded fine-knit cheesecloth. Strain juice through the cheesecloth twice, rinsing cheesecloth as necessary to remove any sediment that blocks the juice flow. (The juice may be strained through a jelly bag instead, if you prefer.) Cover juice and refrigerate for several hours or overnight to allow any remaining sediment to settle to the bottom of the container.

3. Prepare canning jars and lids and bring water in water bath canner to a boil.

4. Place a sieve over a pan or bowl and line it with a piece of damp folded cheesecloth. Ladle or pour juice into the lined sieve, being careful not to disturb any sediment in the bottom of the container. Measure 3½ cups (875 mL) juice.

5. In an 8-quart (8 L) stainless steel stockpot, combine fruit juice, lemon juice and sugar. Bring to a boil over medium heat, stirring constantly until sugar is completely dissolved.

6. Increase heat to medium-high and bring to a full rolling boil, stirring constantly. Stir in pectin. Return to a full rolling boil, stirring constantly, and boil for 1 minute.

✳

7. Remove pot from heat and quickly skim off any foam.

8. Immediately ladle hot jelly into hot jars, leaving ¼ inch (0.5 cm) headspace. Wipe jar rims and threads with a clean, damp paper towel. Center hot lids on jars and screw on bands until fingertip-tight.

9. Place jars in canner, making sure they are covered by at least 1 inch (2.5 cm) of water. Cover and bring to a gentle boil. Process 4-ounce (125 mL) jars and 8-ounce (250 mL) jars for 10 minutes; process 1-pint (500 mL) jars for 15 minutes.

10. Remove jars from canner and place on a wire rack or cloth towel. Let cool for 24 hours, then check seals. Wash and dry jars and store in a cool, dry, dark location.

Blackberry Jelly

✳

*The intense blackberry
flavor and deep color
of this dazzling jelly
are sure to please berry
lovers of all ages.*

Tips: Ripe berries
produce intensely
flavored jellies.
Blackberries that are
dull in appearance are
fully ripe, while shiny
blackberries are
underripe.

The individual juicy
fruit pods or seed
pouches on berries
such as blackberries,
boysenberries and
raspberries are called
drooplets. For the
sweetest berries with
the fullest flavor, choose
blackberries with large
drooplets. The larger
the drooplets on
blackberries, the higher
the sugar content.

12 cups	blackberries, crushed	3 L
3/4 cup	water	175 mL
7 cups	granulated sugar	1.75 L
2	pouches (each 3 oz/85 mL) liquid pectin	2

1. In an 8-quart (8 L) stainless steel stockpot, combine blackberries and water. Bring to a boil over medium-high heat. Reduce heat, cover and simmer gently for 5 minutes. Remove from heat and let stand for 20 minutes.

2. Place a fine-mesh sieve over a pan or bowl. Ladle the cooked blackberries into the sieve and drain the juice from the fruit pulp. Discard the pulp. Rinse the sieve and line it with a piece of damp folded fine-knit cheesecloth. Strain juice through the cheesecloth twice, rinsing cheesecloth as necessary to remove any sediment that blocks the juice flow. (The juice may be strained through a jelly bag instead, if you prefer.) Cover juice and refrigerate for several hours or overnight to allow any remaining sediment to settle to the bottom of the container.

3. Prepare canning jars and lids and bring water in water bath canner to a boil.

4. Place a sieve over a pan or bowl and line it with a piece of damp folded cheesecloth. Ladle or pour juice into the lined sieve, being careful not to disturb any sediment in the bottom of the container. Measure 4¾ cups (1.175 L) juice.

5. In an 8-quart (8 L) stainless steel stockpot, combine blackberry juice and sugar. Bring to a boil over medium heat, stirring constantly until sugar is completely dissolved.

6. Increase heat to medium-high and bring to a full rolling boil, stirring constantly. Stir in pectin. Return to a full rolling boil, stirring constantly, and boil for 1 minute.

7. Remove pot from heat and quickly skim off any foam.

8. Immediately ladle hot jelly into hot jars, leaving $\frac{1}{4}$ inch (0.5 cm) headspace. Wipe jar rims and threads with a clean, damp paper towel. Center hot lids on jars and screw on bands until fingertip-tight.

9. Place jars in canner, making sure they are covered by at least 1 inch (2.5 cm) of water. Cover and bring to a gentle boil. Process 4-ounce (125 mL) jars and 8-ounce (250 mL) jars for 10 minutes; process 1-pint (500 mL) jars for 15 minutes.

10. Remove jars from canner and place on a wire rack or cloth towel. Let cool for 24 hours, then check seals. Wash and dry jars and store in a cool, dry, dark location.

Blueberry Blackberry Jelly

Blueberries and blackberries blend to make a radiant jelly with lots of berry flavor.

Tip: Buy blueberries and blackberries at the peak of the season and freeze them for later use. Frozen blueberries and blackberries make great jellies. Measure frozen berries and let thaw, reserving juice, before crushing.

6 cups	blueberries, crushed	1.5 L
6 cups	blackberries, crushed	1.5 L
1½ cups	water	375 mL
7 cups	granulated sugar	1.75 L
2	pouches (each 3 oz/85 mL) liquid pectin	2

1. In an 8-quart (8 L) stainless steel stockpot, combine blueberries, blackberries and water. Bring to a boil over medium-high heat. Reduce heat, cover and simmer gently for 5 minutes. Remove from heat and let stand for 20 minutes.

2. Place a fine-mesh sieve over a pan or bowl. Ladle the cooked berries into the sieve and drain the juice from the fruit pulp. Discard the pulp. Rinse the sieve and line it with a piece of damp folded fine-knit cheesecloth. Strain juice through the cheesecloth twice, rinsing cheesecloth as necessary to remove any sediment that blocks the juice flow. (The juice may be strained through a jelly bag instead, if you prefer.) Cover juice and refrigerate for several hours or overnight to allow any remaining sediment to settle to the bottom of the container.

3. Prepare canning jars and lids and bring water in water bath canner to a boil.

4. Place a sieve over a pan or bowl and line it with a piece of damp folded cheesecloth. Ladle or pour juice into the lined sieve, being careful not to disturb any sediment in the bottom of the container. Measure 4¾ cups (1.175 L) juice.

5. In an 8-quart (8 L) stainless steel stockpot, combine fruit juice and sugar. Bring to a boil over medium heat, stirring constantly until sugar is completely dissolved.

6. Increase heat to medium-high and bring to a full rolling boil, stirring constantly. Stir in pectin. Return to a full rolling boil, stirring constantly, and boil for 1 minute.

7. Remove pot from heat and quickly skim off any foam.

8. Immediately ladle hot jelly into hot jars, leaving ¼ inch (0.5 cm) headspace. Wipe jar rims and threads with a clean, damp paper towel. Center hot lids on jars and screw on bands until fingertip-tight.

9. Place jars in canner, making sure they are covered by at least 1 inch (2.5 cm) of water. Cover and bring to a gentle boil. Process 4-ounce (125 mL) jars and 8-ounce (250 mL) jars for 10 minutes; process 1-pint (500 mL) jars for 15 minutes.

10. Remove jars from canner and place on a wire rack or cloth towel. Let cool for 24 hours, then check seals. Wash and dry jars and store in a cool, dry, dark location.

Candy Apple Jelly

With a pretty pink color, this jelly blends the flavors of apple cider and cinnamon candies to create a special treat that is spicy, but not too hot.

Variation

If you prefer a stronger cinnamon flavor and deeper color, increase the red hot candies to ½ cup (125 mL).

3¾ cups	unsweetened apple cider	925 mL
6½ cups	granulated sugar	1.625 L
⅓ cup	red hot candies	75 mL
2	pouches (each 3 oz/85 mL) liquid pectin	2

1. Prepare canning jars and lids and bring water in water bath canner to a boil.

2. If the cider contains sediment or pulp, strain it before measuring. To strain cider, place a sieve over a pan or bowl and line it with a piece of damp folded fine-knit cheesecloth. Pour cider into the lined sieve, being careful not to disturb any sediment in the bottom of the container.

3. In an 8-quart (8 L) stainless steel stockpot, combine cider and sugar. Bring to a boil over medium heat, stirring constantly until sugar is completely dissolved. Add red hot candies and stir until completely dissolved.

4. Increase heat to medium-high and bring to a full rolling boil, stirring constantly. Stir in pectin. Return to a full rolling boil, stirring constantly, and boil for 1 minute.

5. Remove pot from heat and quickly skim off any foam.

6. Immediately ladle hot jelly into hot jars, leaving ¼ inch (0.5 cm) headspace. Wipe jar rims and threads with a clean, damp paper towel. Center hot lids on jars and screw on bands until fingertip-tight.

7. Place jars in canner, making sure they are covered by at least 1 inch (2.5 cm) of water. Cover and bring to a gentle boil. Process 4-ounce (125 mL) jars and 8-ounce (250 mL) jars for 10 minutes; process 1-pint (500 mL) jars for 15 minutes.

8. Remove jars from canner and place on a wire rack or cloth towel. Let cool for 24 hours, then check seals. Wash and dry jars and store in a cool, dry, dark location.

Cherry Cider Jelly

3¾ cups	unsweetened cherry cider	925 mL
6½ cups	granulated sugar	1.625 L
2	pouches (each 3 oz/85 mL) liquid pectin	2

*This delightful jelly is
fast and easy to make,
and is a favorite with
kids of all ages.*

Tip: Cherry cider is
popular in cherry-
growing regions, where
it is often sold at U-pick
orchards, produce stands
and local markets. You
can also find it in some
specialty food stores.

1. Prepare canning jars and lids and bring water in water bath canner to a boil.

2. If the cider contains sediment or pulp, strain it before measuring. To strain cider, place a sieve over a pan or bowl and line it with a piece of damp folded fine-knit cheesecloth. Pour cider into the lined sieve, being careful not to disturb any sediment in the bottom of the container.

3. In an 8-quart (8 L) stainless steel stockpot, combine cider and sugar. Bring to a boil over medium heat, stirring constantly until sugar is completely dissolved.

4. Increase heat to medium-high and bring to a full rolling boil, stirring constantly. Stir in pectin. Return to a full rolling boil, stirring constantly, and boil for 1 minute.

5. Remove pot from heat and quickly skim off any foam.

6. Immediately ladle hot jelly into hot jars, leaving ¼ inch (0.5 cm) headspace. Wipe jar rims and threads with a clean, damp paper towel. Center hot lids on jars and screw on bands until fingertip-tight.

7. Place jars in canner, making sure they are covered by at least 1 inch (2.5 cm) of water. Cover and bring to a gentle boil. Process 4-ounce (125 mL) jars and 8-ounce (250 mL) jars for 10 minutes; process 1-pint (500 mL) jars for 15 minutes.

8. Remove jars from canner and place on a wire rack or cloth towel. Let cool for 24 hours, then check seals. Wash and dry jars and store in a cool, dry, dark location.

Cherry Plum Jelly

✳

3½ lbs	sweet cherries, pitted and finely chopped	1.75 kg
3½ lbs	plums, peeled, pitted and finely chopped	1.75 kg
1 cup	water	250 mL
¼ cup	freshly squeezed lemon juice	50 mL
6½ cups	granulated sugar	1.625 L
2	pouches (each 3 oz/85 mL) liquid pectin	2

Makes seven or eight 8-ounce (250 mL) jars

I like to use sweet cherries for this jelly because they blend so well with the flavor of the plums. Sour cherries can also be used instead, if you prefer.

Tips: If using sour cherries, reduce the lemon juice to 1 tbsp (15 mL).

Red plum varieties, such as Santa Rosa, make a nice flavor pairing with both sweet and sour cherries. If preferred, yellow and black plums will also work well.

1. In an 8-quart (8 L) stainless steel stockpot, combine cherries, plums and water. Bring to a boil over medium-high heat. Reduce heat, cover and simmer gently for 10 minutes. Remove from heat and let stand for 20 minutes.

2. Place a fine-mesh sieve over a pan or bowl. Ladle the cooked fruit into the sieve and drain the juice from the fruit pulp. Discard the pulp. Rinse the sieve and line it with a piece of damp folded fine-knit cheesecloth. Strain juice through the cheesecloth twice, rinsing cheesecloth as necessary to remove any sediment that blocks the juice flow. (The juice may be strained through a jelly bag instead, if you prefer.) Cover juice and refrigerate for several hours or overnight to allow any remaining sediment to settle to the bottom of the container.

3. Prepare canning jars and lids and bring water in water bath canner to a boil.

4. Place a sieve over a pan or bowl and line it with a piece of damp folded cheesecloth. Ladle or pour juice into the lined sieve, being careful not to disturb any sediment in the bottom of the container. Measure 4 cups (1 L) juice.

5. In an 8-quart (8 L) stainless steel stockpot, combine fruit juice, lemon juice and sugar. Bring to a boil over medium heat, stirring constantly until sugar is completely dissolved.

6. Increase heat to medium-high and bring to a full rolling boil, stirring constantly. Stir in pectin. Return to a full rolling boil, stirring constantly, and boil for 1 minute.

7. Remove pot from heat and quickly skim off any foam.

Tip: A cherry pitter makes quick work of removing pits from cherries. Handheld cherry pitters are available in most kitchen supply stores and some grocery stores. Many stores also carry more elaborate cherry pitters, which can really come in handy when you're pitting large quantities of cherries.

8. Immediately ladle hot jelly into hot jars, leaving $\frac{1}{4}$ inch (0.5 cm) headspace. Wipe jar rims and threads with a clean, damp paper towel. Center hot lids on jars and screw on bands until fingertip-tight.

9. Place jars in canner, making sure they are covered by at least 1 inch (2.5 cm) of water. Cover and bring to a gentle boil. Process 4-ounce (125 mL) jars and 8-ounce (250 mL) jars for 10 minutes; process 1-pint (500 mL) jars for 15 minutes.

10. Remove jars from canner and place on a wire rack or cloth towel. Let cool for 24 hours, then check seals. Wash and dry jars and store in a cool, dry, dark location.

Crabapple Jelly

✳

Makes eight or nine 8-ounce (250 mL) jars

Crabapples are an excellent fruit to use for making jelly. They often produce a jelly with more intense flavor than regular apples, and red crabapples yield a jelly with a beautiful pink color.

Tip: Use crabapples that are fully ripe and unblemished. Do not use any that have fallen from the tree, as the damaged fruit may contain bacteria that could contaminate the jelly.

5 lbs	crabapples, cored and chopped	2.5 kg
4 cups	water	1 L
7½ cups	granulated sugar	1.875 L
1	pouch (3 oz/85 mL) liquid pectin	1

1. In an 8-quart (8 L) stainless steel stockpot, combine crabapples and water. Bring to a boil over medium-high heat. Reduce heat, cover and simmer gently for 30 minutes. Remove from heat and let stand for 30 minutes.

2. Place a fine-mesh sieve over a pan or bowl. Ladle the cooked crabapples into the sieve and drain the juice from the fruit pulp. Discard the pulp. Rinse the sieve and line it with a piece of damp folded fine-knit cheesecloth. Strain juice through the cheesecloth twice, rinsing cheesecloth as necessary to remove any sediment that blocks the juice flow. (The juice may be strained through a jelly bag instead, if you prefer.) Cover juice and refrigerate for several hours or overnight to allow any remaining sediment to settle to the bottom of the container.

3. Prepare canning jars and lids and bring water in water bath canner to a boil.

4. Place a sieve over a pan or bowl and line it with a piece of damp folded cheesecloth. Ladle or pour juice into the lined sieve, being careful not to disturb any sediment in the bottom of the container. Measure 5 cups (1.25 L) juice.

5. In an 8-quart (8 L) stainless steel stockpot, combine crabapple juice and sugar. Bring to a boil over medium heat, stirring constantly until sugar is completely dissolved.

6. Increase heat to medium-high and bring to a full rolling boil, stirring constantly. Stir in pectin. Return to a full rolling boil, stirring constantly, and boil for 1 minute.

7. Remove pot from heat and quickly skim off any foam.

Tip: To maintain freshness, store liquid pectin in the refrigerator. Bring the pectin to room temperature before using.

8. Immediately ladle hot jelly into hot jars, leaving ¼ inch (0.5 cm) headspace. Wipe jar rims and threads with a clean, damp paper towel. Center hot lids on jars and screw on bands until fingertip-tight.

9. Place jars in canner, making sure they are covered by at least 1 inch (2.5 cm) of water. Cover and bring to a gentle boil. Process 4-ounce (125 mL) jars and 8-ounce (250 mL) jars for 10 minutes; process 1-pint (500 mL) jars for 15 minutes.

10. Remove jars from canner and place on a wire rack or cloth towel. Let cool for 24 hours, then check seals. Wash and dry jars and store in a cool, dry, dark location.

Cranberry Raspberry Jelly

Makes about eight 8-ounce (250 mL) jars

The blending of cranberries and raspberries gives this jewel-like ruby jelly a tantalizing flavor.

Tip: You can use fresh or frozen cranberries and raspberries to make this jelly. Measure frozen berries and let thaw, reserving juice, before crushing.

3 cups	cranberries	750 mL
3½ cups	water	875 mL
8 cups	red raspberries, crushed	2 L
7 cups	granulated sugar	1.75 L
2	pouches (each 3 oz/85 mL) liquid pectin	2

1. In an 8-quart (8 L) stainless steel stockpot, combine cranberries and water. Bring to a boil over medium-high heat. Reduce heat, cover and simmer gently for 10 minutes. Add raspberries. Simmer gently for 5 minutes. Remove from heat and let stand for 30 minutes.

2. Place a fine-mesh sieve over a pan or bowl. Ladle the cooked berries into the sieve and drain the juice from the fruit pulp. Discard the pulp. Rinse the sieve and line it with a piece of damp folded fine-knit cheesecloth. Strain juice through the cheesecloth twice, rinsing cheesecloth as necessary to remove any sediment that blocks the juice flow. (The juice may be strained through a jelly bag instead, if you prefer.) Cover juice and refrigerate for several hours or overnight to allow any remaining sediment to settle to the bottom of the container.

3. Prepare canning jars and lids and bring water in water bath canner to a boil.

4. Place a sieve over a pan or bowl and line it with a piece of damp folded cheesecloth. Ladle or pour juice into the lined sieve, being careful not to disturb any sediment in the bottom of the container. Measure 4½ cups (1.125 L) juice.

5. In an 8-quart (8 L) stainless steel stockpot, combine fruit juice and sugar. Bring to a boil over medium heat, stirring constantly until sugar is completely dissolved.

6. Increase heat to medium-high and bring to a full rolling boil, stirring constantly. Stir in pectin. Return to a full rolling boil, stirring constantly, and boil for 1 minute.

7. Remove pot from heat and quickly skim off any foam.

Tip: Sort fresh or frozen cranberries before making jelly and discard any that are bruised, soft or shriveled.

8. Immediately ladle hot jelly into hot jars, leaving ¼ inch (0.5 cm) headspace. Wipe jar rims and threads with a clean, damp paper towel. Center hot lids on jars and screw on bands until fingertip-tight.

9. Place jars in canner, making sure they are covered by at least 1 inch (2.5 cm) of water. Cover and bring to a gentle boil. Process 4-ounce (125 mL) jars and 8-ounce (250 mL) jars for 10 minutes; process 1-pint (500 mL) jars for 15 minutes.

10. Remove jars from canner and place on a wire rack or cloth towel. Let cool for 24 hours, then check seals. Wash and dry jars and store in a cool, dry, dark location.

Guava Jelly

*With a soft pink color
and delicate flavor,
Guava Jelly has a
charming character.*

Tip: For the fullest flavor,
choose ripe guavas.
A ripe guava will have
a yellow-green skin
that yields to gentle
pressure, an intensely
fragrant aroma and
pinkish-red flesh with
a juicy center.

5 lbs	guavas, thinly sliced	2.5 kg
4½ cups	water	1.125 L
½ cup	freshly squeezed lemon juice	125 mL
6 cups	granulated sugar	1.5 L
1	pouch (3 oz/85 mL) liquid pectin	1

1. In an 8-quart (8 L) stainless steel stockpot, combine guavas and water. Bring to a boil over medium-high heat. Reduce heat, cover and simmer gently for 30 minutes. Remove from heat and let stand for 30 minutes.

2. Place a fine-mesh sieve over a pan or bowl. Ladle the cooked guavas into the sieve and drain the juice from the fruit pulp. Discard the pulp. Rinse the sieve and line it with a piece of damp folded fine-knit cheesecloth. Strain juice through the cheesecloth twice, rinsing cheesecloth as necessary to remove any sediment that blocks the juice flow. (The juice may be strained through a jelly bag instead, if you prefer.) Cover juice and refrigerate for several hours or overnight to allow any remaining sediment to settle to the bottom of the container.

3. Prepare canning jars and lids and bring water in water bath canner to a boil.

4. Place a sieve over a pan or bowl and line it with a piece of damp folded cheesecloth. Ladle or pour juice into the lined sieve, being careful not to disturb any sediment in the bottom of the container. Measure 3½ cups (875 mL) juice.

5. In an 8-quart (8 L) stainless steel stockpot, combine guava juice, lemon juice and sugar. Bring to a boil over medium heat, stirring constantly until sugar is completely dissolved.

6. Increase heat to medium-high and bring to a full rolling boil, stirring constantly. Stir in pectin. Return to a full rolling boil, stirring constantly, and boil for 1 minute.

7. Remove pot from heat and quickly skim off any foam.

Tip: Pineapple guavas make a lovely jelly with a tropical flavor.

8. Immediately ladle hot jelly into hot jars, leaving $\frac{1}{4}$ inch (0.5 cm) headspace. Wipe jar rims and threads with a clean, damp paper towel. Center hot lids on jars and screw on bands until fingertip-tight.

9. Place jars in canner, making sure they are covered by at least 1 inch (2.5 cm) of water. Cover and bring to a gentle boil. Process 4-ounce (125 mL) jars and 8-ounce (250 mL) jars for 10 minutes; process 1-pint (500 mL) jars for 15 minutes.

10. Remove jars from canner and place on a wire rack or cloth towel. Let cool for 24 hours, then check seals. Wash and dry jars and store in a cool, dry, dark location.

Nectarine Jelly

Makes about eight 8-ounce (250 mL) jars

This delightful jelly has a beautiful color and delicate flavor.

Tips: White nectarines have a very mild flavor and are not recommended for making jelly.

To ripen nectarines, place them in a paper bag and let them stand at room temperature for a few days.

6 lbs	nectarines, peeled, pitted and crushed or finely chopped	3 kg
1½ cups	water	375 mL
¼ cup	freshly squeezed lemon juice	50 mL
7½ cups	granulated sugar	1.875 L
2	pouches (each 3 oz/85 mL) liquid pectin	2

1. In an 8-quart (8 L) stainless steel stockpot, combine nectarines and water. Bring to a boil over medium-high heat. Reduce heat, cover and simmer gently for 5 minutes. Remove from heat and let stand for 20 minutes.

2. Place a fine-mesh sieve over a pan or bowl. Ladle the cooked nectarines into the sieve and drain the juice from the fruit pulp. Discard the pulp. Rinse the sieve and line it with a piece of damp folded fine-knit cheesecloth. Strain juice through the cheesecloth twice, rinsing cheesecloth as necessary to remove any sediment that blocks the juice flow. (The juice may be strained through a jelly bag instead, if you prefer.) Cover juice and refrigerate for several hours or overnight to allow any remaining sediment to settle to the bottom of the container.

3. Prepare canning jars and lids and bring water in water bath canner to a boil.

4. Place a sieve over a pan or bowl and line it with a piece of damp folded cheesecloth. Ladle or pour juice into the lined sieve, being careful not to disturb any sediment in the bottom of the container. Measure 3½ cups (875 mL) juice.

5. In an 8-quart (8 L) stainless steel stockpot, combine nectarine juice, lemon juice and sugar. Bring to a boil over medium heat, stirring constantly until sugar is completely dissolved.

6. Increase heat to medium-high and bring to a full rolling boil, stirring constantly. Stir in pectin. Return to a full rolling boil, stirring constantly, and boil for 1 minute.

7. Remove pot from heat and quickly skim off any foam.

Tip: For the best flavor, use ripe nectarines that yield to gentle pressure.

8. Immediately ladle hot jelly into hot jars, leaving ¼ inch (0.5 cm) headspace. Wipe jar rims and threads with a clean, damp paper towel. Center hot lids on jars and screw on bands until fingertip-tight.

9. Place jars in canner, making sure they are covered by at least 1 inch (2.5 cm) of water. Cover and bring to a gentle boil. Process 4-ounce (125 mL) jars and 8-ounce (250 mL) jars for 10 minutes; process 1-pint (500 mL) jars for 15 minutes.

10. Remove jars from canner and place on a wire rack or cloth towel. Let cool for 24 hours, then check seals. Wash and dry jars and store in a cool, dry, dark location.

Nectarine Peach Jelly

Makes about eight 8-ounce (250 mL) jars

The flavors of nectarine and peach enhance each other in this warm and sunny jelly.

Tip: If nectarines and peaches reach ripeness before you are ready to use them, they may be stored in the refrigerator for a few days.

3 lbs	nectarines, peeled, pitted and crushed or finely chopped	1.5 kg
3 lbs	peaches, peeled, pitted and crushed or finely chopped	1.5 kg
1½ cups	water	375 mL
¼ cup	freshly squeezed lemon juice	50 mL
7½ cups	granulated sugar	1.875 L
2	pouches (each 3 oz/85 mL) liquid pectin	2

1. In an 8-quart (8 L) stainless steel stockpot, combine nectarines, peaches and water. Bring to a boil over medium-high heat. Reduce heat, cover and simmer gently for 5 minutes. Remove from heat and let stand for 20 minutes.

2. Place a fine-mesh sieve over a pan or bowl. Ladle the cooked fruit into the sieve and drain the juice from the fruit pulp. Discard the pulp. Rinse the sieve and line it with a piece of damp folded fine-knit cheesecloth. Strain juice through the cheesecloth twice, rinsing cheesecloth as necessary to remove any sediment that blocks the juice flow. (The juice may be strained through a jelly bag instead, if you prefer.) Cover juice and refrigerate for several hours or overnight to allow any remaining sediment to settle to the bottom of the container.

3. Prepare canning jars and lids and bring water in water bath canner to a boil.

4. Place a sieve over a pan or bowl and line it with a piece of damp folded cheesecloth. Ladle or pour juice into the lined sieve, being careful not to disturb any sediment in the bottom of the container. Measure 3½ cups (875 mL) juice.

5. In an 8-quart (8 L) stainless steel stockpot, combine fruit juice, lemon juice and sugar. Bring to a boil over medium heat, stirring constantly until sugar is completely dissolved.

Tip: Yellow-fleshed nectarines and peaches have the strongest flavor and make the best jelly.

6. Increase heat to medium-high and bring to a full rolling boil, stirring constantly. Stir in pectin. Return to a full rolling boil, stirring constantly, and boil for 1 minute.

7. Remove pot from heat and quickly skim off any foam.

8. Immediately ladle hot jelly into hot jars, leaving ¼ inch (0.5 cm) headspace. Wipe jar rims and threads with a clean, damp paper towel. Center hot lids on jars and screw on bands until fingertip-tight.

9. Place jars in canner, making sure they are covered by at least 1 inch (2.5 cm) of water. Cover and bring to a gentle boil. Process 4-ounce (125 mL) jars and 8-ounce (250 mL) jars for 10 minutes; process 1-pint (500 mL) jars for 15 minutes.

10. Remove jars from canner and place on a wire rack or cloth towel. Let cool for 24 hours, then check seals. Wash and dry jars and store in a cool, dry, dark location.

Cranberry Jelly

Bottled cranberry juice makes a lovely red jelly with a tangy flavor. It can be served on toast or alongside meat or poultry dishes.

Tips: Do not use cranberry juice cocktail. That fruit blend is mostly water and contains a lot of sugar, both of which will keep the jelly from setting.

A "not from concentrate" cranberry juice is the preferred choice for this recipe, rather than a reconstituted cranberry juice. The not-from-concentrate juice will have a stronger flavor and a higher natural pectin content. Reconstituted juice, or a juice with a low pectin content, may yield a softer set. Not-from-concentrate juice can be found in many major grocery stores, specialty food stores and health food stores.

3³⁄₄ cups	unsweetened cranberry juice	925 mL
5²⁄₃ cups	granulated sugar	1.4 L
1	pouch (3 oz/85 mL) liquid pectin	1

1. Prepare canning jars and lids and bring water in water bath canner to a boil.

2. If the juice contains sediment or pulp, strain it before measuring. To strain juice, place a sieve over a pan or bowl and line it with a piece of damp folded fine-knit cheesecloth. Pour juice into the lined sieve, being careful not to disturb any sediment in the bottom of the container.

3. In an 8-quart (8 L) stainless steel stockpot, combine cranberry juice and sugar. Bring to a boil over medium heat, stirring constantly until sugar is completely dissolved.

4. Increase heat to medium-high and bring to a full rolling boil, stirring constantly. Stir in pectin. Return to a full rolling boil, stirring constantly, and boil for 1 minute.

5. Remove pot from heat and quickly skim off any foam.

6. Immediately ladle hot jelly into hot jars, leaving ¼ inch (0.5 cm) headspace. Wipe jar rims and threads with a clean, damp paper towel. Center hot lids on jars and screw on bands until fingertip-tight.

7. Place jars in canner, making sure they are covered by at least 1 inch (2.5 cm) of water. Cover and bring to a gentle boil. Process 4-ounce (125 mL) jars and 8-ounce (250 mL) jars for 10 minutes; process 1-pint (500 mL) jars for 15 minutes.

8. Remove jars from canner and place on a wire rack or cloth towel. Let cool for 24 hours, then check seals. Wash and dry jars and store in a cool, dry, dark location.

Apple Cider Jelly (page 105)

Overleaf: Pomegranate Jelly (page 140)

Grape Jelly

✳

3¾ cups	unsweetened Concord grape juice	925 mL
6½ cups	granulated sugar	1.625 L
2	pouches (each 3 oz/85 mL) liquid pectin	2

Grape jelly fans will love this easy recipe. The intense flavor beats any store-bought grape jelly.

Tip: Choose a grape juice with a deep color and no added sugar.

1. Prepare canning jars and lids and bring water in water bath canner to a boil.

2. If the juice contains sediment or pulp, strain it before measuring. To strain juice, place a sieve over a pan or bowl and line it with a piece of damp folded fine-knit cheesecloth. Pour juice into the lined sieve, being careful not to disturb any sediment in the bottom of the container.

3. In an 8-quart (8 L) stainless steel stockpot, combine grape juice and sugar. Bring to a boil over medium heat, stirring constantly until sugar is completely dissolved.

4. Increase heat to medium-high and bring to a full rolling boil, stirring constantly. Stir in pectin. Return to a full rolling boil, stirring constantly, and boil for 1 minute.

5. Remove pot from heat and quickly skim off any foam.

6. Immediately ladle hot jelly into hot jars, leaving ¼ inch (0.5 cm) headspace. Wipe jar rims and threads with a clean, damp paper towel. Center hot lids on jars and screw on bands until fingertip-tight.

7. Place jars in canner, making sure they are covered by at least 1 inch (2.5 cm) of water. Cover and bring to a gentle boil. Process 4-ounce (125 mL) jars and 8-ounce (250 mL) jars for 10 minutes; process 1-pint (500 mL) jars for 15 minutes.

8. Remove jars from canner and place on a wire rack or cloth towel. Let cool for 24 hours, then check seals. Wash and dry jars and store in a cool, dry, dark location.

Overleaf: Sweet Orange Marmalade (page 175), Lemon Marmalade (page 159) and Sunrise Jam (page 99)

Lemon Lime Marmalade (page 160) and Tangelo Marmalade (page 176)

Plum Jelly

Makes about seven 8-ounce (250 mL) jars

Of all the jellies, this recipe is one of the prettiest. I like to use Santa Rosa plums from the tree in my yard for Plum Jelly because of their outstanding flavor and the deep pink color of their juice.

Tip: While I prefer Santa Rosa plums for making plum jelly, almost any variety of plum will work well in this recipe.

7 lbs	plums, peeled, pitted and finely chopped	3.5 kg
1 cup	water	250 mL
1 tbsp	freshly squeezed lemon juice	15 mL
6 cups	granulated sugar	1.5 L
1	pouch (3 oz/85 mL) liquid pectin	1

1. In an 8-quart (8 L) stainless steel stockpot, combine plums and water. Bring to a boil over medium-high heat. Reduce heat, cover and simmer gently for 5 minutes. Remove from heat and let stand for 20 minutes.
2. Place a fine-mesh sieve over a pan or bowl. Ladle the cooked plums into the sieve and drain the juice from the fruit pulp. Discard the pulp. Rinse the sieve and line it with a piece of damp folded fine-knit cheesecloth. Strain juice through the cheesecloth twice, rinsing cheesecloth as necessary to remove any sediment that blocks the juice flow. (The juice may be strained through a jelly bag instead, if you prefer.) Cover juice and refrigerate for several hours or overnight to allow any remaining sediment to settle to the bottom of the container.
3. Prepare canning jars and lids and bring water in water bath canner to a boil.
4. Place a sieve over a pan or bowl and line it with a piece of damp folded cheesecloth. Ladle or pour juice into the lined sieve, being careful not to disturb any sediment in the bottom of the container. Measure 3¾ cups (925 mL) juice.
5. In an 8-quart (8 L) stainless steel stockpot, combine plum juice, lemon juice and sugar. Bring to a boil over medium heat, stirring constantly until sugar is completely dissolved.
6. Increase heat to medium-high and bring to a full rolling boil, stirring constantly. Stir in pectin. Return to a full rolling boil, stirring constantly, and boil for 1 minute.
7. Remove pot from heat and quickly skim off any foam.

8. Immediately ladle hot jelly into hot jars, leaving $\frac{1}{4}$ inch (0.5 cm) headspace. Wipe jar rims and threads with a clean, damp paper towel. Center hot lids on jars and screw on bands until fingertip-tight.

9. Place jars in canner, making sure they are covered by at least 1 inch (2.5 cm) of water. Cover and bring to a gentle boil. Process 4-ounce (125 mL) jars and 8-ounce (250 mL) jars for 10 minutes; process 1-pint (500 mL) jars for 15 minutes.

10. Remove jars from canner and place on a wire rack or cloth towel. Let cool for 24 hours, then check seals. Wash and dry jars and store in a cool, dry, dark location.

Red Raspberry Jelly

Makes about eight 8-ounce (250 mL) jars

This jelly has an intense raspberry flavor and an elegant jewel-tone color. It is one of my favorites!

Tip: Frozen berries make great jellies. As they thaw, they start releasing their flavorful juice, making it easier to extract the juice. If you have an abundance of fresh raspberries, they also make wonderful jelly. You will need about 16 cups (4 L) fresh raspberries to make this jelly.

4	bags (each 12 oz/340 g) frozen unsweetened red raspberries, thawed	4
1½ cups	water	375 mL
7½ cups	granulated sugar	1.875 L
2	pouches (each 3 oz/85 mL) liquid pectin	2

1. In a flat-bottomed pan or bowl, crush raspberries in batches using a vegetable masher or the back of a large spoon.

2. In an 8-quart (8 L) stainless steel stockpot, combine crushed raspberries and water. Bring to a boil over medium-high heat. Reduce heat, cover and simmer gently for 5 minutes. Remove from heat and let stand for 20 minutes.

3. Place a fine-mesh sieve over a pan or bowl. Ladle the cooked raspberries into the sieve and drain the juice from the fruit pulp. Discard the pulp. Rinse the sieve and line it with a piece of damp folded fine-knit cheesecloth. Strain juice through the cheesecloth twice, rinsing cheesecloth as necessary to remove any sediment that blocks the juice flow. (The juice may be strained through a jelly bag instead, if you prefer.) Cover juice and refrigerate for several hours or overnight to allow any remaining sediment to settle to the bottom of the container.

4. Prepare canning jars and lids and bring water in water bath canner to a boil.

5. Place a sieve over a pan or bowl and line it with a piece of damp folded cheesecloth. Ladle or pour juice into the lined sieve, being careful not to disturb any sediment in the bottom of the container. Measure 4 cups (1 L) juice.

6. In an 8-quart (8 L) stainless steel stockpot, combine raspberry juice and sugar. Bring to a boil over medium heat, stirring constantly until sugar is completely dissolved.

7. Increase heat to medium-high and bring to a full rolling boil, stirring constantly. Stir in pectin. Return to a full rolling boil, stirring constantly, and boil for 1 minute.

8. Remove pot from heat and quickly skim off any foam.

9. Immediately ladle hot jelly into hot jars, leaving ¼ inch (0.5 cm) headspace. Wipe jar rims and threads with a clean, damp paper towel. Center hot lids on jars and screw on bands until fingertip-tight.

10. Place jars in canner, making sure they are covered by at least 1 inch (2.5 cm) of water. Cover and bring to a gentle boil. Process 4-ounce (125 mL) jars and 8-ounce (250 mL) jars for 10 minutes; process 1-pint (500 mL) jars for 15 minutes.

11. Remove jars from canner and place on a wire rack or cloth towel. Let cool for 24 hours, then check seals. Wash and dry jars and store in a cool, dry, dark location.

Strawberry Kiwi Jelly

A beautifully balanced jelly with luminous color and a tropical twist.

Tip: Frozen strawberries are not a good choice for making jelly. They are often underripe and lack the strong strawberry flavor needed to make an outstanding strawberry jelly.

8 cups	strawberries, hulled and crushed	2 L
20	medium kiwifruit, peeled, seeded and crushed	20
1 cup	water	250 mL
¼ cup	freshly squeezed lemon juice	50 mL
7 cups	granulated sugar	1.75 L
2	pouches (each 3 oz/85 mL) liquid pectin	2

1. In an 8-quart (8 L) stainless steel stockpot, combine strawberries, kiwis and water. Bring to a boil over medium-high heat. Reduce heat, cover and simmer gently for 10 minutes. Remove from heat and let stand for 20 minutes.

2. Place a fine-mesh sieve over a pan or bowl. Ladle the cooked fruit into the sieve and drain the juice from the fruit pulp. Discard the pulp. Rinse the sieve and line it with a piece of damp folded fine-knit cheesecloth. Strain juice through the cheesecloth twice, rinsing cheesecloth as necessary to remove any sediment that blocks the juice flow. (The juice may be strained through a jelly bag instead, if you prefer.) Cover juice and refrigerate for several hours or overnight to allow any remaining sediment to settle to the bottom of the container.

3. Prepare canning jars and lids and bring water in water bath canner to a boil.

4. Place a sieve over a pan or bowl and line it with a piece of damp folded cheesecloth. Ladle or pour juice into the lined sieve, being careful not to disturb any sediment in the bottom of the container. Measure 4¼ cups (1.05 L) juice.

5. In an 8-quart (8 L) stainless steel stockpot, combine fruit juice, lemon juice and sugar. Bring to a boil over medium heat, stirring constantly until sugar is completely dissolved.

6. Increase heat to medium-high and bring to a full rolling boil, stirring constantly. Stir in pectin. Return to a full rolling boil, stirring constantly, and boil for 1 minute.

Tip: Juicy strawberries make the best jelly. Avoid using strawberries that are very firm, as the jelly will have a mild flavor.

7. Remove pot from heat and quickly skim off any foam.

8. Immediately ladle hot jelly into hot jars, leaving ¼ inch (0.5 cm) headspace. Wipe jar rims and threads with a clean, damp paper towel. Center hot lids on jars and screw on bands until fingertip-tight.

9. Place jars in canner, making sure they are covered by at least 1 inch (2.5 cm) of water. Cover and bring to a gentle boil. Process 4-ounce (125 mL) jars and 8-ounce (250 mL) jars for 10 minutes; process 1-pint (500 mL) jars for 15 minutes.

10. Remove jars from canner and place on a wire rack or cloth towel. Let cool for 24 hours, then check seals. Wash and dry jars and store in a cool, dry, dark location.

Strawberry Pineapple Jelly

✳

**Makes about
seven 8-ounce
(250 mL) jars**

*I love the refreshing
flavor of the blend of
strawberries and
pineapple in this
pretty jelly.*

Tip: Using canned or
bottled pineapple juice
in making jellies is a real
time-saver, and jellies
made with canned or
bottled pineapple juice
set better than those
made with fresh juice.

8 cups	strawberries, hulled and crushed	2 L
2/3 cup	water	150 mL
2 cups	unsweetened pineapple juice	500 mL
1/4 cup	freshly squeezed lemon juice	50 mL
7 cups	granulated sugar	1.75 L
2	pouches (each 3 oz/85 mL) liquid pectin	2

1. In an 8-quart (8 L) stainless steel stockpot, combine strawberries and water. Bring to a boil over medium-high heat. Reduce heat, cover and simmer gently for 10 minutes. Remove from heat and let stand for 20 minutes. Stir in pineapple juice.

2. Place a fine-mesh sieve over a pan or bowl. Ladle the cooked fruit into the sieve and drain the juice from the fruit pulp. Discard the pulp. Rinse the sieve and line it with a piece of damp folded fine-knit cheesecloth. Strain juice through the cheesecloth twice, rinsing cheesecloth as necessary to remove any sediment that blocks the juice flow. (The juice may be strained through a jelly bag instead, if you prefer.) Cover juice and refrigerate for several hours or overnight to allow any remaining sediment to settle to the bottom of the container.

3. Prepare canning jars and lids and bring water in water bath canner to a boil.

4. Place a sieve over a pan or bowl and line it with a piece of damp folded cheesecloth. Ladle or pour juice into the lined sieve, being careful not to disturb any sediment in the bottom of the container. Measure 4 1/4 cups (1.05 L) juice.

5. In an 8-quart (8 L) stainless steel stockpot, combine fruit juice, lemon juice and sugar. Bring to a boil over medium heat, stirring constantly until sugar is completely dissolved.

6. Increase heat to medium-high and bring to a full rolling boil, stirring constantly. Stir in pectin. Return to a full rolling boil, stirring constantly, and boil for 1 minute.

Tip: The quality and freshness of strawberries deteriorate quickly. Whenever possible, use strawberries the same day they are picked.

7. Remove pot from heat and quickly skim off any foam.

8. Immediately ladle hot jelly into hot jars, leaving $\frac{1}{4}$ inch (0.5 cm) headspace. Wipe jar rims and threads with a clean, damp paper towel. Center hot lids on jars and screw on bands until fingertip-tight.

9. Place jars in canner, making sure they are covered by at least 1 inch (2.5 cm) of water. Cover and bring to a gentle boil. Process 4-ounce (125 mL) jars and 8-ounce (250 mL) jars for 10 minutes; process 1-pint (500 mL) jars for 15 minutes.

10. Remove jars from canner and place on a wire rack or cloth towel. Let cool for 24 hours, then check seals. Wash and dry jars and store in a cool, dry, dark location.

Strawberry Raspberry Jelly

✳

Makes about seven 8-ounce (250 mL) jars

This shimmering jelly takes center stage at any breakfast table.

Tip: Unsweetened frozen raspberries may be used instead of fresh raspberries. Measure frozen berries and let thaw, reserving juice, before crushing.

8 cups	strawberries, hulled and crushed	2 L
8 cups	red raspberries, crushed	2 L
1 cup	water	250 mL
3 tbsp	freshly squeezed lemon juice	45 mL
7 cups	granulated sugar	1.75 L
2	pouches (each 3 oz/85 mL) liquid pectin	2

1. In an 8-quart (8 L) stainless steel stockpot, combine strawberries, raspberries and water. Bring to a boil over medium-high heat. Reduce heat, cover and simmer gently for 10 minutes. Remove from heat and let stand for 20 minutes.

2. Place a fine-mesh sieve over a pan or bowl. Ladle the cooked berries into the sieve and drain the juice from the fruit pulp. Discard the pulp. Rinse the sieve and line it with a piece of damp folded fine-knit cheesecloth. Strain juice through the cheesecloth twice, rinsing cheesecloth as necessary to remove any sediment that blocks the juice flow. (The juice may be strained through a jelly bag instead, if you prefer.) Cover juice and refrigerate for several hours or overnight to allow any remaining sediment to settle to the bottom of the container.

3. Prepare canning jars and lids and bring water in water bath canner to a boil.

4. Place a sieve over a pan or bowl and line it with a piece of damp folded cheesecloth. Ladle or pour juice into the lined sieve, being careful not to disturb any sediment in the bottom of the container. Measure 3¾ cups (925 mL) juice.

5. In an 8-quart (8 L) stainless steel stockpot, combine fruit juice, lemon juice and sugar. Bring to a boil over medium heat, stirring constantly until sugar is completely dissolved.

6. Increase heat to medium-high and bring to a full rolling boil, stirring constantly. Stir in pectin. Return to a full rolling boil, stirring constantly, and boil for 1 minute.

Tip: The individual juicy fruit pods or seed pouches on berries such as raspberries, blackberries and boysenberries are called drooplets. For the sweetest berries with the fullest flavor, choose raspberries with large drooplets. The larger the drooplets on raspberries, the higher the sugar and juice content.

7. Remove pot from heat and quickly skim off any foam.

8. Immediately ladle hot jelly into hot jars, leaving ¼ inch (0.5 cm) headspace. Wipe jar rims and threads with a clean, damp paper towel. Center hot lids on jars and screw on bands until fingertip-tight.

9. Place jars in canner, making sure they are covered by at least 1 inch (2.5 cm) of water. Cover and bring to a gentle boil. Process 4-ounce (125 mL) jars and 8-ounce (250 mL) jars for 10 minutes; process 1-pint (500 mL) jars for 15 minutes.

10. Remove jars from canner and place on a wire rack or cloth towel. Let cool for 24 hours, then check seals. Wash and dry jars and store in a cool, dry, dark location.

Pomegranate Jelly

---

*This quick and easy
jelly takes advantage of
bottled pomegranate
juice to save the mess
of seeding and juicing
whole pomegranates.*

Tip: Bottled
pomegranate juice
is available in many
grocery stores, specialty
food stores and health
food stores.

3¾ cups	unsweetened pomegranate juice	925 mL
¼ cup	freshly squeezed lemon juice	50 mL
6½ cups	granulated sugar	1.625 L
1	pouch (3 oz/85 mL) liquid pectin	1

1. Prepare canning jars and lids and bring water in water bath canner to a boil.

2. If the juice contains sediment or pulp, strain it before measuring. To strain juice, place a sieve over a pan or bowl and line it with a piece of damp folded fine-knit cheesecloth. Pour juice into the lined sieve, being careful not to disturb any sediment in the bottom of the container.

3. In an 8-quart (8 L) stainless steel stockpot, combine pomegranate juice, lemon juice and sugar. Bring to a boil over medium heat, stirring constantly until sugar is completely dissolved.

4. Increase heat to medium-high and bring to a full rolling boil, stirring constantly. Stir in pectin. Return to a full rolling boil, stirring constantly, and boil for 1 minute.

5. Remove pot from heat and quickly skim off any foam.

6. Immediately ladle hot jelly into hot jars, leaving ¼ inch (0.5 cm) headspace. Wipe jar rims and threads with a clean, damp paper towel. Center hot lids on jars and screw on bands until fingertip-tight.

7. Place jars in canner, making sure they are covered by at least 1 inch (2.5 cm) of water. Cover and bring to a gentle boil. Process 4-ounce (125 mL) jars and 8-ounce (250 mL) jars for 10 minutes; process 1-pint (500 mL) jars for 15 minutes.

8. Remove jars from canner and place on a wire rack or cloth towel. Let cool for 24 hours, then check seals. Wash and dry jars and store in a cool, dry, dark location.

Marmalades

About Marmalades

A MARMALADE IS A SWEET and tangy spread made from citrus fruit. It usually contains finely chopped pieces of citrus, along with thin strips of the colored outer peel. The fruit and peel are evenly suspended in a shimmering, translucent jelly that will hold its shape and mound up in a spoon. The texture of marmalade is very similar to that of jam.

The term "marmalade" came into usage in the English language in 1480. The term was derived from the French word *marmelade*, which, in turn, came from the Portuguese *marmelada*. The original Portuguese *marmelada* was made from quince (*marmelo*) preserved with honey. The Romans learned from the Greeks that, when quinces were slowly cooked with honey, they would gel when cooled. An early Roman cookbook, attributed to Apicius, includes a recipe for preserving whole quinces with honey.

By the late 1700s, orange marmalade was already a well-known preserve when James Keiller of Dundee, Scotland, and his mother, Janet, opened a factory to produce Dundee Marmalade, a spread made from bitter Seville oranges containing thick chunks of orange peel.

While the most common marmalade flavor is still orange, marmalades can be made with other citrus fruits. Lemons, limes, grapefruit and tangerines all make excellent marmalades, and marmalades made with a combination of citrus fruits are fabulous.

Although marmalades are traditionally made from citrus fruits alone, contemporary versions made with a variety of other fruits combined with the citrus have garnered a whole new crop of marmalade fans. Marmalades can now be made in a host of exciting flavors, such as apricot, strawberry and peach. The colors are beautiful, and the combination of fruit and citrus brings a new dimension of exquisite flavors to a traditional spread.

There are two keys to making an exceptional marmalade. The first is to use only the outer colored portion of the citrus peel, known as the zest, and cut it into very thin strips of $\frac{1}{8}$ inch (0.25 cm) in width or less. Large strips of cooked peel can be very tough and difficult to chew, and they really detract from the texture of the spread. The white portion of the peel, called the pith, is very fibrous and very bitter. Using the pith will give the finished marmalade a bitter flavor. A premium marmalade is made from thin strips of zest without any pith.

A vegetable peeler can be used to remove only the outer colored portion of the peel, and then the peel can be sliced very thin with a sharp knife. However, I prefer to use a handheld zesting tool to remove several thin strips of zest at one time directly from the citrus. A zester usually has five small holes in a row that cut the outer colored portion of the peel from the citrus into thin strips of $1/8$ inch (0.25 cm) or less. Zesters can be found in most kitchen supply stores and are a real time-saver for making marmalade.

The second key to creating a great-tasting marmalade is to section the citrus by cutting the fruit away from the fibrous membrane that surrounds each section. The white membrane is tough and becomes chewy and even tougher when cooked. It detracts from both the flavor and the texture of the marmalade. For marmalade with an intense citrus flavor and tender texture, take the time to section the fruit from the membrane before chopping the fruit.

To separate the fruit from the membrane, after removing the zest, cut a slice off the top and bottom ends of the citrus. Place the citrus on a cutting board, cut side down, and use a sharp knife to cut the peel from the citrus in thick strips. Be sure to remove all of the white pith from the outside. Holding the peeled citrus in your hand, carefully use a small paring knife to cut the citrus sections away from the membrane. Discard the membrane, remove any seeds and finely chop the citrus sections.

Citrus fruits bought at grocery stores and specialty food stores are often coated with vegetable wax to make them shine. While this wax is nontoxic, it should be removed before you zest the fruit for marmalade. If the wax layer is thick, it can cause the peel to turn white when cooked. This is not harmful, but can affect the appearance of the finished marmalade. To remove the wax, use a small vegetable scrub brush to wash the citrus fruit under cool running water. Rinse well and dry before zesting the peel.

Apricot Orange Marmalade

This outstanding fruit marmalade makes a delightful filling for stuffed French toast.

Tips: Choose unblemished apricots with good color. Avoid apricots that are pale yellow, very firm or very soft, as these will not produce spreads with a strong apricot flavor.

For 3½ cups (875 mL) crushed apricots, you'll need about 3½ lbs (1.75 kg) medium apricots.

2	medium Valencia oranges	2
3½ cups	crushed pitted peeled apricots	875 mL
⅓ cup	freshly squeezed lemon juice	75 mL
⅓ cup	freshly squeezed orange juice	75 mL
½ tsp	unsalted butter (optional)	2 mL
5½ cups	granulated sugar	1.375 L
1	pouch (3 oz/85 mL) liquid pectin	1

1. Prepare canning jars and lids and bring water in water bath canner to a boil.

2. Using a zester, remove only the outer colored portion of the peel from the oranges in very thin strips. Coarsely chop the zested peel. (The colored zest may also be removed from the fruit using a vegetable peeler, then cut into very thin strips with a sharp knife and coarsely chopped.) Peel the oranges, removing all of the white pith. Cut the fruit sections away from the membrane and remove any seeds. Discard the pith and membrane. Finely chop the fruit. Set aside.

3. In a bowl, combine apricots and lemon juice. Stir gently until apricots are completely coated with lemon juice. Cover and set aside.

4. In an 8-quart (8 L) stainless steel stockpot, combine chopped oranges and orange juice. Bring to a boil over medium-high heat. Reduce heat, cover and simmer gently for 3 minutes. Stir in orange zest until well distributed. Cover and simmer for 3 minutes. Add apricot mixture and butter, if using.

5. Gradually stir in sugar. Increase heat to medium-high and bring to a full rolling boil, stirring constantly. Stir in pectin. Return to a full rolling boil, stirring constantly, and boil for 1 minute.

6. Remove pot from heat and skim off any foam. Let marmalade cool in the pot for 5 minutes, stirring occasionally.

7. Ladle hot marmalade into hot jars, leaving ¼ inch (0.5 cm) headspace. Remove any air bubbles. Wipe jar rims and threads with a clean, damp paper towel. Center hot lids on jars and screw on bands until fingertip-tight.

8. Place jars in canner, making sure they are covered by at least 1 inch (2.5 cm) of water. Cover and bring to a gentle boil. Process 4-ounce (125 mL) jars and 8-ounce (250 mL) jars for 10 minutes; process 1-pint (500 mL) jars for 15 minutes.

9. Remove jars from canner and place on a wire rack or cloth towel. Let cool for 24 hours, then check seals. Wash and dry jars and store in a cool, dry, dark location.

Apricot Pineapple Marmalade

*The classic pairing of
apricots and pineapple
gets an extra flavor
boost when combined
with oranges.*

Tips: Liquid and
powdered pectins
have different setting
properties and are not
interchangeable.

For 2½ cups
(625 mL) chopped
apricots, you'll need
about 2½ lbs (1.25 kg)
medium apricots.

2	medium Valencia oranges	2
2½ cups	finely chopped pitted peeled apricots	625 mL
¼ cup	freshly squeezed lemon juice	50 mL
¼ cup	freshly squeezed orange juice	50 mL
1 cup	drained canned juice-packed crushed pineapple	250 mL
½ tsp	unsalted butter (optional)	2 mL
5½ cups	granulated sugar	1.375 L
1	pouch (3 oz/85 mL) liquid pectin	1

1. Prepare canning jars and lids and bring water in water bath canner to a boil.

2. Using a zester, remove only the outer colored portion of the peel from the oranges in very thin strips. Coarsely chop the zested peel. (The colored zest may also be removed from the fruit using a vegetable peeler, then cut into very thin strips with a sharp knife and coarsely chopped.) Peel the oranges, removing all of the white pith. Cut the fruit sections away from the membrane and remove any seeds. Discard the pith and membrane. Finely chop the fruit. Set aside.

3. In a bowl, combine apricots and lemon juice. Stir gently until apricots are completely coated with lemon juice. Cover and set aside.

4. In an 8-quart (8 L) stainless steel stockpot, combine chopped oranges and orange juice. Bring to a boil over medium-high heat. Reduce heat, cover and simmer gently for 3 minutes. Stir in orange zest until well distributed. Cover and simmer for 3 minutes. Add apricot mixture, pineapple and butter, if using.

5. Gradually stir in sugar. Increase heat to medium-high and bring to a full rolling boil, stirring constantly. Stir in pectin. Return to a full rolling boil, stirring constantly, and boil for 1 minute.

6. Remove pot from heat and skim off any foam. Let marmalade cool in the pot for 5 minutes, stirring occasionally.

7. Ladle hot marmalade into hot jars, leaving ¼ inch (0.5 cm) headspace. Remove any air bubbles. Wipe jar rims and threads with a clean, damp paper towel. Center hot lids on jars and screw on bands until fingertip-tight.

8. Place jars in canner, making sure they are covered by at least 1 inch (2.5 cm) of water. Cover and bring to a gentle boil. Process 4-ounce (125 mL) jars and 8-ounce (250 mL) jars for 10 minutes; process 1-pint (500 mL) jars for 15 minutes.

9. Remove jars from canner and place on a wire rack or cloth towel. Let cool for 24 hours, then check seals. Wash and dry jars and store in a cool, dry, dark location.

Bing Cherry Marmalade

*Bing cherries make an
amazing marmalade
and an incredible treat
to serve to guests.*

Tips: A cherry pitter
makes quick work of
removing pits from
cherries. Handheld
cherry pitters are
available in most kitchen
supply stores and some
grocery stores. Many
stores also carry more
elaborate cherry pitters,
which can really come in
handy when you're
pitting large quantities
of cherries.

For 3½ cups (875 mL)
quartered cherries,
you'll need about 3 lbs
(1.5 kg) cherries.

2	medium Valencia oranges	2
3½ cups	quartered pitted fresh Bing cherries	875 mL
¼ cup	freshly squeezed lemon juice	50 mL
⅓ cup	freshly squeezed orange juice	75 mL
½ tsp	unsalted butter (optional)	2 mL
4 cups	granulated sugar	1 L
1	pouch (3 oz/85 mL) liquid pectin	1

1. Prepare canning jars and lids and bring water in water bath canner to a boil.

2. Using a zester, remove only the outer colored portion of the peel from the oranges in very thin strips. Coarsely chop the zested peel. (The colored zest may also be removed from the fruit using a vegetable peeler, then cut into very thin strips with a sharp knife and coarsely chopped.) Peel the oranges, removing all of the white pith. Cut the fruit sections away from the membrane and remove any seeds. Discard the pith and membrane. Finely chop the fruit. Set aside.

3. In a bowl, combine cherries and lemon juice. Stir gently until cherries are completely coated with lemon juice. Cover and set aside.

4. In an 8-quart (8 L) stainless steel stockpot, combine chopped oranges and orange juice. Bring to a boil over medium-high heat. Reduce heat, cover and simmer gently for 3 minutes. Stir in orange zest until well distributed. Cover and simmer for 3 minutes. Add cherry mixture and butter, if using.

5. Gradually stir in sugar. Increase heat to medium-high and bring to a full rolling boil, stirring constantly. Stir in pectin. Return to a full rolling boil, stirring constantly, and boil for 1 minute.

6. Remove pot from heat and skim off any foam. Let marmalade cool in the pot for 5 minutes, stirring occasionally.

Tip: Lamberts, Black Giants or other sweet cherry varieties may be used if Bing cherries are not available.

7. Ladle hot marmalade into hot jars, leaving ¼ inch (0.5 cm) headspace. Remove any air bubbles. Wipe jar rims and threads with a clean, damp paper towel. Center hot lids on jars and screw on bands until fingertip-tight.

8. Place jars in canner, making sure they are covered by at least 1 inch (2.5 cm) of water. Cover and bring to a gentle boil. Process 4-ounce (125 mL) jars and 8-ounce (250 mL) jars for 10 minutes; process 1-pint (500 mL) jars for 15 minutes.

9. Remove jars from canner and place on a wire rack or cloth towel. Let cool for 24 hours, then check seals. Wash and dry jars and store in a cool, dry, dark location.

Cherry Apricot Marmalade

2	medium Valencia oranges	2
1¾ cups	finely chopped pitted peeled apricots	425 mL
1⅔ cups	finely chopped pitted fresh cherries	400 mL
¼ cup	freshly squeezed lemon juice	50 mL
⅓ cup	freshly squeezed orange juice	75 mL
½ tsp	unsalted butter (optional)	2 mL
4¾ cups	granulated sugar	1.175 L
1	pouch (3 oz/85 mL) liquid pectin	1

Makes five or six 8-ounce (250 mL) jars

Apricots and cherries make a delightful combination and blend beautifully in this superb marmalade.

Tips: Ripe sweet cherries have the most flavor and make the best marmalades.

For 1¾ cups (425 mL) finely chopped apricots, you'll need about 2 lbs (1 kg) medium apricots. For 1⅔ cups (400 mL) finely chopped cherries, you'll need about 1½ lbs (750 g) cherries.

1. Prepare canning jars and lids and bring water in water bath canner to a boil.

2. Using a zester, remove only the outer colored portion of the peel from the oranges in very thin strips. Coarsely chop the zested peel. (The colored zest may also be removed from the fruit using a vegetable peeler, then cut into very thin strips with a sharp knife and coarsely chopped.) Peel the oranges, removing all of the white pith. Cut the fruit sections away from the membrane and remove any seeds. Discard the pith and membrane. Finely chop the fruit. Set aside.

3. In a bowl, combine apricots, cherries and lemon juice. Stir gently until apricots and cherries are completely coated with lemon juice. Cover and set aside.

4. In an 8-quart (8 L) stainless steel stockpot, combine chopped oranges and orange juice. Bring to a boil over medium-high heat. Reduce heat, cover and simmer gently for 3 minutes. Stir in orange zest until well distributed. Cover and simmer for 3 minutes. Add apricot and cherry mixture and butter, if using.

5. Gradually stir in sugar. Increase heat to medium-high and bring to a full rolling boil, stirring constantly. Stir in pectin. Return to a full rolling boil, stirring constantly, and boil for 1 minute.

6. Remove pot from heat and skim off any foam. Let marmalade cool in the pot for 5 minutes, stirring occasionally.

*

Tips: For the best flavor, use ripe apricots that yield to gentle pressure.

To ripen apricots, place them in paper bag and let them stand at room temperature for a few days.

7. Ladle hot marmalade into hot jars, leaving ¼ inch (0.5 cm) headspace. Remove any air bubbles. Wipe jar rims and threads with a clean, damp paper towel. Center hot lids on jars and screw on bands until fingertip-tight.

8. Place jars in canner, making sure they are covered by at least 1 inch (2.5 cm) of water. Cover and bring to a gentle boil. Process 4-ounce (125 mL) jars and 8-ounce (250 mL) jars for 10 minutes; process 1-pint (500 mL) jars for 15 minutes.

9. Remove jars from canner and place on a wire rack or cloth towel. Let cool for 24 hours, then check seals. Wash and dry jars and store in a cool, dry, dark location.

Citrus Trio Marmalade

✳

Makes about five 8-ounce (250 mL) jars

The delicate strips of citrus peel suspended in the shimmering jelly make a beautiful presentation.

Tip: Doubling marmalade recipes is not advised. If the pan is too full, not enough liquid will boil off during cooking and the marmalade likely will not set properly.

6 to 8	medium Valencia oranges	6 to 8
1 to 2	medium pink or ruby grapefruit	1 to 2
2 to 3	large lemons	2 to 3
1/8 tsp	baking soda	0.5 mL
5 cups	granulated sugar	1.25 L
1/2 tsp	unsalted butter (optional)	2 mL
1	pouch (3 oz/85 mL) liquid pectin	1

1. Prepare canning jars and lids and bring water in water bath canner to a boil.

2. Using a zester, remove only the outer colored portion of the peel in very thin strips from 3 of the oranges, 1 grapefruit and 2 of the lemons. Coarsely chop the zested peel. (The colored zest may also be removed from the fruit using a vegetable peeler, then cut into very thin strips with a sharp knife and coarsely chopped.) Peel all of the oranges, grapefruit and lemons, removing all of the outer white pith. Cut the fruit sections away from the membrane and remove any seeds. Discard the pith and membrane. Finely chop the fruit and measure 1¾ cups (425 mL) oranges, ¾ cup (175 mL) grapefruit, and ½ cup (125 mL) lemons.

3. In an 8-quart (8 L) stainless steel stockpot, combine chopped oranges and baking soda. Bring to a boil over medium-high heat. Reduce heat, cover and simmer gently for 5 minutes. Stir in chopped grapefruit, chopped lemons and orange zest, grapefruit zest and lemon zest until well distributed. Cover and simmer for 3 minutes.

4. Gradually stir in sugar and butter, if using. Increase heat to medium-high and bring to a full rolling boil, stirring constantly. Stir in pectin. Return to a full rolling boil, stirring constantly, and boil for 1 minute.

5. Remove pot from heat and skim off any foam. Let marmalade cool in the pot for 5 minutes, stirring occasionally.

Tip: Pink or ruby grapefruit add a lovely color and flavor to this marmalade, but white grapefruit may be used as well.

6. Ladle hot marmalade into hot jars, leaving ¼ inch (0.5 cm) headspace. Remove any air bubbles. Wipe jar rims and threads with a clean, damp paper towel. Center hot lids on jars and screw on bands until fingertip-tight.

7. Place jars in canner, making sure they are covered by at least 1 inch (2.5 cm) of water. Cover and bring to a gentle boil. Process 4-ounce (125 mL) jars and 8-ounce (250 mL) jars for 10 minutes; process 1-pint (500 mL) jars for 15 minutes.

8. Remove jars from canner and place on a wire rack or cloth towel. Let cool for 24 hours, then check seals. Wash and dry jars and store in a cool, dry, dark location.

Grapefruit Cranberry Marmalade

---

5 to 7	medium pink or ruby grapefruit	5 to 7
⅔ cup	unsweetened cranberry juice	150 mL
½ cup	freshly squeezed lemon juice	125 mL
⅛ tsp	baking soda	0.5 mL
5 cups	granulated sugar	1.25 L
½ tsp	unsalted butter (optional)	2 mL
1	pouch (3 oz/85 mL) liquid pectin	1

1. Prepare canning jars and lids and bring water in water bath canner to a boil.

2. Using a zester, remove only the outer colored portion of the peel in very thin strips from 3 of the grapefruit. Coarsely chop the zested peel. (The colored zest may also be removed from the fruit using a vegetable peeler, then cut into very thin strips with a sharp knife and coarsely chopped.) Peel all of the grapefruit, removing all of the outer white pith. Cut the fruit sections away from the membrane and remove any seeds. Discard the pith and membrane. Finely chop the fruit and measure 1⅔ cups (400 mL).

3. In an 8-quart (8 L) stainless steel stockpot, combine chopped grapefruit, grapefruit zest, cranberry juice, lemon juice and baking soda. Bring to a boil over medium-high heat. Reduce heat, cover and simmer gently for 3 minutes.

4. Gradually stir in sugar and butter, if using. Increase heat to medium-high and bring to a full rolling boil, stirring constantly. Stir in pectin. Return to a full rolling boil, stirring constantly, and boil for 1 minute.

5. Remove pot from heat and skim off any foam. Let marmalade cool in the pot for 5 minutes, stirring occasionally.

6. Ladle hot marmalade into hot jars, leaving ¼ inch (0.5 cm) headspace. Remove any air bubbles. Wipe jar rims and threads with a clean, damp paper towel. Center hot lids on jars and screw on bands until fingertip-tight.

Tip: Do not use cranberry juice cocktail. That fruit blend is mostly water and contains a lot of sugar, both of which will keep the marmalade from setting.

7. Place jars in canner, making sure they are covered by at least 1 inch (2.5 cm) of water. Cover and bring to a gentle boil. Process 4-ounce (125 mL) jars and 8-ounce (250 mL) jars for 10 minutes; process 1-pint (500 mL) jars for 15 minutes.

8. Remove jars from canner and place on a wire rack or cloth towel. Let cool for 24 hours, then check seals. Wash and dry jars and store in a cool, dry, dark location.

Grapefruit Lime Marmalade

This refreshing citrus marmalade has lots of zip and zing.

Tip: White grapefruit are preferred for this recipe because the flavor and color blend well with the limes, but pink or ruby grapefruit will also work well.

5 to 7	medium white grapefruit	5 to 7
8 to 10	medium limes	8 to 10
2 tbsp	freshly squeezed lemon juice	30 mL
1/8 tsp	baking soda	0.5 mL
5 cups	granulated sugar	1.25 L
1/2 tsp	unsalted butter (optional)	2 mL
1	pouch (3 oz/85 mL) liquid pectin	1

1. Prepare canning jars and lids and bring water in water bath canner to a boil.

2. Using a zester, remove only the outer colored portion of the peel in very thin strips from 2 of the grapefruit and 3 of the limes. Coarsely chop the zested peel. (The colored zest may also be removed from the fruit using a vegetable peeler, then cut into very thin strips with a sharp knife and coarsely chopped.) Peel all of the grapefruit and limes, removing all of the outer white pith. Cut the fruit sections away from the membrane and remove any seeds. Discard the pith and membrane. Finely chop the fruit and measure 2 cups (500 mL) grapefruit and 1 cup (250 mL) limes.

3. In an 8-quart (8 L) stainless steel stockpot, combine chopped limes, lemon juice and baking soda. Bring to a boil over medium-high heat. Reduce heat, cover and simmer gently for 5 minutes. Stir in chopped grapefruit, grapefruit zest and lime zest until well distributed. Cover and simmer for 3 minutes.

4. Gradually stir in sugar and butter, if using. Increase heat to medium-high and bring to a full rolling boil, stirring constantly. Stir in pectin. Return to a full rolling boil, stirring constantly, and boil for 1 minute.

5. Remove pot from heat and skim off any foam. Let marmalade cool in the pot for 5 minutes, stirring occasionally.

Tip: Bearss limes, a type of Persian or Tahitian lime and the most common large green lime found in grocery stores, have an intense lime flavor and are the best choice for making marmalades and other spreads.

6. Ladle hot marmalade into hot jars, leaving $\frac{1}{4}$ inch (0.5 cm) headspace. Remove any air bubbles. Wipe jar rims and threads with a clean, damp paper towel. Center hot lids on jars and screw on bands until fingertip-tight.

7. Place jars in canner, making sure they are covered by at least 1 inch (2.5 cm) of water. Cover and bring to a gentle boil. Process 4-ounce (125 mL) jars and 8-ounce (250 mL) jars for 10 minutes; process 1-pint (500 mL) jars for 15 minutes.

8. Remove jars from canner and place on a wire rack or cloth towel. Let cool for 24 hours, then check seals. Wash and dry jars and store in a cool, dry, dark location.

Pink Grapefruit Marmalade

✳

*Pink grapefruit make a
flavorful marmalade
with a beautiful,
shimmering color.*

Tip: White grapefruit
may be substituted for
the pink grapefruit in
this recipe.

6 to 8	medium pink or ruby grapefruit	6 to 8
½ cup	freshly squeezed lemon juice	125 mL
⅛ tsp	baking soda	0.5 mL
5 cups	granulated sugar	1.25 L
½ tsp	unsalted butter (optional)	2 mL
1	pouch (3 oz/85 mL) liquid pectin	1

1. Prepare canning jars and lids and bring water in water bath canner to a boil.

2. Using a zester, remove only the outer colored portion of the peel in very thin strips from 3 of the grapefruit. Coarsely chop the zested peel. (The colored zest may also be removed from the fruit using a vegetable peeler, then cut into very thin strips with a sharp knife and coarsely chopped.) Peel all of the grapefruit, removing all of the outer white pith. Cut the fruit sections away from the membrane and remove any seeds. Discard the pith and membrane. Finely chop the fruit and measure 2⅓ cups (575 mL).

3. In an 8-quart (8 L) stainless steel stockpot, combine chopped grapefruit, grapefruit zest, lemon juice and baking soda. Bring to a boil over medium-high heat. Reduce heat, cover and simmer gently for 3 minutes.

4. Gradually stir in sugar and butter, if using. Increase heat to medium-high and bring to a full rolling boil, stirring constantly. Stir in pectin. Return to a full rolling boil, stirring constantly, and boil for 1 minute.

5. Remove pot from heat and skim off any foam. Let marmalade cool in the pot for 5 minutes, stirring occasionally.

6. Ladle hot marmalade into hot jars, leaving ¼ inch (0.5 cm) headspace. Remove any air bubbles. Wipe jar rims and threads with a clean, damp paper towel. Center hot lids on jars and screw on bands until fingertip-tight.

7. Place jars in canner, making sure they are covered by at least 1 inch (2.5 cm) of water. Cover and bring to a gentle boil. Process 4-ounce (125 mL) jars and 8-ounce (250 mL) jars for 10 minutes; process 1-pint (500 mL) jars for 15 minutes.

8. Remove jars from canner and place on a wire rack or cloth towel. Let cool for 24 hours, then check seals. Wash and dry jars and store in a cool, dry, dark location.

Lemon Marmalade

**Makes about
five 8-ounce
(250 mL) jars**

*I love the flavor of
lemons, and this
beautiful marmalade
is one of my favorites.*

Tips: For the best
flavor, the lemons
should be fully ripe,
juicy and have a peel
with a good yellow
color without any hints
of green. Underripe
lemons will make a
very tart marmalade.

Meyer lemons make
wonderful marmalade!
If you have access to
Meyer lemons, they
are a great choice for
this marmalade.

16 to 20	medium lemons	16 to 20
1/8 tsp	baking soda	0.5 mL
5 cups	granulated sugar	1.25 L
1/2 tsp	unsalted butter (optional)	2 mL
1	pouch (3 oz/85 mL) liquid pectin	1

1. Prepare canning jars and lids and bring water in water bath canner to a boil.

2. Using a zester, remove only the outer colored portion of the peel in very thin strips from 6 of the lemons. Coarsely chop the zested peel. (The colored zest may also be removed from the fruit using a vegetable peeler, then cut into very thin strips with a sharp knife and coarsely chopped.) Peel all of the lemons, removing all of the outer white pith. Cut the fruit sections away from the membrane and remove any seeds. Discard the pith and membrane. Finely chop the fruit and measure 3 cups (750 mL).

3. In an 8-quart (8 L) stainless steel stockpot, combine chopped lemons, lemon zest and baking soda. Bring to a boil over medium-high heat. Reduce heat, cover and simmer gently for 3 minutes.

4. Gradually stir in sugar and butter, if using. Increase heat to medium-high and bring to a full rolling boil, stirring constantly. Stir in pectin. Return to a full rolling boil, stirring constantly, and boil for 1 minute.

5. Remove pot from heat and skim off any foam. Let marmalade cool in the pot for 5 minutes, stirring occasionally.

6. Ladle hot marmalade into hot jars, leaving 1/4 inch (0.5 cm) headspace. Remove any air bubbles. Wipe jar rims and threads with a clean, damp paper towel. Center hot lids on jars and screw on bands until fingertip-tight.

7. Place jars in canner, making sure they are covered by at least 1 inch (2.5 cm) of water. Cover and bring to a gentle boil. Process 4-ounce (125 mL) jars and 8-ounce (250 mL) jars for 10 minutes; process 1-pint (500 mL) jars for 15 minutes.

8. Remove jars from canner and place on a wire rack or cloth towel. Let cool for 24 hours, then check seals. Wash and dry jars and store in a cool, dry, dark location.

Lemon Lime Marmalade

✳

Makes about five 8-ounce (250 mL) jars

The tangy, refreshing flavor of the lemons and limes gives this marmalade its special zing.

Tip: Baking soda is added to citrus marmalades to help balance the acidity.

7 to 10	medium lemons	7 to 10
12 to 15	medium limes	12 to 15
1/2 cup	water	125 mL
1/8 tsp	baking soda	0.5 mL
5 cups	granulated sugar	1.25 L
1/2 tsp	unsalted butter (optional)	2 mL
1	pouch (3 oz/85 mL) liquid pectin	1

1. Prepare canning jars and lids and bring water in water bath canner to a boil.

2. Using a zester, remove only the outer colored portion of the peel in very thin strips from 4 of the lemons and 6 of the limes. Coarsely chop the zested peel. (The colored zest may also be removed from the fruit using a vegetable peeler, then cut into very thin strips with a sharp knife and coarsely chopped.) Peel all of the lemons and limes, removing all of the outer white pith. Cut the fruit sections away from the membrane and remove any seeds. Discard the pith and membrane. Finely chop the fruit and measure 1 1/2 cups (375 mL) lemons and 1 1/2 cups (375 mL) limes.

3. In an 8-quart (8 L) stainless steel stockpot, combine chopped limes, water and baking soda. Bring to a boil over medium-high heat. Reduce heat, cover and simmer gently for 5 minutes. Stir in chopped lemons, lemon zest and lime zest until well distributed. Cover and simmer for 3 minutes.

4. Gradually stir in sugar and butter, if using. Increase heat to medium-high and bring to a full rolling boil, stirring constantly. Stir in pectin. Return to a full rolling boil, stirring constantly, and boil for 1 minute.

5. Remove pot from heat and skim off any foam. Let marmalade cool in the pot for 5 minutes, stirring occasionally.

Tip: Use only the zest, the colored portion of the citrus peel, when making marmalades. The white pith is very bitter and will give the marmalade an unpleasant flavor.

6. Ladle hot marmalade into hot jars, leaving ¼ inch (0.5 cm) headspace. Remove any air bubbles. Wipe jar rims and threads with a clean, damp paper towel. Center hot lids on jars and screw on bands until fingertip-tight.

7. Place jars in canner, making sure they are covered by at least 1 inch (2.5 cm) of water. Cover and bring to a gentle boil. Process 4-ounce (125 mL) jars and 8-ounce (250 mL) jars for 10 minutes; process 1-pint (500 mL) jars for 15 minutes.

8. Remove jars from canner and place on a wire rack or cloth towel. Let cool for 24 hours, then check seals. Wash and dry jars and store in a cool, dry, dark location.

Tangy Lime Marmalade

✳

Makes about five 8-ounce (250 mL) jars

This remarkable citrus marmalade has an intense lime flavor.

Tips: A few drops of green food coloring added to the water intensifies the color of the marmalade. The food coloring may be omitted, if you prefer.

Bearss limes, a type of Persian or Tahitian lime and the most common large green lime found in grocery stores, have an intense lime flavor and are the best choice for making marmalades and other spreads.

24 to 30	medium limes	24 to 30
3 to 4	drops green food coloring (optional)	3 to 4
1/2 cup	water	125 mL
1/8 tsp	baking soda	0.5 mL
5 cups	granulated sugar	1.25 L
1/2 tsp	unsalted butter (optional)	2 mL
1	pouch (3 oz/85 mL) liquid pectin	1

1. Prepare canning jars and lids and bring water in water bath canner to a boil.

2. Using a zester, remove only the outer colored portion of the peel in very thin strips from 12 of the limes. Coarsely chop the zested peel. (The colored zest may also be removed from the fruit using a vegetable peeler, then cut into very thin strips with a sharp knife and coarsely chopped.) Peel all of the limes, removing all of the outer white pith. Cut the fruit sections away from the membrane and remove any seeds. Discard the pith and membrane. Finely chop the fruit and measure 3 cups (750 mL). Set aside.

3. If using green food coloring, add to the water and stir to combine.

4. In an 8-quart (8 L) stainless steel stockpot, combine chopped limes, water and baking soda. Bring to a boil over medium-high heat. Reduce heat, cover and simmer gently for 5 minutes. Stir in lime zest until well distributed. Cover and simmer for 3 minutes.

5. Gradually stir in sugar and butter, if using. Increase heat to medium-high and bring to a full rolling boil, stirring constantly. Stir in pectin. Return to a full rolling boil, stirring constantly, and boil for 1 minute.

6. Remove pot from heat and skim off any foam. Let marmalade cool in the pot for 5 minutes, stirring occasionally.

Tip: To maintain freshness, store liquid pectin in the refrigerator. Bring the pectin to room temperature before using.

7. Ladle hot marmalade into hot jars, leaving $\frac{1}{4}$ inch (0.5 cm) headspace. Remove any air bubbles. Wipe jar rims and threads with a clean, damp paper towel. Center hot lids on jars and screw on bands until fingertip-tight.

8. Place jars in canner, making sure they are covered by at least 1 inch (2.5 cm) of water. Cover and bring to a gentle boil. Process 4-ounce (125 mL) jars and 8-ounce (250 mL) jars for 10 minutes; process 1-pint (500 mL) jars for 15 minutes.

9. Remove jars from canner and place on a wire rack or cloth towel. Let cool for 24 hours, then check seals. Wash and dry jars and store in a cool, dry, dark location.

Nectarine Marmalade

*Combined with
oranges, nectarines
make a delectable
golden marmalade.*

Tips: Choose
nectarines that have
smooth skin and are
free of blemishes,
soft spots or bruises.

For 3½ cups (875 mL)
crushed nectarines,
you'll need about
4 lbs (2 kg) or about
12 medium nectarines.

2	medium Valencia oranges	2
1	large lemon	1
3½ cups	crushed pitted peeled nectarines	875 mL
¼ cup	freshly squeezed lemon juice	50 mL
⅓ cup	freshly squeezed orange juice	75 mL
½ tsp	unsalted butter (optional)	2 mL
5½ cups	granulated sugar	1.375 L
1	pouch (3 oz/85 mL) liquid pectin	1

1. Prepare canning jars and lids and bring water in water bath canner to a boil.

2. Using a zester, remove only the outer colored portion of the peel from the oranges and lemon in very thin strips. Coarsely chop the zested peel. (The colored zest may also be removed from the fruit using a vegetable peeler, then cut into very thin strips with a sharp knife and coarsely chopped.) Peel the oranges and lemon, removing all of the white pith. Cut the fruit sections away from the membrane and remove any seeds. Discard the pith and membrane. Finely chop the fruit. Set aside.

3. In a bowl, combine nectarines and lemon juice. Stir gently until nectarines are completely coated with lemon juice. Cover and set aside.

4. In an 8-quart (8 L) stainless steel stockpot, combine chopped oranges, chopped lemon and orange juice. Bring to a boil over medium-high heat. Reduce heat, cover and simmer gently for 3 minutes. Stir in orange zest and lemon zest until well distributed. Cover and simmer for 3 minutes. Add nectarine mixture and butter, if using.

5. Gradually stir in sugar. Increase heat to medium-high and bring to a full rolling boil, stirring constantly. Stir in pectin. Return to a full rolling boil, stirring constantly, and boil for 1 minute.

6. Remove pot from heat and skim off any foam. Let marmalade cool in the pot for 5 minutes, stirring occasionally.

Tip: For the best flavor, use ripe nectarines that yield to gentle pressure.

7. Ladle hot marmalade into hot jars, leaving $\frac{1}{4}$ inch (0.5 cm) headspace. Remove any air bubbles. Wipe jar rims and threads with a clean, damp paper towel. Center hot lids on jars and screw on bands until fingertip-tight.

8. Place jars in canner, making sure they are covered by at least 1 inch (2.5 cm) of water. Cover and bring to a gentle boil. Process 4-ounce (125 mL) jars and 8-ounce (250 mL) jars for 10 minutes; process 1-pint (500 mL) jars for 15 minutes.

9. Remove jars from canner and place on a wire rack or cloth towel. Let cool for 24 hours, then check seals. Wash and dry jars and store in a cool, dry, dark location.

Peach Marmalade

**Makes about
five 8-ounce
(250 mL) jars**

*This stunning
marmalade tastes
as good as it looks!*

Tips: Make Peach
Marmalade when fresh
peaches are at the peak
of their season and
have the best flavor.

For 3½ cups (875 mL)
crushed peaches, you'll
need about 4 lbs (2 kg)
or about 12 medium
peaches.

2	medium Valencia oranges	2
1	large lemon	1
3½ cups	crushed pitted peeled peaches	875 mL
¼ cup	freshly squeezed lemon juice	50 mL
⅓ cup	freshly squeezed orange juice	75 mL
½ tsp	unsalted butter (optional)	2 mL
5½ cups	granulated sugar	1.375 L
1	pouch (3 oz/85 mL) liquid pectin	1

1. Prepare canning jars and lids and bring water in water bath canner to a boil.

2. Using a zester, remove only the outer colored portion of the peel from the oranges and lemon in very thin strips. Coarsely chop the zested peel. (The colored zest may also be removed from the fruit using a vegetable peeler, then cut into very thin strips with a sharp knife and coarsely chopped.) Peel the oranges and lemon, removing all of the white pith. Cut the fruit sections away from the membrane and remove any seeds. Discard the pith and membrane. Finely chop the fruit. Set aside.

3. In a bowl, combine peaches and lemon juice. Stir gently until peaches are completely coated with lemon juice. Cover and set aside.

4. In an 8-quart (8 L) stainless steel stockpot, combine chopped oranges, chopped lemon and orange juice. Bring to a boil over medium-high heat. Reduce heat, cover and simmer gently for 3 minutes. Stir in orange zest and lemon zest until well distributed. Cover and simmer for 3 minutes. Add peach mixture and butter, if using.

5. Gradually stir in sugar. Increase heat to medium-high and bring to a full rolling boil, stirring constantly. Stir in pectin. Return to a full rolling boil, stirring constantly, and boil for 1 minute.

6. Remove pot from heat and skim off any foam. Let marmalade cool in the pot for 5 minutes, stirring occasionally.

7. Ladle hot marmalade into hot jars, leaving ¼ inch (0.5 cm) headspace. Remove any air bubbles. Wipe jar rims and threads with a clean, damp paper towel. Center hot lids on jars and screw on bands until fingertip-tight.

8. Place jars in canner, making sure they are covered by at least 1 inch (2.5 cm) of water. Cover and bring to a gentle boil. Process 4-ounce (125 mL) jars and 8-ounce (250 mL) jars for 10 minutes; process 1-pint (500 mL) jars for 15 minutes.

9. Remove jars from canner and place on a wire rack or cloth towel. Let cool for 24 hours, then check seals. Wash and dry jars and store in a cool, dry, dark location.

Peach Nectarine Marmalade

*Picked at the peak
of the season and
transformed into
this radiant, classy
marmalade, peaches
and nectarines add
style to any breakfast
table.*

Tips: To ripen peaches
and nectarines, place
them in a paper bag
and let them stand at
room temperature
for a few days.

For 1¾ cups (425 mL)
crushed peaches, you'll
need about 2 lbs (1 kg)
or about 6 medium
peaches. For 1¾ cups
(425 mL) crushed
nectarines, you'll need
about 2 lbs (1 kg) or
about 6 medium
nectarines.

2	medium Valencia oranges	2
1	large lemon	1
1¾ cups	crushed pitted peeled peaches	425 mL
1¾ cups	crushed pitted peeled nectarines	425 mL
¼ cup	freshly squeezed lemon juice	50 mL
⅓ cup	freshly squeezed orange juice	75 mL
½ tsp	unsalted butter (optional)	2 mL
5½ cups	granulated sugar	1.375 L
1	pouch (3 oz/85 mL) liquid pectin	1

1. Prepare canning jars and lids and bring water in water bath canner to a boil.

2. Using a zester, remove only the outer colored portion of the peel from the oranges and lemon in very thin strips. Coarsely chop the zested peel. (The colored zest may also be removed from the fruit using a vegetable peeler, then cut into very thin strips with a sharp knife and coarsely chopped.) Peel the oranges and lemon, removing all of the white pith. Cut the fruit sections away from the membrane and remove any seeds. Discard the pith and membrane. Finely chop the fruit. Set aside.

3. In a bowl, combine peaches, nectarines and lemon juice. Stir gently until peaches and nectarines are completely coated with lemon juice. Cover and set aside.

4. In an 8-quart (8 L) stainless steel stockpot, combine chopped oranges, chopped lemon and orange juice. Bring to a boil over medium-high heat. Reduce heat, cover and simmer gently for 3 minutes. Stir in orange zest and lemon zest until well distributed. Cover and simmer for 3 minutes. Add peach and nectarine mixture and butter, if using.

5. Gradually stir in sugar. Increase heat to medium-high and bring to a full rolling boil, stirring constantly. Stir in pectin. Return to a full rolling boil, stirring constantly, and boil for 1 minute.

Tips: If nectarines or peaches reach ripeness before you are ready to use them, they may be stored in the refrigerator for a few days.

Yellow-fleshed peaches and nectarines make the best-tasting marmalade. White-fleshed peaches and nectarines make a mild-flavored marmalade with a softer set.

6. Remove pot from heat and skim off any foam. Let marmalade cool in the pot for 5 minutes, stirring occasionally.

7. Ladle hot marmalade into hot jars, leaving ¼ inch (0.5 cm) headspace. Remove any air bubbles. Wipe jar rims and threads with a clean, damp paper towel. Center hot lids on jars and screw on bands until fingertip-tight.

8. Place jars in canner, making sure they are covered by at least 1 inch (2.5 cm) of water. Cover and bring to a gentle boil. Process 4-ounce (125 mL) jars and 8-ounce (250 mL) jars for 10 minutes; process 1-pint (500 mL) jars for 15 minutes.

9. Remove jars from canner and place on a wire rack or cloth towel. Let cool for 24 hours, then check seals. Wash and dry jars and store in a cool, dry, dark location.

Pineapple Marmalade

*The tropical flavors
of this marmalade
make a lovely pairing
with both shrimp
and chicken.*

Tips: Fresh pineapples
contain an enzyme that
inhibits marmalades
from setting. It is best
to use canned pineapple
in spread recipes to
achieve a proper set.

If using a can size other
than 20 oz (567 mL),
you will need 1 ⅛ cups
(280 mL) drained
crushed pineapple
for this recipe.

4	medium Valencia oranges	4
2	medium lemons	2
1	can (20 oz/567 g) juice-packed crushed pineapple, drained (see tips, at left)	1
5 cups	granulated sugar	1.25 L
½ tsp	unsalted butter (optional)	2 mL
1	pouch (3 oz/85 mL) liquid pectin	1

1. Prepare canning jars and lids and bring water in water bath canner to a boil.

2. Using a zester, remove only the outer colored portion of the peel from the oranges and lemons in very thin strips. Coarsely chop the zested peel. (The colored zest may also be removed from the fruit using a vegetable peeler, then cut into very thin strips with a sharp knife and coarsely chopped.) Peel the oranges and lemons, removing all of the white pith. Cut the fruit sections away from the membrane and remove any seeds. Discard the pith and membrane. Finely chop the fruit.

3. In an 8-quart (8 L) stainless steel stockpot, combine chopped oranges, chopped lemons and pineapple. Bring to a boil over medium-high heat. Reduce heat, cover and simmer gently for 5 minutes. Stir in orange zest and lemon zest until well distributed. Cover and simmer for 3 minutes.

4. Gradually stir in sugar and butter, if using. Increase heat to medium-high and bring to a full rolling boil, stirring constantly. Stir in pectin. Return to a full rolling boil, stirring constantly, and boil for 1 minute.

5. Remove pot from heat and skim off any foam. Let marmalade cool in the pot for 5 minutes, stirring occasionally.

6. Ladle hot marmalade into hot jars, leaving ¼ inch (0.5 cm) headspace. Remove any air bubbles. Wipe jar rims and threads with a clean, damp paper towel. Center hot lids on jars and screw on bands until fingertip-tight.

7. Place jars in canner, making sure they are covered by at least 1 inch (2.5 cm) of water. Cover and bring to a gentle boil. Process 4-ounce (125 mL) jars and 8-ounce (250 mL) jars for 10 minutes; process 1-pint (500 mL) jars for 15 minutes.

8. Remove jars from canner and place on a wire rack or cloth towel. Let cool for 24 hours, then check seals. Wash and dry jars and store in a cool, dry, dark location.

Raspberry Marmalade

A delectable spread for scones or toast, this rosy marmalade is loaded with flavor.

Tips: To reduce the amount of seeds in the finished marmalade, press about half the raspberry pulp through a fine-mesh sieve to remove the seeds before measuring.

For 3 cups (750 mL) crushed raspberries, you'll need about 2 lbs (1 kg) or 8 cups (2 L) raspberries.

4	medium lemons	4
1/8 tsp	baking soda	0.5 mL
3 cups	crushed raspberries	750 mL
1/2 tsp	unsalted butter (optional)	2 mL
6 cups	granulated sugar	1.5 L
1	pouch (3 oz/85 mL) liquid pectin	1

1. Prepare canning jars and lids and bring water in water bath canner to a boil.

2. Using a zester, remove only the outer colored portion of the peel from the lemons in very thin strips. Coarsely chop the zested peel. (The colored zest may also be removed from the fruit using a vegetable peeler, then cut into very thin strips with a sharp knife and coarsely chopped.) Peel the lemons, removing all of the white pith. Cut the fruit sections away from the membrane and remove any seeds. Discard the pith and membrane. Finely chop the fruit.

3. In an 8-quart (8 L) stainless steel stockpot, combine chopped lemons, lemon zest and baking soda. Bring to a boil over medium-high heat. Reduce heat, cover and simmer gently for 3 minutes. Add raspberries and butter, if using.

4. Gradually stir in sugar. Increase heat to medium-high and bring to a full rolling boil, stirring constantly. Stir in pectin. Return to a full rolling boil, stirring constantly, and boil for 1 minute.

5. Remove pot from heat and skim off any foam. Let marmalade cool in the pot for 5 minutes, stirring occasionally.

6. Ladle hot marmalade into hot jars, leaving 1/4 inch (0.5 cm) headspace. Remove any air bubbles. Wipe jar rims and threads with a clean, damp paper towel. Center hot lids on jars and screw on bands until fingertip-tight.

7. Place jars in canner, making sure they are covered by at least 1 inch (2.5 cm) of water. Cover and bring to a gentle boil. Process 4-ounce (125 mL) jars and 8-ounce (250 mL) jars for 10 minutes; process 1-pint (500 mL) jars for 15 minutes.

8. Remove jars from canner and place on a wire rack or cloth towel. Let cool for 24 hours, then check seals. Wash and

Strawberry Marmalade

Makes about eight 8-ounce (250 mL) jars

A family favorite for years, this superb marmalade has amazing color and luscious fruit flavor.

Tips: Use a tomato huller or strawberry huller to remove the leaves, stems and white hulls from strawberries before cutting and crushing the berries.

For 3½ cups (875 mL) crushed strawberries, you'll need about 2½ lbs (1.25 kg) or 7 cups (1.75 L) strawberries.

2	medium Valencia oranges	2
1	large lemon	1
3½ cups	crushed hulled strawberries	875 mL
2 tbsp	freshly squeezed lemon juice	30 mL
⅓ cup	freshly squeezed orange juice	75 mL
½ tsp	unsalted butter (optional)	2 mL
7 cups	granulated sugar	1.75 L
1	pouch (3 oz/85 mL) liquid pectin	1

1. Prepare canning jars and lids and bring water in water bath canner to a boil.

2. Using a zester, remove only the outer colored portion of the peel from the oranges and lemon in very thin strips. Coarsely chop the zested peel. (The colored zest may also be removed from the fruit using a vegetable peeler, then cut into very thin strips with a sharp knife and coarsely chopped.) Peel the oranges and lemon, removing all of the white pith. Cut the fruit sections away from the membrane and remove any seeds. Discard the pith and membrane. Finely chop the fruit. Set aside.

3. In a bowl, combine strawberries and lemon juice. Stir gently until strawberries are completely coated with lemon juice. Cover and set aside.

4. In an 8-quart (8 L) stainless steel stockpot, combine chopped oranges, chopped lemon and orange juice. Bring to a boil over medium-high heat. Reduce heat, cover and simmer gently for 3 minutes. Stir in orange zest and lemon zest until well distributed. Cover and simmer for 3 minutes. Add strawberry mixture and butter, if using.

5. Gradually stir in sugar. Increase heat to medium-high and bring to a full rolling boil, stirring constantly. Stir in pectin. Return to a full rolling boil, stirring constantly, and boil for 1 minute.

6. Remove pot from heat and skim off any foam. Let marmalade cool in the pot for 5 minutes, stirring occasionally.

7. Ladle hot marmalade into hot jars, leaving $1/4$ inch (0.5 cm) headspace. Remove any air bubbles. Wipe jar rims and threads with a clean, damp paper towel. Center hot lids on jars and screw on bands until fingertip-tight.

8. Place jars in canner, making sure they are covered by at least 1 inch (2.5 cm) of water. Cover and bring to a gentle boil. Process 4-ounce (125 mL) jars and 8-ounce (250 mL) jars for 10 minutes; process 1-pint (500 mL) jars for 15 minutes.

9. Remove jars from canner and place on a wire rack or cloth towel. Let cool for 24 hours, then check seals. Wash and dry jars and store in a cool, dry, dark location.

Sunshine Marmalade

Makes about five 8-ounce (250 mL) jars

A vibrant golden color and superb blending of flavors are the special rewards for making this marmalade.

Tip: Butter is added to marmalade recipes to help reduce the amount of foam created when the fruit boils. The butter is an optional ingredient and may be eliminated, if you prefer.

10 to 12	medium Valencia oranges	10 to 12
6 to 8	medium lemons	6 to 8
$1/8$ tsp	baking soda	0.5 mL
5 cups	granulated sugar	1.25 L
$1/2$ tsp	unsalted butter (optional)	2 mL
1	pouch (3 oz/85 mL) liquid pectin	1

1. Prepare canning jars and lids and bring water in water bath canner to a boil.

2. Using a zester, remove only the outer colored portion of the peel in very thin strips from 4 of the oranges and 2 of the lemons. Coarsely chop the zested peel. (The colored zest may also be removed from the fruit using a vegetable peeler, then cut into very thin strips with a sharp knife and coarsely chopped.) Peel all of the oranges and lemons, removing all of the outer white pith. Cut the fruit sections away from the membrane and remove any seeds. Discard the pith and membrane. Finely chop the fruit and measure 2 cups (500 mL) oranges and 1 cup (250 mL) lemons.

3. In an 8-quart (8 L) stainless steel stockpot, combine chopped oranges and baking soda. Bring to a boil over medium-high heat. Reduce heat, cover and simmer gently for 8 minutes. Stir in chopped lemons, orange zest and lemon zest until well distributed. Cover and simmer for 3 minutes.

4. Gradually stir in sugar and butter, if using. Increase heat to medium-high and bring to a full rolling boil, stirring constantly. Stir in pectin. Return to a full rolling boil, stirring constantly, and boil for 1 minute.

5. Remove pot from heat and skim off any foam. Let marmalade cool in the pot for 5 minutes, stirring occasionally.

6. Ladle hot marmalade into hot jars, leaving $1/4$ inch (0.5 cm) headspace. Remove any air bubbles. Wipe jar rims and threads with a clean, damp paper towel. Center hot lids on jars and screw on bands until fingertip-tight.

7. Place jars in canner, making sure they are covered by at least 1 inch (2.5 cm) of water. Cover and bring to a gentle boil. Process 4-ounce (125 mL) jars and 8-ounce (250 mL) jars for 10 minutes; process 1-pint (500 mL) jars for 15 minutes.

8. Remove jars from canner and place on a wire rack or cloth towel. Let cool for 24 hours, then check seals. Wash and dry jars and store in a cool, dry, dark location.

Sweet Orange Marmalade

12 to 14	medium Valencia oranges	12 to 14
1/4 cup	freshly squeezed lemon juice	50 mL
1/8 tsp	baking soda	0.5 mL
5 cups	granulated sugar	1.25 L
1/2 tsp	unsalted butter (optional)	2 mL
1	pouch (3 oz/85 mL) liquid pectin	1

Makes about five 8-ounce (250 mL) jars

Made without the bitter white pith found in most marmalades, this fragrant marmalade has an intense orange flavor and a pleasing texture.

Tip: Do not use navel oranges for making marmalade. Navel oranges become tough when cooked, and they contain an enzyme that will cause the fruit to turn bitter during storage.

1. Prepare canning jars and lids and bring water in water bath canner to a boil.

2. Using a zester, remove only the outer colored portion of the peel in very thin strips from 6 of the oranges. Coarsely chop the zested peel. (The colored zest may also be removed from the fruit using a vegetable peeler, then cut into very thin strips with a sharp knife and coarsely chopped.) Peel all of the oranges, removing all of the outer white pith. Cut the fruit sections away from the membrane and remove any seeds. Discard the pith and membrane. Finely chop the fruit and measure 2⅔ cups (650 mL).

3. In an 8-quart (8 L) stainless steel stockpot, combine chopped oranges, lemon juice and baking soda. Bring to a boil over medium-high heat. Reduce heat, cover and simmer gently for 8 minutes. Stir in orange zest until well distributed. Cover and simmer for 3 minutes.

4. Gradually stir in sugar and butter, if using. Increase heat to medium-high and bring to a full rolling boil, stirring constantly. Stir in pectin. Return to a full rolling boil, stirring constantly, and boil for 1 minute.

5. Remove pot from heat and skim off any foam. Let marmalade cool in the pot for 5 minutes, stirring occasionally.

6. Ladle hot marmalade into hot jars, leaving 1/4 inch (0.5 cm) headspace. Remove any air bubbles. Wipe jar rims and threads with a clean, damp paper towel. Center hot lids on jars and screw on bands until fingertip-tight.

7. Place jars in canner, making sure they are covered by at least 1 inch (2.5 cm) of water. Cover and bring to a gentle boil. Process 4-ounce (125 mL) jars and 8-ounce (250 mL) jars for 10 minutes; process 1-pint (500 mL) jars for 15 minutes.

8. Remove jars from canner and place on a wire rack or cloth towel. Let cool for 24 hours, then check seals. Wash and dry jars and store in a cool, dry, dark location.

Tangelo Marmalade

**Makes about
five 8-ounce
(250 mL) jars**

*Deep orange in
color, this fragrant
marmalade is sure to
delight marmalade
fans looking for
something special.*

Tip: Tangelos are a cross
between a tangerine
and an orange.
Minneola tangelos are
the most common and
are available in most
grocery stores from late
fall through early spring.

14 to 18	tangelos	14 to 18
1/3 cup	freshly squeezed lemon juice	75 mL
1/8 tsp	baking soda	0.5 mL
5 cups	granulated sugar	1.25 L
1/2 tsp	unsalted butter (optional)	2 mL
1	pouch (3 oz/85 mL) liquid pectin	1

1. Prepare canning jars and lids and bring water in water bath canner to a boil.

2. Using a zester, remove only the outer colored portion of the peel in very thin strips from 6 of the tangelos. Coarsely chop the zested peel. (The colored zest may also be removed from the fruit using a vegetable peeler, then cut into very thin strips with a sharp knife and coarsely chopped.) Peel all of the tangelos, removing all of the outer white pith. Cut the fruit sections away from the membrane and remove any seeds. Discard the pith and membrane. Finely chop the fruit and measure 2⅔ cups (650 mL).

3. In an 8-quart (8 L) stainless steel stockpot, combine chopped tangelos, lemon juice and baking soda. Bring to a boil over medium-high heat. Reduce heat, cover and simmer gently for 5 minutes. Stir in tangelo zest until well distributed. Cover and simmer for 3 minutes.

4. Gradually stir in sugar and butter, if using. Increase heat to medium-high and bring to a full rolling boil, stirring constantly. Stir in pectin. Return to a full rolling boil, stirring constantly, and boil for 1 minute.

5. Remove pot from heat and skim off any foam. Let marmalade cool in the pot for 5 minutes, stirring occasionally.

6. Ladle hot marmalade into hot jars, leaving ¼ inch (0.5 cm) headspace. Remove any air bubbles. Wipe jar rims and threads with a clean, damp paper towel. Center hot lids on jars and screw on bands until fingertip-tight.

7. Place jars in canner, making sure they are covered by at least 1 inch (2.5 cm) of water. Cover and bring to a gentle boil. Process 4-ounce (125 mL) jars and 8-ounce (250 mL) jars for 10 minutes; process 1-pint (500 mL) jars for 15 minutes.

8. Remove jars from canner and place on a wire rack or cloth towel. Let cool for 24 hours, then check seals. Wash and dry jars and store in a cool, dry, dark location.

Preserves & Conserves

✳

About Preserves

THE TERM "PRESERVES" has two meanings in home canning. In the general sense, it refers to any product that has been preserved by home canning, such as jam, fruit or even sauces and pickles. It also refers to a specific type of soft spread that has its own unique and wonderful characteristics. In this book, we are talking about the soft spread type of preserves.

Preserves are made with large, uniform pieces of fruit or with small whole fruits. The cooked fruit holds its shape, and the fruit pieces are evenly distributed in the jar and suspended in a soft jelly or very thick syrup. During the cooking process, dissolved sugar penetrates the fruit cells, giving the fruit pieces a luminous, semi-transparent appearance.

The crown jewel of soft spreads, perfect preserves contain brightly colored, translucent fruit with intense flavor. The fruit is tender and glistens, making preserves completely irresistible. Preserves enthusiasts love the luscious pieces of fruit suspended in the shimmering jelly. When it comes to elegance, preserves are hard to beat!

While preserves have traditionally been made from just one kind of fruit, as with jams, mixed-fruit preserves are rapidly gaining in popularity among home canners. One, two or even three fruits can be used together in a preserve to create a unique flavor combination.

Floating Fruit

The distinguishing trait of quality preserves is that the fruit is perfectly distributed throughout the jar after the preserves have cooled and set. As with jams, floating fruit in preserves is a common problem for some home canners. There are a few techniques to help prevent floating fruit in preserves. The first is to choose fully ripe fruit that is not overly juicy. Some fruit is juicier than others. Take strawberries, for example. Some strawberry varieties are very soft and juicy, while others are firmer but still full of flavor. The firmer, flavorful strawberries are a better choice for preserves because the berries will hold their shape, release less juice and be far less likely to float in the finished preserve.

When making preserves, the fruit and a portion of the sugar are combined and set aside to stand for a period of time before the preserve is cooked. The fruit and sugar are then slowly heated until the sugar is completely dissolved. This allows the fruit to absorb some of the sugar and release air from its cells. When the air is released, it is replaced with dissolved sugar and the fruit becomes heavier, enabling it to remain suspended in the jelly rather than separating from the jelly and rising to the top of the jar. Absorption of sugar also turns the fruit translucent, makes it shimmer, and unifies the flavor and texture of the preserves.

Another technique that helps prevent floating fruit is letting the preserves stand in the pot for 5 minutes after removing the pot from the heat and before filling the jars. Gently stirring the preserves every minute or so will help distribute the fruit evenly through the jelly. This standing time allows the fruit pieces to continue cooking, without overcooking, and to fully absorb the syrup.

Pectin

Be sure to use the specific type of pectin called for in the recipe. Liquid and powdered pectins have different formulations and different setting properties and are not interchangeable. Because powdered pectin is designed to be combined with the fruit and boiled before the sugar is added, it is not suitable for making preserves where the fruit and sugar need to be combined first. Using a different type of pectin than the one called for in the recipe will result in a preserve that does not set.

If liquid pectin has been stored in the refrigerator, let it come to room temperature before using. Be sure to squeeze out the entire contents of the liquid pectin pouch into the pan.

About Conserves

AS HOME CANNERS EXPAND beyond basic jams and jellies, many are discovering the wonderful world of conserves. A conserve, you say? What is a conserve? Conserves are delightful soft spreads with a texture similar to that of jam. They are prepared basically the same way jam is made. What sets conserves apart is that they traditionally contain two or more fruits and nuts. Conserves may be made with fresh or dried fruits, or a combination of both. Dried fruits, such as raisins or currants, are frequent additions to conserves. Dried cranberries are especially nice in conserves, and coconut can give a tropical conserve a wonderful flavor and texture.

The addition of chopped nuts gives conserves a unique texture and a rich flavor. Large nut pieces will make the conserve too chunky, so chop nuts into small pieces to give the conserve a smoother texture. When making conserves, make sure the nuts you use are fresh. Taste them before making the conserve, just to be sure. Nothing ruins a conserve quite like the taste of stale or rancid nuts. For the best flavor and texture, add the nuts to the conserve just before the final boil.

Some home canners prefer the flavor of lightly toasted nuts in their conserves. To lightly toast nuts, preheat the oven to 350°F (180°C). Line a baking sheet with foil and spread the chopped nuts over the foil in a single layer. Bake for 5 minutes, stirring halfway through. Remove the nuts from the pan and let cool completely before using.

All of the techniques that apply to making single-fruit and mixed-fruit jams also apply to making conserves. Like jams, conserves are thick in texture and should mound up in a spoon, hold their shape and spread easily. There should be no separation of the fruit and nuts from the juice in the spread, and the conserve should not be runny.

Each type of fruit has a different level of natural pectin and different requirements in order for the conserve to set. The proportions of each type of fruit in these recipes, along with the proportions of sugar, pectin and acid, have been balanced to achieve a good set. Altering the proportions may prevent the conserve from setting.

Apple Preserves

✳

Makes about six 8-ounce (250 mL) jars

The flavor of these preserves is reminiscent of apple pie. Use any variety of apple that holds its shape when cooked, such as Granny Smith.

Tips: Apple cider adds an extra depth of flavor to apple preserves. If you cannot find apple cider, you may substitute unsweetened apple juice.

For 7 cups (1.75 L) chopped apples, you'll need about 3 lbs (1.5 kg) or about 8 medium apples.

7 cups	chopped cored peeled apples	1.75 L
2 tbsp	freshly squeezed lemon juice	30 mL
1 cup	unsweetened apple cider	250 mL
5 cups	granulated sugar, divided	1.25 L
1½ tsp	ground cinnamon	7 mL
¼ tsp	ground nutmeg	1 mL
½ tsp	unsalted butter (optional)	2 mL
1	pouch (3 oz/85 mL) liquid pectin	1

1. Prepare canning jars and lids and bring water in water bath canner to a boil.

2. In an 8-quart (8 L) stainless steel stockpot, combine apples and lemon juice. Stir gently until apples are completely coated with lemon juice. Stir in apple cider. Add 2 cups (500 mL) of the sugar and stir just until combined. Cover and let stand for 1 hour.

3. Gradually stir in the remaining sugar, cinnamon, nutmeg and butter, if using. Heat, uncovered, over medium heat until sugar is mostly dissolved, stirring frequently to prevent sticking. Bring to a gentle boil and simmer gently for 10 minutes, stirring frequently.

4. Increase heat to medium-high and bring to a full rolling boil, stirring constantly. Stir in pectin. Return to a full rolling boil, stirring constantly, and boil for 1 minute.

5. Remove pot from heat and skim off any foam. Let preserves cool in the pot for 5 minutes, stirring occasionally.

6. Ladle hot preserves into hot jars, leaving ¼ inch (0.5 cm) headspace. Remove any air bubbles. Wipe jar rims and threads with a clean, damp paper towel. Center hot lids on jars and screw on bands until fingertip-tight.

7. Place jars in canner, making sure they are covered by at least 1 inch (2.5 cm) of water. Cover and bring to a gentle boil. Process 4-ounce (125 mL) jars and 8-ounce (250 mL) jars for 10 minutes; process 1-pint (500 mL) jars for 15 minutes.

8. Remove jars from canner and place on a wire rack or cloth towel. Let cool for 24 hours, then check seals. Wash and dry jars and store in a cool, dry, dark location.

Apple Pear Preserves

＊

Refreshing fruit flavors highlight these delicious preserves, which make a superb filling for crêpes.

Tips: When making preserves, choose cooking apples that have good flavor and hold their shape when cooked, such as Granny Smith, Jonathan, Rome Beauty, Winesap, Northern Spy or Braeburn.

Use a pear variety that holds its shape well when cooked, such as Bartlett, for making preserves.

For 3½ cups (875 mL) chopped apples, you'll need about 1½ lbs (750 g) or about 4 medium apples. For 2½ cups (625 mL) chopped pears, you'll need about 2½ lbs (1.25 kg) or about 7 medium pears.

3½ cups	chopped cored peeled apples	875 mL
2½ cups	chopped cored peeled pears	625 mL
3 tbsp	freshly squeezed lemon juice	45 mL
4½ cups	granulated sugar, divided	1.125 L
½ tsp	unsalted butter (optional)	2 mL
1	pouch (3 oz/85 mL) liquid pectin	1

1. Prepare canning jars and lids and bring water in water bath canner to a boil.

2. In an 8-quart (8 L) stainless steel stockpot, combine apples, pears and lemon juice. Stir gently until apples and pears are completely coated with lemon juice. Add 2 cups (500 mL) of the sugar and stir just until combined. Cover and let stand for 1 hour.

3. Gradually stir in the remaining sugar and butter, if using. Heat, uncovered, over medium heat until sugar is mostly dissolved, stirring frequently to prevent sticking. Bring to a gentle boil and simmer gently for 5 minutes, stirring frequently.

4. Increase heat to medium-high and bring to a full rolling boil, stirring constantly. Stir in pectin. Return to a full rolling boil, stirring constantly, and boil for 1 minute.

5. Remove pot from heat and skim off any foam. Let preserves cool in the pot for 5 minutes, stirring occasionally.

6. Ladle hot preserves into hot jars, leaving ¼ inch (0.5 cm) headspace. Remove any air bubbles. Wipe jar rims and threads with a clean, damp paper towel. Center hot lids on jars and screw on bands until fingertip-tight.

7. Place jars in canner, making sure they are covered by at least 1 inch (2.5 cm) of water. Cover and bring to a gentle boil. Process 4-ounce (125 mL) jars and 8-ounce (250 mL) jars for 10 minutes; process 1-pint (500 mL) jars for 15 minutes.

8. Remove jars from canner and place on a wire rack or cloth towel. Let cool for 24 hours, then check seals. Wash and dry jars and store in a cool, dry, dark location.

Apricot Cherry Preserves

2 cups	halved pitted fresh sweet cherries	500 mL
2 cups	sliced pitted peeled apricots	500 mL
6 tbsp	freshly squeezed lemon juice	90 mL
4 cups	granulated sugar, divided	1 L
½ tsp	unsalted butter (optional)	2 mL
1	pouch (3 oz/85 mL) liquid pectin	1

**Makes about
five 8-ounce
(250 mL) jars**

*The combination of
cherries and apricots
produces exquisitely
flavored preserves.*

Tips: Combining the
fruit and sugar and
then letting the mixture
stand for a period of
time allows the fruit to
release juice and absorb
some of the sugar.

For 2 cups (500 mL)
halved cherries, you'll
need about 1¾ lbs
(875 g) cherries. For
2 cups (500 mL) sliced
apricots, you'll need
about 1½ lbs (750 g)
medium apricots.

1. Prepare canning jars and lids and bring water in water
   bath canner to a boil.

2. In an 8-quart (8 L) stainless steel stockpot, combine
   cherries, apricots and lemon juice. Stir gently until cherries
   and apricots are completely coated with lemon juice. Add
   2 cups (500 mL) of the sugar and stir just until combined.
   Cover and let stand for 20 minutes.

3. Gradually stir in the remaining sugar and butter, if using.
   Heat, uncovered, over medium heat until sugar is mostly
   dissolved, stirring frequently to prevent sticking. Bring to
   a gentle boil and simmer gently for 5 minutes, stirring
   frequently.

4. Increase heat to medium-high and bring to a full rolling
   boil, stirring constantly. Stir in pectin. Return to a full
   rolling boil, stirring constantly, and boil for 1 minute.

5. Remove pot from heat and skim off any foam. Let preserves
   cool in the pot for 5 minutes, stirring occasionally.

6. Ladle hot preserves into hot jars, leaving ¼ inch (0.5 cm)
   headspace. Remove any air bubbles. Wipe jar rims and
   threads with a clean, damp paper towel. Center hot lids
   on jars and screw on bands until fingertip-tight.

7. Place jars in canner, making sure they are covered by at
   least 1 inch (2.5 cm) of water. Cover and bring to a gentle
   boil. Process 4-ounce (125 mL) jars and 8-ounce (250 mL)
   jars for 10 minutes; process 1-pint (500 mL) jars for
   15 minutes.

8. Remove jars from canner and place on a wire rack or cloth
   towel. Let cool for 24 hours, then check seals. Wash and
   dry jars and store in a cool, dry, dark location.

Apricot Pineapple Preserves

✳

*I like to use pineapple
tidbits for preserves
because the pieces are
larger than crushed
pineapple but not as
large as pineapple
chunks. If you cannot
find pineapple tidbits,
crushed pineapple
may be substituted.*

Tips: If the apricots are
very large, cut them
into sixths or eighths
instead of quarters.

If using a can size other
than 20 oz (567 mL),
you will need 1⅓ cups
(325 mL) drained
pineapple tidbits for
this recipe.

For 3¾ cups (925 mL)
quartered apricots,
you'll need about 3 lbs
(1.5 kg) medium
apricots.

1	can (20 oz/567 mL) juice-packed pineapple tidbits, drained (see tip, at left)	1
4½ cups	granulated sugar, divided	1.125 L
3¾ cups	quartered pitted peeled apricots	925 mL
½ cup	freshly squeezed lemon juice	125 mL
½ tsp	unsalted butter (optional)	2 mL
1	pouch (3 oz/85 mL) liquid pectin	1

1. Prepare canning jars and lids and bring water in water bath canner to a boil.

2. In an 8-quart (8 L) stainless steel stockpot, combine pineapple and 1½ cups (375 mL) of the sugar and stir just until combined. Cover and let stand for 1 hour.

3. In a bowl, combine apricots and lemon juice. Stir gently until apricots are completely coated with lemon juice.

4. Add apricot mixture to the pineapple mixture and stir just until combined. Gradually stir in the remaining sugar and butter, if using. Heat, uncovered, over medium heat until sugar is mostly dissolved, stirring frequently to prevent sticking. Bring to a gentle boil and simmer gently for 5 minutes, stirring frequently.

5. Increase heat to medium-high and bring to a full rolling boil, stirring constantly. Stir in pectin. Return to a full rolling boil, stirring constantly, and boil for 1 minute.

6. Remove pot from heat and skim off any foam. Let preserves cool in the pot for 5 minutes, stirring occasionally.

7. Ladle hot preserves into hot jars, leaving ¼ inch (0.5 cm) headspace. Remove any air bubbles. Wipe jar rims and threads with a clean, damp paper towel. Center hot lids on jars and screw on bands until fingertip-tight.

8. Place jars in canner, making sure they are covered by at least 1 inch (2.5 cm) of water. Cover and bring to a gentle boil. Process 4-ounce (125 mL) jars and 8-ounce (250 mL) jars for 10 minutes; process 1-pint (500 mL) jars for 15 minutes.

9. Remove jars from canner and place on a wire rack or cloth towel. Let cool for 24 hours, then check seals. Wash and dry jars and store in a cool, dry, dark location.

Blueberry Apricot Preserves

*

**Makes about
six 8-ounce
(250 mL) jars**

*Succulent blueberries
and lively apricots
tantalize the senses in
these exciting preserves.*

Tips: To freeze fresh
blueberries for later use,
spread them in a single
layer on a foil-lined
baking sheet. Freeze
for several hours or
overnight. Pack frozen
blueberries into labeled
zippered freezer bags
and store in the freezer
until ready to use.

For 2 1/2 cups (625 mL)
blueberries, you'll
need about 1 lb (500 g).
For 2 1/2 cups (625 mL)
quartered apricots,
you'll need about 2 lbs
(1 kg) medium apricots.

2 1/2 cups	blueberries	625 mL
2 1/2 cups	quartered pitted peeled apricots	625 mL
1/3 cup	freshly squeezed lemon juice	75 mL
5 1/2 cups	granulated sugar, divided	1.375 L
1/2 tsp	unsalted butter (optional)	2 mL
1	pouch (3 oz/85 mL) liquid pectin	1

1. Prepare canning jars and lids and bring water in water bath canner to a boil.

2. In an 8-quart (8 L) stainless steel stockpot, combine blueberries, apricots and lemon juice. Stir gently until blueberries and apricots are completely coated with lemon juice. Add 2 cups (500 mL) of the sugar and stir just until combined. Cover and let stand for 30 minutes.

3. Gradually stir in the remaining sugar and butter, if using. Heat, uncovered, over medium heat until sugar is mostly dissolved, stirring frequently to prevent sticking. Bring to a gentle boil and simmer gently for 3 minutes, stirring frequently.

4. Increase heat to medium-high and bring to a full rolling boil, stirring constantly. Stir in pectin. Return to a full rolling boil, stirring constantly, and boil for 1 minute.

5. Remove pot from heat and skim off any foam. Let preserves cool in the pot for 5 minutes, stirring occasionally.

6. Ladle hot preserves into hot jars, leaving 1/4 inch (0.5 cm) headspace. Remove any air bubbles. Wipe jar rims and threads with a clean, damp paper towel. Center hot lids on jars and screw on bands until fingertip-tight.

7. Place jars in canner, making sure they are covered by at least 1 inch (2.5 cm) of water. Cover and bring to a gentle boil. Process 4-ounce (125 mL) jars and 8-ounce (250 mL) jars for 10 minutes; process 1-pint (500 mL) jars for 15 minutes.

8. Remove jars from canner and place on a wire rack or cloth towel. Let cool for 24 hours, then check seals. Wash and dry jars and store in a cool, dry, dark location.

Blueberry Pie Preserves

Mmmmm! Blueberries and a hint of cinnamon — what a delightful flavor combination!

Tips: Fresh or frozen blueberries can be used. If using frozen blueberries, do not rinse or defrost them before making the preserves.

For 6 cups (1.5 L) blueberries, you'll need about 2½ lbs (1.25 kg).

6 cups	blueberries	1.5 L
¼ cup	water	50 mL
7 cups	granulated sugar, divided	1.75 L
½ tsp	ground cinnamon	2 mL
½ tsp	unsalted butter (optional)	2 mL
1	pouch (3 oz/85 mL) liquid pectin	1

1. Prepare canning jars and lids and bring water in water bath canner to a boil.

2. In an 8-quart (8 L) stainless steel stockpot, combine blueberries and water. Add 2 cups (500 mL) of the sugar and stir just until combined. Cover and let stand for 30 minutes.

3. Uncover and heat over medium heat until sugar is mostly dissolved, stirring frequently to prevent sticking. Gradually stir in the remaining sugar, cinnamon and butter, if using.

4. Increase heat to medium-high and bring to a full rolling boil, stirring constantly. Stir in pectin. Return to a full rolling boil, stirring constantly, and boil for 1 minute.

5. Remove pot from heat and skim off any foam. Let preserves cool in the pot for 5 minutes, stirring occasionally.

6. Ladle hot preserves into hot jars, leaving ¼ inch (0.5 cm) headspace. Remove any air bubbles. Wipe jar rims and threads with a clean, damp paper towel. Center hot lids on jars and screw on bands until fingertip-tight.

7. Place jars in canner, making sure they are covered by at least 1 inch (2.5 cm) of water. Cover and bring to a gentle boil. Process 4-ounce (125 mL) jars and 8-ounce (250 mL) jars for 10 minutes; process 1-pint (500 mL) jars for 15 minutes.

8. Remove jars from canner and place on a wire rack or cloth towel. Let cool for 24 hours, then check seals. Wash and dry jars and store in a cool, dry, dark location.

Boysenberry Preserves

✳

Makes about six 8-ounce (250 mL) jars

These preserves, with luscious, intense berry flavor and a deep, dark color, are simply divine.

Tips: Frozen boysenberries make delicious preserves, and there's no need to thaw them — just combine the frozen berries and sugar in the pot.

For 6½ cups (1.625 L) boysenberries, you'll need about 3 lbs (1.5 kg).

Variation

Blackberry Preserves: Substitute fresh or frozen blackberries for the boysenberries.

6½ cups	boysenberries	1.625 L
6 cups	granulated sugar, divided	1.5 L
½ tsp	unsalted butter (optional)	2 mL
1	pouch (3 oz/85 mL) liquid pectin	1

1. Prepare canning jars and lids and bring water in water bath canner to a boil.

2. In an 8-quart (8 L) stainless steel stockpot, combine boysenberries and 2 cups (500 mL) of the sugar and stir just until combined. Cover and let stand for 30 minutes.

3. Uncover and heat over medium heat until sugar is mostly dissolved, stirring frequently to prevent sticking. Gradually stir in the remaining sugar and butter, if using.

4. Increase heat to medium-high and bring to a full rolling boil, stirring constantly. Stir in pectin. Return to a full rolling boil, stirring constantly, and boil for 1 minute.

5. Remove pot from heat and skim off any foam. Let preserves cool in the pot for 5 minutes, stirring occasionally.

6. Ladle hot preserves into hot jars, leaving ¼ inch (0.5 cm) headspace. Remove any air bubbles. Wipe jar rims and threads with a clean, damp paper towel. Center hot lids on jars and screw on bands until fingertip-tight.

7. Place jars in canner, making sure they are covered by at least 1 inch (2.5 cm) of water. Cover and bring to a gentle boil. Process 4-ounce (125 mL) jars and 8-ounce (250 mL) jars for 10 minutes; process 1-pint (500 mL) jars for 15 minutes.

8. Remove jars from canner and place on a wire rack or cloth towel. Let cool for 24 hours, then check seals. Wash and dry jars and store in a cool, dry, dark location.

Cherry Almond Preserves

Sweet Bing cherries make exquisite preserves, and the hint of almond gives them a special flavor.

Tips: Lamberts, Black Giants or other sweet cherry varieties may be used if Bing cherries are not available.

For 4 cups (1 L) halved cherries, you'll need about 3 lbs (1.5 kg) cherries.

4 cups	halved pitted fresh Bing cherries	1 L
3 tbsp	freshly squeezed lemon juice	45 mL
1/2 cup	light corn syrup	125 mL
4 cups	granulated sugar, divided	1 L
1/2 tsp	unsalted butter (optional)	2 mL
1	pouch (3 oz/85 mL) liquid pectin	1
1 tsp	pure almond extract	5 mL

1. Prepare canning jars and lids and bring water in water bath canner to a boil.

2. In an 8-quart (8 L) stainless steel stockpot, combine cherries and lemon juice. Stir gently until cherries are completely coated with lemon juice. Stir in corn syrup. Add 2 cups (500 mL) of the sugar and stir just until combined. Cover and let stand for 10 minutes.

3. Uncover and heat over medium heat until sugar is mostly dissolved, stirring frequently to prevent sticking. Gradually stir in the remaining sugar and butter, if using.

4. Increase heat to medium-high and bring to a full rolling boil, stirring constantly. Stir in pectin. Return to a full rolling boil, stirring constantly, and boil for 1 minute.

5. Remove pot from heat and skim off any foam. Let preserves cool in the pot for 5 minutes, stirring occasionally.

6. Ladle hot preserves into hot jars, leaving 1/4 inch (0.5 cm) headspace. Remove any air bubbles. Wipe jar rims and threads with a clean, damp paper towel. Center hot lids on jars and screw on bands until fingertip-tight.

7. Place jars in canner, making sure they are covered by at least 1 inch (2.5 cm) of water. Cover and bring to a gentle boil. Process 4-ounce (125 mL) jars and 8-ounce (250 mL) jars for 10 minutes; process 1-pint (500 mL) jars for 15 minutes.

8. Remove jars from canner and place on a wire rack or cloth towel. Let cool for 24 hours, then check seals. Wash and dry jars and store in a cool, dry, dark location.

Nectarine Papaya Preserves

✳

*The exotic flavor
of papaya combined
with nectarine creates
marvelous preserves.*

Tips: Choose papayas
that are mostly yellow
to orange in color and
yield to gentle pressure.

For 2¼ cups (550 mL)
chopped nectarines,
you'll need about 2 lbs
(1 kg) or about 6
medium nectarines. For
2¼ cups (550 mL)
chopped papayas, you'll
need about 3 medium
papayas.

2¼ cups	chopped pitted peeled nectarines	550 mL
2¼ cups	chopped seeded peeled papayas	550 mL
3 tbsp	freshly squeezed lemon juice	45 mL
4 cups	granulated sugar, divided	1 L
½ tsp	unsalted butter (optional)	2 mL
1	pouch (3 oz/85 mL) liquid pectin	1

1. Prepare canning jars and lids and bring water in water bath canner to a boil.

2. In an 8-quart (8 L) stainless steel stockpot, combine nectarines, papayas and lemon juice. Stir gently until nectarines and papayas are completely coated with lemon juice. Add 2 cups (500 mL) of the sugar and stir just until combined. Cover and let stand for 1 hour.

3. Gradually stir in the remaining sugar and butter, if using. Heat, uncovered, over medium heat until sugar is mostly dissolved, stirring frequently to prevent sticking. Bring to a gentle boil and simmer gently for 5 minutes, stirring frequently.

4. Increase heat to medium-high and bring to a full rolling boil, stirring constantly. Stir in pectin. Return to a full rolling boil, stirring constantly, and boil for 1 minute.

5. Remove pot from heat and skim off any foam. Let preserves cool in the pot for 5 minutes, stirring occasionally.

6. Ladle hot preserves into hot jars, leaving ¼ inch (0.5 cm) headspace. Remove any air bubbles. Wipe jar rims and threads with a clean, damp paper towel. Center hot lids on jars and screw on bands until fingertip-tight.

7. Place jars in canner, making sure they are covered by at least 1 inch (2.5 cm) of water. Cover and bring to a gentle boil. Process 4-ounce (125 mL) jars and 8-ounce (250 mL) jars for 10 minutes; process 1-pint (500 mL) jars for 15 minutes.

8. Remove jars from canner and place on a wire rack or cloth towel. Let cool for 24 hours, then check seals. Wash and dry jars and store in a cool, dry, dark location.

Peach Pie Preserves

Makes about five 8-ounce (250 mL) jars

The subtle, warm flavors of the spices blend beautifully with the sweet, fragrant peaches, making these preserves a wonderful treat.

Tips: Make Peach Pie Preserves when fresh peaches are at the peak of the season and have the best flavor.

For 4¾ cups (1.175 L) chopped peaches, you'll need about 4 lbs (2 kg) or about 12 medium peaches.

4¾ cups	chopped pitted peeled peaches	1.175 L
¼ cup	freshly squeezed lemon juice	50 mL
4 cups	granulated sugar, divided	1 L
1 tsp	ground cinnamon	5 mL
¼ tsp	ground nutmeg	1 mL
½ tsp	unsalted butter (optional)	2 mL
1	pouch (3 oz/85 mL) liquid pectin	1

1. Prepare canning jars and lids and bring water in water bath canner to a boil.

2. In an 8-quart (8 L) stainless steel stockpot, combine peaches and lemon juice. Stir gently until peaches are completely coated with lemon juice. Add 2 cups (500 mL) of the sugar and stir just until combined. Cover and let stand for 1 hour.

3. Gradually stir in the remaining sugar, cinnamon, nutmeg and butter, if using. Heat, uncovered, over medium heat until sugar is mostly dissolved, stirring frequently to prevent sticking. Bring to a gentle boil and simmer gently for 5 minutes, stirring frequently.

4. Increase heat to medium-high and bring to a full rolling boil, stirring constantly. Stir in pectin. Return to a full rolling boil, stirring constantly, and boil for 1 minute.

5. Remove pot from heat and skim off any foam. Let preserves cool in the pot for 5 minutes, stirring occasionally.

6. Ladle hot preserves into hot jars, leaving ¼ inch (0.5 cm) headspace. Remove any air bubbles. Wipe jar rims and threads with a clean, damp paper towel. Center hot lids on jars and screw on bands until fingertip-tight.

7. Place jars in canner, making sure they are covered by at least 1 inch (2.5 cm) of water. Cover and bring to a gentle boil. Process 4-ounce (125 mL) jars and 8-ounce (250 mL) jars for 10 minutes; process 1-pint (500 mL) jars for 15 minutes.

8. Remove jars from canner and place on a wire rack or cloth towel. Let cool for 24 hours, then check seals. Wash and dry jars and store in a cool, dry, dark location.

Peach Apricot Preserves

✱

Makes about five 8-ounce (250 mL) jars

Open these vibrant preserves on a cold winter morning and enjoy the taste of summer in a jar.

Tips: To quickly and easily peel peaches and apricots, gently drop the fruit, a few at a time, into a pot of boiling water for 30 seconds. Using a slotted spoon, remove the fruit from the boiling water and immediately plunge them into a bowl or pan of ice water for 1 to 2 minutes to stop the cooking process. Drain the fruit and use a small, sharp paring knife to remove the peels.

For 2¼ cups (550 mL) chopped peaches, you'll need about 2 lbs (1 kg) or about 6 medium peaches. For 2¼ cups (550 mL) chopped apricots, you'll need about 2 lbs (1 kg) medium apricots.

2¼ cups	chopped pitted peeled peaches	550 mL
2¼ cups	chopped pitted peeled apricots	550 mL
½ cup	freshly squeezed lemon juice	125 mL
4 cups	granulated sugar, divided	1 L
½ tsp	unsalted butter (optional)	2 mL
1	pouch (3 oz/85 mL) liquid pectin	1

1. Prepare canning jars and lids and bring water in water bath canner to a boil.

2. In an 8-quart (8 L) stainless steel stockpot, combine peaches, apricots and lemon juice. Stir gently until peaches and apricots are completely coated with lemon juice. Add 2 cups (500 mL) of the sugar and stir just until combined. Cover and let stand for 1 hour.

3. Gradually stir in the remaining sugar and butter, if using. Heat, uncovered, over medium heat until sugar is mostly dissolved, stirring frequently to prevent sticking. Bring to a gentle boil and simmer gently for 5 minutes, stirring frequently.

4. Increase heat to medium-high and bring to a full rolling boil, stirring constantly. Stir in pectin. Return to a full rolling boil, stirring constantly, and boil for 1 minute.

5. Remove pot from heat and skim off any foam. Let preserves cool in the pot for 5 minutes, stirring occasionally.

6. Ladle hot preserves into hot jars, leaving ¼ inch (0.5 cm) headspace. Remove any air bubbles. Wipe jar rims and threads with a clean, damp paper towel. Center hot lids on jars and screw on bands until fingertip-tight.

7. Place jars in canner, making sure they are covered by at least 1 inch (2.5 cm) of water. Cover and bring to a gentle boil. Process 4-ounce (125 mL) jars and 8-ounce (250 mL) jars for 10 minutes; process 1-pint (500 mL) jars for 15 minutes.

8. Remove jars from canner and place on a wire rack or cloth towel. Let cool for 24 hours, then check seals. Wash and dry jars and store in a cool, dry, dark location.

Peach Nectarine Preserves

**Makes about
five 8-ounce
(250 mL) jars**

*These glistening
preserves make an
outstanding gift.*

Tips: White peaches
and nectarines have
a mild flavor and soft
texture and are not
recommended for
making preserves.

For 2¼ cups (550 mL)
chopped peaches, you'll
need about 2 lbs (1 kg)
or about 6 medium
peaches. For 2¼ cups
(550 mL) chopped
nectarines, you'll need
about 2 lbs (1 kg) or
about 6 medium
nectarines.

2¼ cups	chopped pitted peeled peaches	550 mL
2¼ cups	chopped pitted peeled nectarines	550 mL
¼ cup	freshly squeezed lemon juice	50 mL
4 cups	granulated sugar, divided	1 L
½ tsp	unsalted butter (optional)	2 mL
1	pouch (3 oz/85 mL) liquid pectin	1

1. Prepare canning jars and lids and bring water in water bath canner to a boil.

2. In an 8-quart (8 L) stainless steel stockpot, combine peaches, nectarines and lemon juice. Stir gently until peaches and nectarines are completely coated with lemon juice. Add 2 cups (500 mL) of the sugar and stir just until combined. Cover and let stand for 1 hour.

3. Gradually stir in the remaining sugar and butter, if using. Heat, uncovered, over medium heat until sugar is mostly dissolved, stirring frequently to prevent sticking. Bring to a gentle boil and simmer gently for 5 minutes, stirring frequently.

4. Increase heat to medium-high and bring to a full rolling boil, stirring constantly. Stir in pectin. Return to a full rolling boil, stirring constantly, and boil for 1 minute.

5. Remove pot from heat and skim off any foam. Let preserves cool in the pot for 5 minutes, stirring occasionally.

6. Ladle hot preserves into hot jars, leaving ¼ inch (0.5 cm) headspace. Remove any air bubbles. Wipe jar rims and threads with a clean, damp paper towel. Center hot lids on jars and screw on bands until fingertip-tight.

7. Place jars in canner, making sure they are covered by at least 1 inch (2.5 cm) of water. Cover and bring to a gentle boil. Process 4-ounce (125 mL) jars and 8-ounce (250 mL) jars for 10 minutes; process 1-pint (500 mL) jars for 15 minutes.

8. Remove jars from canner and place on a wire rack or cloth towel. Let cool for 24 hours, then check seals. Wash and dry jars and store in a cool, dry, dark location.

Cherry Almond Preserves (page 188)
Overleaf: Apricot Cranberry Conserve (page 199)

Pear Peach Preserves

✳

**Makes about
five 8-ounce
(250 mL) jars**

*Set aside a few jars
of these charming
preserves for special
occasions.*

Tips: For the best
flavor, use ripe pears
and peaches that yield
to gentle pressure.

Use a pear variety that
holds its shape well
when cooked, such as
Bartlett, for making
preserves.

For 2¼ cups (550 mL)
chopped pears, you'll
need about 2 lbs (1 kg)
or about 6 medium
pears. For 2¼ cups
(550 mL) chopped
peaches, you'll need
about 2 lbs (1 kg) or
about 6 medium
peaches.

2¼ cups	chopped cored peeled pears	550 mL
2¼ cups	chopped pitted peeled peaches	550 mL
¼ cup	freshly squeezed lemon juice	50 mL
4 cups	granulated sugar, divided	1 L
½ tsp	unsalted butter (optional)	2 mL
1	pouch (3 oz/85 mL) liquid pectin	1

1. Prepare canning jars and lids and bring water in water bath canner to a boil.

2. In an 8-quart (8 L) stainless steel stockpot, combine pears, peaches and lemon juice. Stir gently until pears and peaches are completely coated with lemon juice. Add 2 cups (500 mL) of the sugar and stir just until combined. Cover and let stand for 1 hour.

3. Gradually stir in the remaining sugar and butter, if using. Heat, uncovered, over medium heat until sugar is mostly dissolved, stirring frequently to prevent sticking. Bring to a gentle boil and simmer gently for 5 minutes, stirring frequently.

4. Increase heat to medium-high and bring to a full rolling boil, stirring constantly. Stir in pectin. Return to a full rolling boil, stirring constantly, and boil for 1 minute.

5. Remove pot from heat and skim off any foam. Let preserves cool in the pot for 5 minutes, stirring occasionally.

6. Ladle hot preserves into hot jars, leaving ¼ inch (0.5 cm) headspace. Remove any air bubbles. Wipe jar rims and threads with a clean, damp paper towel. Center hot lids on jars and screw on bands until fingertip-tight.

7. Place jars in canner, making sure they are covered by at least 1 inch (2.5 cm) of water. Cover and bring to a gentle boil. Process 4-ounce (125 mL) jars and 8-ounce (250 mL) jars for 10 minutes; process 1-pint (500 mL) jars for 15 minutes.

8. Remove jars from canner and place on a wire rack or cloth towel. Let cool for 24 hours, then check seals. Wash and dry jars and store in a cool, dry, dark location.

Overleaf: Apple Butter
(page 212)

Orange Juice Curd
(page 223)

Plum Apricot Preserves

✳

These tantalizing preserves are loaded with luscious pieces of fruit.

Tips: Cut the plums and apricots into pieces of uniform size.

Santa Rosa plums are a good choice for this conserve, but almost any variety of red, purple or yellow plum will work well.

For 3⅓ cups (825 mL) chopped plums, you'll need about 2½ lbs (1.25 kg) medium plums. For 2¼ cups (550 mL) chopped apricots, you'll need about 2 lbs (1 kg) medium apricots

3⅓ cups	chopped pitted peeled plums	825 mL
2¼ cups	chopped pitted peeled apricots	550 mL
⅓ cup	freshly squeezed lemon juice	75 mL
5 cups	granulated sugar, divided	1.25 L
½ tsp	unsalted butter (optional)	2 mL
1	pouch (3 oz/85 mL) liquid pectin	1

1. Prepare canning jars and lids and bring water in water bath canner to a boil.

2. In an 8-quart (8 L) stainless steel stockpot, combine plums, apricots and lemon juice. Stir gently until plums and apricots are completely coated with lemon juice. Add 2 cups (500 mL) of the sugar and stir just until combined. Cover and let stand for 30 minutes.

3. Gradually stir in the remaining sugar and butter, if using. Heat, uncovered, over medium heat until sugar is mostly dissolved, stirring frequently to prevent sticking. Bring to a gentle boil and simmer gently for 5 minutes, stirring frequently.

4. Increase heat to medium-high and bring to a full rolling boil, stirring constantly. Stir in pectin. Return to a full rolling boil, stirring constantly, and boil for 1 minute.

5. Remove pot from heat and skim off any foam. Let preserves cool in the pot for 5 minutes, stirring occasionally.

6. Ladle hot preserves into hot jars, leaving ¼ inch (0.5 cm) headspace. Remove any air bubbles. Wipe jar rims and threads with a clean, damp paper towel. Center hot lids on jars and screw on bands until fingertip-tight.

7. Place jars in canner, making sure they are covered by at least 1 inch (2.5 cm) of water. Cover and bring to a gentle boil. Process 4-ounce (125 mL) jars and 8-ounce (250 mL) jars for 10 minutes; process 1-pint (500 mL) jars for 15 minutes.

8. Remove jars from canner and place on a wire rack or cloth towel. Let cool for 24 hours, then check seals. Wash and dry jars and store in a cool, dry, dark location.

Strawberry Preserves

Makes about seven 8-ounce (250 mL) jars

Strawberry is one of my favorite flavors of preserves. I love the large, flavorful pieces of strawberry suspended in the tender jelly.

Tips: If the strawberries are large, cut them into quarters rather than in half. Strawberries that are very small may be left whole.

For 6 cups (1.5 L) halved strawberries, you'll need about 3 lbs (1.5 kg) small strawberries.

6 cups	halved small hulled strawberries	1.5 L
1/3 cup	freshly squeezed lemon juice	75 mL
6 cups	granulated sugar, divided	1.5 L
1/2 tsp	unsalted butter (optional)	2 mL
1	pouch (3 oz/85 mL) liquid pectin	1

1. Prepare canning jars and lids and bring water in water bath canner to a boil.

2. In an 8-quart (8 L) stainless steel stockpot, combine strawberries and lemon juice. Stir gently until strawberries are completely coated with lemon juice. Add 2 cups (500 mL) of the sugar and stir just until combined. Cover and let stand for 2 hours.

3. Gradually stir in the remaining sugar and butter, if using. Heat, uncovered, over medium heat until sugar is mostly dissolved, stirring frequently to prevent sticking. Bring to a gentle boil and simmer gently for 5 minutes, stirring frequently.

4. Increase heat to medium-high and bring to a full rolling boil, stirring constantly. Stir in pectin. Return to a full rolling boil, stirring constantly, and boil for 1 minute.

5. Remove pot from heat and skim off any foam. Let preserves cool in the pot for 5 minutes, stirring occasionally.

6. Ladle hot preserves into hot jars, leaving 1/4 inch (0.5 cm) headspace. Remove any air bubbles. Wipe jar rims and threads with a clean, damp paper towel. Center hot lids on jars and screw on bands until fingertip-tight.

7. Place jars in canner, making sure they are covered by at least 1 inch (2.5 cm) of water. Cover and bring to a gentle boil. Process 4-ounce (125 mL) jars and 8-ounce (250 mL) jars for 10 minutes; process 1-pint (500 mL) jars for 15 minutes.

8. Remove jars from canner and place on a wire rack or cloth towel. Let cool for 24 hours, then check seals. Wash and dry jars and store in a cool, dry, dark location.

Strawberry Peach Preserves

*The flavor of these
superb preserves is
simply divine!*

Tips: The quality
and freshness
of strawberries
deteriorate quickly.
Whenever possible,
use strawberries
the same day they
are picked.

For 3 cups (750 mL)
quartered strawberries,
you'll need about
2 lbs (1 kg) small
strawberries. For
2¼ cups (550 mL)
chopped peaches,
you'll need about
2 lbs (1 kg) or about
6 medium peaches.

3 cups	quartered small hulled strawberries	750 mL
2¼ cups	chopped pitted peeled peaches	550 mL
⅓ cup	freshly squeezed lemon juice	75 mL
5 cups	granulated sugar, divided	1.25 L
½ tsp	unsalted butter (optional)	2 mL
1	pouch (3 oz/85 mL) liquid pectin	1

1. Prepare canning jars and lids and bring water in water bath canner to a boil.

2. In an 8-quart (8 L) stainless steel stockpot, combine strawberries, peaches and lemon juice. Stir gently until strawberries and peaches are completely coated with lemon juice. Add 2 cups (500 mL) of the sugar and stir just until combined. Cover and let stand for 1½ hours.

3. Gradually stir in the remaining sugar and butter, if using. Heat, uncovered, over medium heat until sugar is mostly dissolved, stirring frequently to prevent sticking. Bring to a gentle boil and simmer gently for 5 minutes, stirring frequently.

4. Increase heat to medium-high and bring to a full rolling boil, stirring constantly. Stir in pectin. Return to a full rolling boil, stirring constantly, and boil for 1 minute.

5. Remove pot from heat and skim off any foam. Let preserves cool in the pot for 5 minutes, stirring occasionally.

6. Ladle hot preserves into hot jars, leaving ¼ inch (0.5 cm) headspace. Remove any air bubbles. Wipe jar rims and threads with a clean, damp paper towel. Center hot lids on jars and screw on bands until fingertip-tight.

7. Place jars in canner, making sure they are covered by at least 1 inch (2.5 cm) of water. Cover and bring to a gentle boil. Process 4-ounce (125 mL) jars and 8-ounce (250 mL) jars for 10 minutes; process 1-pint (500 mL) jars for 15 minutes.

8. Remove jars from canner and place on a wire rack or cloth towel. Let cool for 24 hours, then check seals. Wash and dry jars and store in a cool, dry, dark location.

Apple Raisin Conserve

✳

*A perfect conserve
for fall canning!*

Tips: Granny Smith,
Jonathan and Rome
Beauty apples are all
good choices for
this conserve.

For the best flavor
and texture, use
fresh, plump raisins in
conserves. Dried-out,
shriveled raisins will
be tough and chewy.

For 3 cups (750 mL)
finely chopped apples,
you'll need about
1½ lbs (750 g) or about
4 medium apples.

¾ cup	unsweetened apple juice	175 mL
½ cup	raisins	125 mL
3 cups	finely chopped cored peeled apples	750 mL
¼ cup	freshly squeezed lemon juice	50 mL
3 cups	granulated sugar	750 mL
2 cups	firmly packed light brown sugar	500 mL
½ tsp	unsalted butter (optional)	2 mL
½ cup	chopped walnuts	125 mL
1	pouch (3 oz/85 mL) liquid pectin	1

1. Prepare canning jars and lids and bring water in water bath canner to a boil.

2. In a small saucepan, combine apple juice and raisins. Heat over medium heat until apple juice is warm. Remove from heat, cover and let stand for 30 minutes.

3. In an 8-quart (8 L) stainless steel stockpot, combine apple juice mixture, apples and lemon juice. Bring to a boil over medium heat, stirring frequently. Reduce heat, cover and simmer for 5 minutes. Gradually stir in granulated sugar, brown sugar and butter, if using. Bring to a boil over medium heat, stirring constantly until sugar is completely dissolved. Stir in walnuts.

4. Increase heat to medium-high and bring to a full rolling boil, stirring constantly. Stir in pectin. Return to a full rolling boil, stirring constantly, and boil for 1 minute.

5. Remove pot from heat and skim off any foam. Let conserve cool in the pot for 5 minutes, stirring occasionally.

6. Ladle hot conserve into hot jars, leaving ¼ inch (0.5 cm) headspace. Remove any air bubbles. Wipe jar rims and threads with a clean, damp paper towel. Center hot lids on jars and screw on bands until fingertip-tight.

7. Place jars in canner, making sure they are covered by at least 1 inch (2.5 cm) of water. Cover and bring to a gentle boil. Process 4-ounce (125 mL) jars and 8-ounce (250 mL) jars for 10 minutes; process 1-pint (500 mL) jars for 15 minutes.

8. Remove jars from canner and place on a wire rack or cloth towel. Let cool for 24 hours, then check seals. Wash and dry jars and store in a cool, dry, dark location.

Apricot Conserve

*This vibrant conserve
beautifully blends
gleaming apricots and
crunchy almonds.*

Tips: For the best
flavor, use ripe apricots
that yield to gentle
pressure.

For 3½ cups (875 mL)
crushed apricots, you'll
need about 3½ lbs
(1.75 kg) medium
apricots.

2	medium Valencia oranges	2
3½ cups	crushed pitted peeled apricots	875 mL
⅓ cup	freshly squeezed lemon juice	75 mL
1	package (1.75 oz/49 to 57 g) regular powdered fruit pectin	1
6¼ cups	granulated sugar, divided	1.55 L
½ tsp	unsalted butter (optional)	2 mL
½ cup	coarsely chopped slivered almonds	125 mL

1. Prepare canning jars and lids and bring water in water bath canner to a boil.

2. Grate 1 tsp (5 mL) zest from one of the oranges. Peel both oranges, removing all of the white pith. Cut the fruit sections away from the membrane and remove any seeds. Discard the pith and membrane. Finely chop the fruit.

3. In an 8-quart (8 L) stainless steel stockpot, combine chopped oranges, orange zest, apricots and lemon juice.

4. In a small bowl, combine pectin and ¼ cup (50 mL) of the sugar. Gradually stir into fruit. Add butter, if using.

5. Bring fruit mixture to a full rolling boil over medium-high heat, stirring constantly. Gradually stir in the remaining sugar. Stir in almonds. Return to a full rolling boil, stirring constantly, and boil for 1 minute.

6. Remove pot from heat and skim off any foam. Let conserve cool in the pot for 5 minutes, stirring occasionally.

7. Ladle hot conserve into hot jars, leaving ¼ inch (0.5 cm) headspace. Remove any air bubbles. Wipe jar rims and threads with a clean, damp paper towel. Center hot lids on jars and screw on bands until fingertip-tight.

8. Place jars in canner, making sure they are covered by at least 1 inch (2.5 cm) of water. Cover and bring to a gentle boil. Process 4-ounce (125 mL) jars and 8-ounce (250 mL) jars for 10 minutes; process 1-pint (500 mL) jars for 15 minutes.

9. Remove jars from canner and place on a wire rack or cloth towel. Let cool for 24 hours, then check seals. Wash and dry jars and store in a cool, dry, dark location.

Apricot Cranberry Conserve

✳

Makes about eight 8-ounce (250 mL) jars

The crunch of the almonds provides an appealing texture to this fun and tasty conserve.

Tips: Soaking the cranberries in the warm orange juice softens them and keeps them from floating in the finished conserve.

For 3 cups (750 mL) crushed apricots, you'll need about 3 lbs (1.5 kg) medium apricots.

1 cup	dried cranberries	250 mL
1 tbsp	grated orange zest	15 mL
½ cup	freshly squeezed orange juice	125 mL
3 cups	crushed pitted peeled apricots	750 mL
½ cup	freshly squeezed lemon juice	125 mL
6 cups	granulated sugar	1.5 L
½ tsp	unsalted butter (optional)	2 mL
½ cup	coarsely chopped slivered almonds	125 mL
2	pouches (each 3 oz/85 mL) liquid pectin	2

1. Prepare canning jars and lids and bring water in water bath canner to a boil.

2. In a small saucepan, combine dried cranberries and orange juice. Heat over medium heat until orange juice is warm. Remove from heat, cover and let stand for 1 hour.

3. In an 8-quart (8 L) stainless steel stockpot, combine apricots and lemon juice. Stir in cranberry mixture and orange zest. Gradually stir in sugar and butter, if using. Bring to a boil over medium heat, stirring constantly until sugar is completely dissolved. Stir in almonds.

4. Increase heat to medium-high and bring to a full rolling boil, stirring constantly. Stir in pectin. Return to a full rolling boil, stirring constantly, and boil for 1 minute.

5. Remove pot from heat and skim off any foam. Let conserve cool in the pot for 5 minutes, stirring occasionally.

6. Ladle hot conserve into hot jars, leaving ¼ inch (0.5 cm) headspace. Remove any air bubbles. Wipe jar rims and threads with a clean, damp paper towel. Center hot lids on jars and screw on bands until fingertip-tight.

7. Place jars in canner, making sure they are covered by at least 1 inch (2.5 cm) of water. Cover and bring to a gentle boil. Process 4-ounce (125 mL) jars and 8-ounce (250 mL) jars for 10 minutes; process 1-pint (500 mL) jars for 15 minutes.

8. Remove jars from canner and place on a wire rack or cloth towel. Let cool for 24 hours, then check seals. Wash and dry jars and store in a cool, dry, dark location.

Cherry Conserve

✳

*Family and friends will
line up to receive jars
of this incredible
conserve.*

Tips: Some people
prefer toasted nuts in
their conserves. To
lightly toast nuts,
preheat oven to 350°F
(180°C). Line a baking
sheet with foil and
spread nuts over the
foil in a single layer.
Bake for 5 minutes,
stirring halfway through.
Let cool completely
before using.

For 3½ cups (875 mL)
finely chopped cherries,
you'll need about 3 lbs
(1.5 kg) cherries.

3½ cups	finely chopped pitted fresh sweet cherries	875 mL
½ cup	freshly squeezed lemon juice	125 mL
1	package (1.75 oz/49 to 57 g) regular powdered fruit pectin	1
4½ cups	granulated sugar, divided	1.125 L
½ tsp	unsalted butter (optional)	2 mL
½ cup	chopped walnuts	125 mL
½ tsp	pure almond extract (optional)	2 mL

1. Prepare canning jars and lids and bring water in water bath canner to a boil.

2. In an 8-quart (8 L) stainless steel stockpot, combine cherries and lemon juice.

3. In a small bowl, combine pectin and ¼ cup (50 mL) of the sugar. Gradually stir into fruit. Add butter, if using.

4. Bring fruit mixture to a full rolling boil over medium-high heat, stirring constantly. Gradually stir in the remaining sugar. Stir in walnuts. Return to a full rolling boil, stirring constantly, and boil for 1 minute.

5. Remove pot from heat and skim off any foam. Stir in almond extract, if using. Let conserve cool in the pot for 5 minutes, stirring occasionally

6. Ladle hot conserve into hot jars, leaving ¼ inch (0.5 cm) headspace. Remove any air bubbles. Wipe jar rims and threads with a clean, damp paper towel. Center hot lids on jars and screw on bands until fingertip-tight.

7. Place jars in canner, making sure they are covered by at least 1 inch (2.5 cm) of water. Cover and bring to a gentle boil. Process 4-ounce (125 mL) jars and 8-ounce (250 mL) jars for 10 minutes; process 1-pint (500 mL) jars for 15 minutes.

8. Remove jars from canner and place on a wire rack or cloth towel. Let cool for 24 hours, then check seals. Wash and dry jars and store in a cool, dry, dark location.

Cherry Plum Conserve

✳

*The sweetness and
tang of the cherries
and plums harmonize
with the richness and
crunch of the pecans
in this lively conserve.*

Tips: The flavor of
Santa Rosa plums pairs
nicely with cherries, but
you may use any variety
of red or purple plum
in this recipe.

Chopped walnuts are
also a good choice
for this recipe.

For 1¾ cups (425 mL)
finely chopped cherries,
you'll need about 2 lbs
(1 kg) cherries. For
1¾ cups (425 mL)
crushed plums, you'll
need about 2 lbs (1 kg)
medium plums.

1¾ cups	finely chopped pitted fresh sweet cherries	425 mL
1¾ cups	crushed pitted peeled plums	425 mL
¼ cup	freshly squeezed lemon juice	50 mL
5½ cups	granulated sugar	1.375 L
½ tsp	unsalted butter (optional)	2 mL
½ cup	chopped pecans	125 mL
1	pouch (3 oz/85 mL) liquid pectin	1

1. Prepare canning jars and lids and bring water in water bath canner to a boil.

2. In an 8-quart (8 L) stainless steel stockpot, combine cherries, plums and lemon juice. Gradually stir in sugar and butter, if using. Bring to a boil over medium heat, stirring constantly until sugar is completely dissolved. Stir in pecans.

3. Increase heat to medium-high and bring to a full rolling boil, stirring constantly. Stir in pectin. Return to a full rolling boil, stirring constantly, and boil for 1 minute.

4. Remove pot from heat and skim off any foam. Let conserve cool in the pot for 5 minutes, stirring occasionally.

5. Ladle hot conserve into hot jars, leaving ¼ inch (0.5 cm) headspace. Remove any air bubbles. Wipe jar rims and threads with a clean, damp paper towel. Center hot lids on jars and screw on bands until fingertip-tight.

6. Place jars in canner, making sure they are covered by at least 1 inch (2.5 cm) of water. Cover and bring to a gentle boil. Process 4-ounce (125 mL) jars and 8-ounce (250 mL) jars for 10 minutes; process 1-pint (500 mL) jars for 15 minutes.

7. Remove jars from canner and place on a wire rack or cloth towel. Let cool for 24 hours, then check seals. Wash and dry jars and store in a cool, dry, dark location.

Cranberry Orange Conserve

✳

*This festive, ruby-colored conserve is
perfect for holiday
gift-giving.*

Tips: Use only top-quality cranberries in
home canning. Discard
any berries that are
deformed, immature,
soft or bruised. Buy
a few extra bags of
cranberries during the
holiday season and toss
them in the freezer so
they are ready and
waiting when canning
season rolls around.

For 1½ cups (375 mL)
finely chopped Valencia
oranges, you'll need 9 to
12 medium oranges.

1½ cups	finely chopped sectioned peeled Valencia oranges	375 mL
1 cup	coarsely chopped cranberries	250 mL
⅓ cup	freshly squeezed lemon juice	75 mL
4 cups	granulated sugar	1 L
½ tsp	unsalted butter (optional)	2 mL
½ cup	chopped walnuts or almonds	125 mL
1	pouch (3 oz/85 mL) liquid pectin	1

1. Prepare canning jars and lids and bring water in water bath canner to a boil.

2. In an 8-quart (8 L) stainless steel stockpot, combine oranges, cranberries and lemon juice. Bring to a boil over medium heat, stirring frequently. Reduce heat, cover and simmer gently for 5 minutes. Gradually stir in sugar and butter, if using. Bring to a boil over medium heat, stirring constantly until sugar is completely dissolved. Stir in walnuts.

3. Increase heat to medium-high and bring to a full rolling boil, stirring constantly. Stir in pectin. Return to a full rolling boil, stirring constantly, and boil for 1 minute.

4. Remove pot from heat and skim off any foam. Let conserve cool in the pot for 5 minutes, stirring occasionally.

5. Ladle hot conserve into hot jars, leaving ¼ inch (0.5 cm) headspace. Remove any air bubbles. Wipe jar rims and threads with a clean, damp paper towel. Center hot lids on jars and screw on bands until fingertip-tight.

6. Place jars in canner, making sure they are covered by at least 1 inch (2.5 cm) of water. Cover and bring to a gentle boil. Process 4-ounce (125 mL) jars and 8-ounce (250 mL) jars for 10 minutes; process 1-pint (500 mL) jars for 15 minutes.

7. Remove jars from canner and place on a wire rack or cloth towel. Let cool for 24 hours, then check seals. Wash and dry jars and store in a cool, dry, dark location.

CranRaspberry Conserve

The combination of raspberries and cranberries makes a delightful conserve.

Tip: Frozen cranberries can also be used. Thaw them along with the raspberries before making the conserve.

2	bags (each 12 oz/340 g) frozen unsweetened raspberries, thawed	2
1	bag (12 oz/340 g) fresh cranberries, coarsely chopped	1
2 tbsp	freshly squeezed lemon juice	30 mL
1	package (1.75 oz/49 to 57 g) regular powdered fruit pectin	1
6 cups	granulated sugar, divided	1.5 L
½ tsp	unsalted butter (optional)	2 mL
½ cup	coarsely chopped slivered almonds	125 mL

1. Prepare canning jars and lids and bring water in water bath canner to a boil.

2. In an 8-quart (8 L) stainless steel stockpot, combine raspberries, cranberries and lemon juice.

3. In a small bowl, combine pectin and ¼ cup (50 mL) of the sugar. Gradually stir into fruit. Add butter, if using.

4. Bring fruit mixture to a full rolling boil over medium-high heat, stirring constantly. Gradually stir in the remaining sugar. Stir in almonds. Return to a full rolling boil, stirring constantly, and boil for 1 minute.

5. Remove pot from heat and skim off any foam. Let conserve cool in the pot for 5 minutes, stirring occasionally.

6. Ladle hot conserve into hot jars, leaving ¼ inch (0.5 cm) headspace. Remove any air bubbles. Wipe jar rims and threads with a clean, damp paper towel. Center hot lids on jars and screw on bands until fingertip-tight.

7. Place jars in canner, making sure they are covered by at least 1 inch (2.5 cm) of water. Cover and bring to a gentle boil. Process 4-ounce (125 mL) jars and 8-ounce (250 mL) jars for 10 minutes; process 1-pint (500 mL) jars for 15 minutes.

8. Remove jars from canner and place on a wire rack or cloth towel. Let cool for 24 hours, then check seals. Wash and dry jars and store in a cool, dry, dark location.

Peach Cocktail Conserve

—✳—

Makes about seven 8-ounce (250 mL) jars

This enchanting conserve is packed with flavor.

Tips: Bartlett pears are a good choice for this conserve because their flavor pairs well with the peaches, pineapple and maraschino cherries.

If using a can size other than 8 oz (227 mL), you will need ½ cup (125 mL) drained crushed pineapple for this recipe.

Always taste nuts before using them to make sure they are not stale or rancid. Use only fresh nuts in making conserves.

For 1⅓ cups (325 mL) crushed peaches, you'll need about 1½ lbs (750 g) or about 5 medium peaches. For 1⅓ cups (325 mL) finely chopped pears, you'll need about 1½ lbs (750 g) or about 5 medium pears.

1⅓ cups	crushed pitted peeled peaches	325 mL
1⅓ cups	finely chopped pitted peeled pears	325 mL
1	can (8 oz/227 mL) juice-packed crushed pineapple, drained (see tip, at left)	1
¼ cup	chopped drained maraschino cherries	50 mL
¼ cup	freshly squeezed lemon juice	50 mL
1	package (1.75 oz/49 to 57 g) regular powdered fruit pectin	1
5 cups	granulated sugar, divided	1.25 L
½ tsp	unsalted butter (optional)	2 mL
½ cup	coarsely chopped slivered almonds	125 mL

1. Prepare canning jars and lids and bring water in water bath canner to a boil.

2. In an 8-quart (8 L) stainless steel stockpot, combine peaches, pears, pineapple, maraschino cherries and lemon juice.

3. In a small bowl, combine pectin and ¼ cup (50 mL) of the sugar. Gradually stir into fruit. Add butter, if using.

4. Bring fruit mixture to a full rolling boil over medium-high heat, stirring constantly. Gradually stir in the remaining sugar. Stir in almonds. Return to a full rolling boil, stirring constantly, and boil for 1 minute.

5. Remove pot from heat and skim off any foam. Let conserve cool in the pot for 5 minutes, stirring occasionally.

6. Ladle hot conserve into hot jars, leaving ¼ inch (0.5 cm) headspace. Remove any air bubbles. Wipe jar rims and threads with a clean, damp paper towel. Center hot lids on jars and screw on bands until fingertip-tight.

7. Place jars in canner, making sure they are covered by at least 1 inch (2.5 cm) of water. Cover and bring to a gentle boil. Process 4-ounce (125 mL) jars and 8-ounce (250 mL) jars for 10 minutes; process 1-pint (500 mL) jars for 15 minutes.

8. Remove jars from canner and place on a wire rack or cloth towel. Let cool for 24 hours, then check seals. Wash and dry jars and store in a cool, dry, dark location.

Pear Peach Conserve

✳

Jars of this glorious conserve have a habit of disappearing fast.

Tips: Bartlett pears make excellent conserves.

When making conserves, chop nuts into small pieces for a smoother texture.

For 1¾ cups (425 mL) finely chopped pears, you'll need about 2 lbs (1 kg) or about 6 medium pears. For 1¾ cups (425 mL) crushed peaches, you'll need about 2 lbs (1 kg) or about 6 medium peaches.

1¾ cups	finely chopped cored peeled pears	425 mL
1¾ cups	crushed pitted peeled peaches	425 mL
2 tbsp	freshly squeezed lemon juice	30 mL
1	package (1.75 oz/49 to 57 g) regular powdered fruit pectin	1
5 cups	granulated sugar, divided	1.25 L
½ tsp	unsalted butter (optional)	2 mL
½ cup	coarsely chopped slivered almonds	125 mL

1. Prepare canning jars and lids and bring water in water bath canner to a boil.

2. In an 8-quart (8 L) stainless steel stockpot, combine pears, peaches and lemon juice.

3. In a small bowl, combine pectin and ¼ cup (50 mL) of the sugar. Gradually stir into fruit. Add butter, if using.

4. Bring fruit mixture to a full rolling boil over medium-high heat, stirring constantly. Gradually stir in the remaining sugar. Stir in almonds. Return to a full rolling boil, stirring constantly, and boil for 1 minute.

5. Remove pot from heat and skim off any foam. Let conserve cool in the pot for 5 minutes, stirring occasionally.

6. Ladle hot conserve into hot jars, leaving ¼ inch (0.5 cm) headspace. Remove any air bubbles. Wipe jar rims and threads with a clean, damp paper towel. Center hot lids on jars and screw on bands until fingertip-tight.

7. Place jars in canner, making sure they are covered by at least 1 inch (2.5 cm) of water. Cover and bring to a gentle boil. Process 4-ounce (125 mL) jars and 8-ounce (250 mL) jars for 10 minutes; process 1-pint (500 mL) jars for 15 minutes.

8. Remove jars from canner and place on a wire rack or cloth towel. Let cool for 24 hours, then check seals. Wash and dry jars and store in a cool, dry, dark location.

Pineapple Apricot Conserve

✳

Makes six or seven 8-ounce (250 mL) jars

This luscious golden conserve is excellent spooned over ice cream for a delectable dessert.

Tips: Using canned crushed pineapple saves you the work of chopping the pineapple into small pieces.

If using a can size other than 20 oz (567 mL), you will need 1⅛ cups (280 mL) drained crushed pineapple for this recipe.

For 2 cups (500 mL) crushed apricots, you'll need about 2 lbs (1 kg) medium apricots.

2 cups	crushed pitted peeled apricots	500 mL
1	can (20 oz/567 mL) juice-packed crushed pineapple, drained (see tip, at left)	1
⅓ cup	freshly squeezed lemon juice	75 mL
1	package (1.75 oz/49 to 57 g) regular powdered fruit pectin	1
6 cups	granulated sugar, divided	1.5 L
½ tsp	unsalted butter (optional)	2 mL
½ cup	coarsely chopped shredded or flaked sweetened coconut	125 mL
½ cup	chopped macadamia nuts	125 mL

1. Prepare canning jars and lids and bring water in water bath canner to a boil.

2. In an 8-quart (8 L) stainless steel stockpot, combine apricots, pineapple and lemon juice.

3. In a small bowl, combine pectin and ¼ cup (50 mL) of the sugar. Gradually stir into fruit. Add butter, if using.

4. Bring fruit mixture to a full rolling boil over medium-high heat, stirring constantly. Gradually stir in the remaining sugar. Stir in coconut and macadamia nuts. Return to a full rolling boil, stirring constantly, and boil for 1 minute.

5. Remove pot from heat and skim off any foam. Let conserve cool in the pot for 5 minutes, stirring occasionally.

6. Ladle hot conserve into hot jars, leaving ¼ inch (0.5 cm) headspace. Remove any air bubbles. Wipe jar rims and threads with a clean, damp paper towel. Center hot lids on jars and screw on bands until fingertip-tight.

7. Place jars in canner, making sure they are covered by at least 1 inch (2.5 cm) of water. Cover and bring to a gentle boil. Process 4-ounce (125 mL) jars and 8-ounce (250 mL) jars for 10 minutes; process 1-pint (500 mL) jars for 15 minutes.

8. Remove jars from canner and place on a wire rack or cloth towel. Let cool for 24 hours, then check seals. Wash and dry jars and store in a cool, dry, dark location.

Butters
& Curds

✳

About Butters

FRUIT BUTTERS ARE CLASSIC, old-fashioned soft spreads made by slowly cooking fruit pulp and sugar to a thick but spreadable consistency. The texture and flavor of a butter are more rustic than, and not as delicate as, those of a jam or a jelly. Butters can be made from single fruits or, for a more complex flavor, from a combination of a couple of fruits. Spices may be added, or butters may be left plain to let the fruit flavor shine through. The choice is yours, and butters can easily be adapted to suit your personal taste.

Butters are thick fruit purées cooked gently until they hold their shape. The texture is achieved not by cooking the fruit with sugar, pectin and acid to make it set, as in a jam, but rather by slowly cooking the puréed fruit until enough liquid evaporates that it becomes very thick and spreadable. This slow cooking concentrates the fruit and creates a smooth, creamy texture similar to a rustic, country-style butter — hence the name of the spread.

Because butters are slow-cooked, they are more forgiving in terms of timing. You don't have to get the spread off the stove at just the right moment for fear that it won't gel. In fact, fruit butters do not gel at all. Instead, they thicken naturally as they cook down.

Butters are made by cooking chopped fruit with a small amount of liquid until the fruit is soft and tender. The fruit is then pressed through a food mill or fine-mesh sieve to purée it and remove any fibrous pieces. The puréed fruit is then returned to the pan, sugar is added and the mixture is cooked slowly until it is very thick.

When making butters, use a wide, heavy-bottomed pan that distributes heat evenly. It is important to stir the butter frequently while it is simmering to prevent sticking, especially as it starts to thicken. If the heat under the pan is too high or the butter is not stirred often enough, the fruit can scorch. If this happens, the butter will lose its fruity flavor and the entire mixture will develop an unpleasant burned flavor that cannot be corrected. Another thing to avoid is overcooking the butter. An overcooked butter will solidify and have a rubbery texture when cooled. A butter should hold its shape when spooned out of a jar, but it should not be firm and cut like a jelly.

The butter is done when it is very thick and spreadable and it holds its shape. To test the doneness of a butter, place a spoonful on a plate. If it holds its shape and no liquid seeps from it, it is done. If the butter spreads across the plate or a ring of liquid forms around the edge, then it needs to be cooked a bit longer. Depending on the juice content of the fruit and how rapidly it simmers, the butter may need to cook for slightly shorter or longer than the time indicated in the recipe. Start checking the doneness about 5 minutes before the specified time to avoid overcooking the butter.

Some cooks like to make butters in a slow cooker (Crock-Pot) as there is less chance of the butter burning. This is true, although spreads cooked by this method often do not thicken enough to be called a butter. It may be necessary to transfer the mixture to a pan over direct heat for the final stage of cooking in order to cook off enough liquid so that the butter does not separate.

When you add spices to butters, the taste of the spices should be subtle, enhancing the flavor of the fruit without overpowering it. The flavor of spices intensifies during storage, so don't overdo it. One spice to be very careful of is cloves. Cloves can be very intense and can easily overpower every other flavor in a butter. If you use cloves in your butters, use them sparingly.

While Apple Butter is still the most common, butter flavors have expanded well beyond the traditional. New flavor combinations have renewed home canners' interest in this smooth spread, and butters are once again seeing a rise in popularity.

You will notice that there is no recipe for pumpkin butter in this book. While pumpkin butter is a popular flavor, the USDA no longer considers it safe for home canning. Pumpkin purée is too dense to allow heat to penetrate to the spread in the center of the jar. This means that the contents of the jar do not get hot enough to kill any bacteria or deactivate any enzymes that may be present inside. If you make pumpkin butter, it *must* be stored in the refrigerator and used within 1 month of being made.

About Curds

CURDS ARE ELEGANT, silky smooth, rich and luxurious citrus spreads that are similar to soft custard. The basic ingredients in a curd are beaten eggs and egg yolks, sugar, butter and citrus juice and zest, which are gently cooked together until thick and then allowed to cool, forming a soft, smooth, intensely flavored spread.

In England during the late 19th and early 20th centuries, homemade lemon curd was served as an alternative to jam at afternoon tea with breads and scones. The British also use this traditional spread as a filling for tarts, small pastries and cakes and as a dessert topping. Lemon pie, made with lemon curd and topped with a baked meringue, has been a favorite dessert in Britain since the 19th century.

Lemon curd is different, though, from a standard lemon filling or dessert custard in that it contains a higher proportion of lemon juice and zest, which gives it a more intense lemon flavor. Lemon curd also contains butter and has a smoother, creamier texture than either lemon filling or custard, both of which contain little or no butter and use cornstarch or flour as the thickening agent. In a curd, it is the eggs that thicken the spread.

Once considered a gourmet delicacy, curds are a rapidly growing category of soft spread. As home canners learn that these creamy citrus spreads are actually quite easy to make at home, curds are quickly being added to home canning repertoires. While lemon is still the most common and most popular flavor, interest in making a variety of citrus curds has grown significantly. It is difficult to find commercially made curds in flavors other than lemon; however, many flavors can readily be made at home, with excellent results. Any variety of citrus fruit will make a wonderful curd. Orange curds have a soft, lovely citrus flavor, while lime curds have a bold, tangy flavor.

The trick with curds is to get the eggs to thicken but keep them from curdling. This is accomplished by cooking the curd in the top of a double boiler over boiling water that does not touch the bottom of the top pan. Cooking over direct heat would cause the bottom of the pan to get too hot and cook the eggs too fast, making them curdle or scorch. Never let a curd boil, as this will definitely cause the eggs to curdle. Stir the curd constantly with a heatproof spatula or spoon to cook it evenly and attain the thick, silky texture that makes a curd sublime.

If you do not have a double boiler, you can make one with a metal or tempered glass bowl that fits snugly in the top of a large saucepan. Just make sure the bottom of the bowl does not touch the boiling water. The acid in citrus juice can react with aluminum, so be sure to use a nonreactive container, such as stainless steel, for making curds.

After cooking, strain the hot curd to remove the citrus zest and any little bits of egg that may have curdled in the pan. Straining ensures that the curd will be smooth and creamy, with a luxurious texture.

Because curds contain eggs and butter, they have a much shorter storage life than jams and other soft spreads. Use only 8-ounce (250 mL) or smaller jars for canning curds. After water bath processing, store curds in the refrigerator for up to 3 months. Any curd that starts to turn brown on the surface, shows any other signs of discoloration or spoilage, or has an "off" smell should not be eaten. If you give a jar of curd as a gift, be sure to let the recipient know to store it in the refrigerator and the date it needs to be used by.

Curds can also be stored in the refrigerator, covered tightly, for up to 1 month without water bath processing. As jars of curd in my home never last 3 months, I usually store curd in a small bowl in the refrigerator, where it is ready and waiting to be spread on biscuits for breakfast, to fill individual tarts for a heavenly dessert or to be spooned onto fresh berries any time of day. When the curd is gone, I simply make more. Curds that I plan to give as gifts go into the water bath.

Many state and county fairs in the United States have competition classes for canned curds. The jar size requirement is usually 8-ounce (250 mL) or smaller. If you plan to enter curds at a fair, the jars must be water bath processed or they will not be accepted for judging. Process 8-ounce (250 mL) and 4-ounce (125 mL) jars for 15 minutes or as indicated in the fair's exhibitor handbook.

Apple Butter

✴

*With a hint of
cinnamon and nutmeg,
this butter has lots of
apple flavor. If you
prefer a spicier butter,
increase the amount
of cinnamon to suit
your taste.*

Tip: Granny Smith
apples are a good choice
for making butters.

4 lbs	apples, peeled, cored and chopped	2 kg
2 tbsp	freshly squeezed lemon juice	30 mL
2 cups	unsweetened apple juice or water	500 mL
2½ cups	granulated sugar	625 mL
1 tsp	ground cinnamon	5 mL
¼ tsp	ground nutmeg	1 mL

1. Prepare canning jars and lids and bring water in water bath canner to a boil.

2. In an 8-quart (8 L) stainless steel stockpot, combine apples and lemon juice. Stir in apple juice. Bring to a boil over medium heat, stirring frequently. Reduce heat, cover and simmer for 30 minutes, or until apples are soft, stirring frequently to prevent sticking. Remove pot from heat and skim off any foam.

3. Press cooked apples and juice through a food mill or a fine-meshed sieve into a heatproof bowl or pan.

4. Return strained apple pulp to the pot. Stir in sugar, cinnamon and nutmeg. Bring to a gentle boil over medium heat, stirring until the sugar is completely dissolved. Reduce heat and simmer until mixture is thick, about 30 minutes, stirring frequently to prevent sticking or scorching. Remove pot from heat and skim off any foam.

5. Ladle hot butter into hot jars, leaving ¼ inch (0.5 cm) headspace. Remove any air bubbles. Wipe jar rims and threads with a clean, damp paper towel. Center hot lids on jars and screw on bands until fingertip-tight.

6. Place jars in canner, making sure they are covered by at least 1 inch (2.5 cm) of water. Cover and bring to a gentle boil. Process 4-ounce (125 mL) jars and 8-ounce (250 mL) jars for 10 minutes; process 1-pint (500 mL) jars for 15 minutes.

7. Remove jars from canner and place on a wire rack or cloth towel. Let cool for 24 hours, then check seals. Wash and dry jars and store in a cool, dry, dark location.

Apricot Plum Butter

Makes about six 8-ounce (250 mL) jars

This pretty butter is a great way to use up the last of the harvest.

Tip: Do not reduce the amount of lemon juice in a recipe. A specific acidity level is needed for safe canning and to ensure safe storage after canning.

2½ lbs	apricots, peeled, pitted and chopped	1.25 kg
1½ lbs	plums, peeled, pitted and chopped	750 g
3 tbsp	freshly squeezed lemon juice	45 mL
½ cup	freshly squeezed orange juice	125 mL
3 cups	granulated sugar	750 mL

1. Prepare canning jars and lids and bring water in water bath canner to a boil.

2. In an 8-quart (8 L) stainless steel stockpot, combine apricots, plums and lemon juice. Stir in orange juice. Bring to a boil over medium heat, stirring frequently. Reduce heat, cover and simmer for 10 minutes, or until apricots and plums are soft, stirring frequently to prevent sticking. Remove pot from heat and skim off any foam.

3. Press cooked fruit and juice through a food mill or a fine-meshed sieve into a heatproof bowl or pan.

4. Return strained fruit pulp to the pot. Stir in sugar. Bring to a gentle boil over medium heat, stirring until the sugar is completely dissolved. Reduce heat and simmer until mixture is thick, 25 to 30 minutes, stirring frequently to prevent sticking or scorching. Remove pot from heat and skim off any foam.

5. Ladle hot butter into hot jars, leaving ¼ inch (0.5 cm) headspace. Remove any air bubbles. Wipe jar rims and threads with a clean, damp paper towel. Center hot lids on jars and screw on bands until fingertip-tight.

6. Place jars in canner, making sure they are covered by at least 1 inch (2.5 cm) of water. Cover and bring to a gentle boil. Process 4-ounce (125 mL) jars and 8-ounce (250 mL) jars for 10 minutes; process 1-pint (500 mL) jars for 15 minutes.

7. Remove jars from canner and place on a wire rack or cloth towel. Let cool for 24 hours, then check seals. Wash and dry jars and store in a cool, dry, dark location.

Nectarine Butter

✳

This smooth fruit butter is a luxurious spread for breakfast toast and is equally delicious spooned over ice cream.

Tip: To ripen nectarines, place them in a paper bag and let them stand at room temperature for a few days.

4 lbs	nectarines, peeled, pitted and chopped	2 kg
3 tbsp	freshly squeezed lemon juice	45 mL
½ cup	freshly squeezed orange juice	125 mL
3 cups	granulated sugar	750 mL
½ tsp	ground cinnamon	2 mL

1. Prepare canning jars and lids and bring water in water bath canner to a boil.

2. In an 8-quart (8 L) stainless steel stockpot, combine nectarines and lemon juice. Stir in orange juice. Bring to a boil over medium heat, stirring frequently. Reduce heat, cover and simmer for 10 minutes, or until nectarines are soft, stirring frequently to prevent sticking. Remove pot from heat and skim off any foam.

3. Press cooked nectarines and juice through a food mill or a fine-meshed sieve into a heatproof bowl or pan.

4. Return strained nectarine pulp to the pot. Stir in sugar and cinnamon. Bring to a gentle boil over medium heat, stirring until the sugar is completely dissolved. Reduce heat and simmer until mixture is thick, 20 to 30 minutes, stirring frequently to prevent sticking or scorching. Remove pot from heat and skim off any foam.

5. Ladle hot butter into hot jars, leaving ¼ inch (0.5 cm) headspace. Remove any air bubbles. Wipe jar rims and threads with a clean, damp paper towel. Center hot lids on jars and screw on bands until fingertip-tight.

6. Place jars in canner, making sure they are covered by at least 1 inch (2.5 cm) of water. Cover and bring to a gentle boil. Process 4-ounce (125 mL) jars and 8-ounce (250 mL) jars for 10 minutes; process 1-pint (500 mL) jars for 15 minutes.

7. Remove jars from canner and place on a wire rack or cloth towel. Let cool for 24 hours, then check seals. Wash and dry jars and store in a cool, dry, dark location.

Nectarine Peach Butter

✳

2 lbs	nectarines, peeled, pitted and chopped	1 kg
2 lbs	peaches, peeled, pitted and chopped	1 kg
3 tbsp	freshly squeezed lemon juice	45 mL
½ cup	freshly squeezed orange juice	125 mL
3 cups	granulated sugar	750 mL

Makes about six 8-ounce (250 mL) jars

The pretty golden-orange color of this butter is reflected in its warm, comforting flavor.

Tip: If nectarines or peaches reach ripeness before you are ready to use them, they may be stored in the refrigerator for a few days.

1. Prepare canning jars and lids and bring water in water bath canner to a boil.

2. In an 8-quart (8 L) stainless steel stockpot, combine nectarines, peaches and lemon juice. Stir in orange juice. Bring to a boil over medium heat, stirring frequently. Reduce heat, cover and simmer for 10 minutes, or until nectarines and peaches are soft, stirring frequently to prevent sticking. Remove pot from heat and skim off any foam.

3. Press cooked fruit and juice through a food mill or a fine-meshed sieve into a heatproof bowl or pan.

4. Return strained fruit pulp to the pot. Stir in sugar. Bring to a gentle boil over medium heat, stirring until the sugar is completely dissolved. Reduce heat and simmer until mixture is thick, 20 to 30 minutes, stirring frequently to prevent sticking or scorching. Remove pot from heat and skim off any foam.

5. Ladle hot butter into hot jars, leaving ¼ inch (0.5 cm) headspace. Remove any air bubbles. Wipe jar rims and threads with a clean, damp paper towel. Center hot lids on jars and screw on bands until fingertip-tight.

6. Place jars in canner, making sure they are covered by at least 1 inch (2.5 cm) of water. Cover and bring to a gentle boil. Process 4-ounce (125 mL) jars and 8-ounce (250 mL) jars for 10 minutes; process 1-pint (500 mL) jars for 15 minutes.

7. Remove jars from canner and place on a wire rack or cloth towel. Let cool for 24 hours, then check seals. Wash and dry jars and store in a cool, dry, dark location.

Peach Orange Butter

Makes four or five 8-ounce (250 mL) jars

The glowing, fruity flavors of peach and orange are infused together in this balanced, aromatic butter.

Tip: For a richer flavor, use yellow peaches rather than white peaches.

3 lbs	peaches, peeled, pitted and chopped	1.5 kg
3 tbsp	freshly squeezed lemon juice	45 mL
	Thinly sliced zest of 2 oranges	
⅔ cup	freshly squeezed orange juice	150 mL
3 cups	granulated sugar	750 mL
3 tbsp	frozen orange juice concentrate, thawed	45 mL

1. Prepare canning jars and lids and bring water in water bath canner to a boil.

2. In an 8-quart (8 L) stainless steel stockpot, combine peaches and lemon juice. Stir in orange zest and orange juice. Bring to a boil over medium heat, stirring frequently. Reduce heat, cover and simmer for 10 minutes, or until peaches are soft, stirring frequently to prevent sticking. Remove pot from heat and skim off any foam.

3. Press cooked peaches and juice through a food mill or a fine-meshed sieve into a heatproof bowl or pan.

4. Return strained peach pulp to the pot. Stir in sugar and orange juice concentrate. Bring to a gentle boil over medium heat, stirring until the sugar is completely dissolved. Reduce heat and simmer until mixture is thick, 20 to 30 minutes, stirring frequently to prevent sticking or scorching. Remove pot from heat and skim off any foam.

5. Ladle hot butter into hot jars, leaving ¼ inch (0.5 cm) headspace. Remove any air bubbles. Wipe jar rims and threads with a clean, damp paper towel. Center hot lids on jars and screw on bands until fingertip-tight.

6. Place jars in canner, making sure they are covered by at least 1 inch (2.5 cm) of water. Cover and bring to a gentle boil. Process 4-ounce (125 mL) jars and 8-ounce (250 mL) jars for 10 minutes; process 1-pint (500 mL) jars for 15 minutes.

7. Remove jars from canner and place on a wire rack or cloth towel. Let cool for 24 hours, then check seals. Wash and dry jars and store in a cool, dry, dark location.

Pear Apple Butter

✳

The delicate pear flavor blends beautifully with the apple in this lovely butter.

Tips: To keep from masking the delicate pear flavor, the only spice added to this butter is a touch of nutmeg. A pinch of cinnamon may also be added, if you like.

Bartlett pears are a good choice for making butters.

3 lbs	pears, peeled, cored and chopped	1.5 kg
2 lbs	apples, peeled, cored and finely chopped	1 kg
	Thinly sliced zest of 1 lemon	
3 tbsp	freshly squeezed lemon juice	45 mL
	Thinly sliced zest of 1 orange	
½ cup	freshly squeezed orange juice	125 mL
2½ cups	granulated sugar	625 mL
½ tsp	ground nutmeg	2 mL

1. Prepare canning jars and lids and bring water in water bath canner to a boil.

2. In an 8-quart (8 L) stainless steel stockpot, combine pears, apples and lemon juice. Stir in lemon zest, orange zest and orange juice. Bring to a boil over medium heat, stirring frequently. Reduce heat, cover and simmer for 20 minutes, or until pears and apples are soft, stirring frequently to prevent sticking. Remove pot from heat and skim off any foam.

3. Press cooked fruit and juice through a food mill or a fine-meshed sieve into a heatproof bowl or pan.

4. Return strained fruit pulp to the pot. Stir in sugar and nutmeg. Bring to a gentle boil over medium heat, stirring until the sugar is completely dissolved. Reduce heat and simmer until mixture is thick, 25 to 30 minutes, stirring frequently to prevent sticking or scorching. Remove pot from heat and skim off any foam.

5. Ladle hot butter into hot jars, leaving ¼ inch (0.5 cm) headspace. Remove any air bubbles. Wipe jar rims and threads with a clean, damp paper towel. Center hot lids on jars and screw on bands until fingertip-tight.

6. Place jars in canner, making sure they are covered by at least 1 inch (2.5 cm) of water. Cover and bring to a gentle boil. Process 4-ounce (125 mL) jars and 8-ounce (250 mL) jars for 10 minutes; process 1-pint (500 mL) jars for 15 minutes.

7. Remove jars from canner and place on a wire rack or cloth towel. Let cool for 24 hours, then check seals. Wash and dry jars and store in a cool, dry, dark location.

Grapefruit Curd

Grapefruit Curd has a bright, refreshing citrus flavor.

Tips: White grapefruit have a more intense flavor and a higher acidity level than pink grapefruit, both of which are important factors in making curds.

As an alternative to water bath processing, curds may be stored in the refrigerator in a tightly covered container. Gently press a piece of plastic wrap on the surface of the curd to prevent a skin from forming. The curd will maintain its flavor and texture in the refrigerator for up to 1 month.

3	large eggs	3
3	large egg yolks	3
1¼ cups	superfine sugar	300 mL
2 tbsp	very thinly sliced white grapefruit zest	30 mL
½ cup	strained freshly squeezed white grapefruit juice	125 mL
⅓ cup	cold unsalted butter, cut into pieces	75 mL

1. Prepare canning jars and lids and bring water in water bath canner to a boil.

2. In the top pan of a stainless steel double boiler, using a wire whisk, lightly beat together eggs and egg yolks. Add sugar and beat until well blended. Gradually whisk in grapefruit juice. Add grapefruit zest and butter.

3. Place pan over boiling water. Make sure the water does not touch the bottom of the pan; otherwise, the curd may cook too quickly and cause the eggs to curdle. Stirring constantly to prevent scorching, cook until the mixture will thickly coat the back of a metal spoon or heatproof spatula, about 7 minutes. Do not let boil.

4. Place a fine-mesh strainer over a heatproof bowl or pan and pour hot curd through the strainer to remove the zest and any lumps.

5. Ladle hot curd into hot jars, leaving ¼ inch (0.5 cm) headspace. Remove any air bubbles. Wipe jar rims and threads with a clean, damp paper towel. Center hot lids on jars and screw on bands until fingertip-tight.

6. Place jars in canner, making sure they are covered by at least 1 inch (2.5 cm) of water. Cover and bring to a gentle boil. Process 4-ounce (125 mL) jars and 8-ounce (250 mL) jars for 15 minutes.

7. Remove jars from canner and place on a wire rack or cloth towel. Let cool for 24 hours, then check seals. Wash and dry jars and store in the refrigerator for up to 3 months.

Lemon Curd

✳

Lemon is the traditional flavor for curd, and it is hard to beat. If you have Meyer lemons, they are the perfect choice for this luscious curd.

Tips: A stainless steel pan or bowl is recommended for making curds, because aluminum and copper pans can react adversely with the eggs and lemon juice.

As an alternative to water bath processing, curds may be stored in the refrigerator in a tightly covered container. Gently press a piece of plastic wrap on the surface of the curd to prevent a skin from forming. The curd will maintain its flavor and texture in the refrigerator for up to 1 month.

3	large eggs	3
3	large egg yolks	3
1¾ cups	superfine sugar	425 mL
2 tbsp	very thinly sliced lemon zest	30 mL
½ cup	strained freshly squeezed lemon juice	125 mL
⅓ cup	cold unsalted butter, cut into pieces	75 mL

1. Prepare canning jars and lids and bring water in water bath canner to a boil.

2. In the top pan of a stainless steel double boiler, using a wire whisk, lightly beat together eggs and egg yolks. Add sugar and beat until well blended. Gradually whisk in lemon juice. Add lemon zest and butter.

3. Place pan over boiling water. Make sure the water does not touch the bottom of the pan; otherwise, the curd may cook too quickly and cause the eggs to curdle. Stirring constantly to prevent scorching, cook until the mixture will thickly coat the back of a metal spoon or heatproof spatula, about 7 minutes. Do not let boil.

4. Place a fine-mesh strainer over a heatproof bowl or pan and pour hot curd through the strainer to remove the zest and any lumps.

5. Ladle hot curd into hot jars, leaving ¼ inch (0.5 cm) headspace. Remove any air bubbles. Wipe jar rims and threads with a clean, damp paper towel. Center hot lids on jars and screw on bands until fingertip-tight.

6. Place jars in canner, making sure they are covered by at least 1 inch (2.5 cm) of water. Cover and bring to a gentle boil. Process 4-ounce (125 mL) jars and 8-ounce (250 mL) jars for 15 minutes.

7. Remove jars from canner and place on a wire rack or cloth towel. Let cool for 24 hours, then check seals. Wash and dry jars and store in the refrigerator for up to 3 months.

Lemon Lime Curd

✳

Makes about two 8-ounce (250 mL) jars or five 4-ounce (125 mL) jars

The bright citrus flavor of this curd is delightful on cream scones and evokes images of elegant English teas.

Tips: Straining the lemon and lime juices removes the pulp so the finished curd will be silky smooth.

As an alternative to water bath processing, curds may be stored in the refrigerator in a tightly covered container. Gently press a piece of plastic wrap on the surface of the curd to prevent a skin from forming. The curd will maintain its flavor and texture in the refrigerator for up to 1 month.

3	large eggs	3
3	large egg yolks	3
1½ cups	superfine sugar	375 mL
1 tbsp	very thinly sliced lemon zest	15 mL
¼ cup	strained freshly squeezed lemon juice	50 mL
1 tbsp	very thinly sliced lime zest	15 mL
¼ cup	strained freshly squeezed lime juice	50 mL
⅓ cup	cold unsalted butter, cut into pieces	75 mL

1. Prepare canning jars and lids and bring water in water bath canner to a boil.

2. In the top pan of a stainless steel double boiler, using a wire whisk, lightly beat together eggs and egg yolks. Add sugar and beat until well blended. Gradually whisk in lemon juice and lime juice. Add lemon zest, lime zest and butter.

3. Place pan over boiling water. Make sure the water does not touch the bottom of the pan; otherwise, the curd may cook too quickly and cause the eggs to curdle. Stirring constantly to prevent scorching, cook until the mixture will thickly coat the back of a metal spoon or heatproof spatula, about 7 minutes. Do not let boil.

4. Place a fine-mesh strainer over a heatproof bowl or pan and pour hot curd through the strainer to remove the zest and any lumps.

5. Ladle hot curd into hot jars, leaving ¼ inch (0.5 cm) headspace. Remove any air bubbles. Wipe jar rims and threads with a clean, damp paper towel. Center hot lids on jars and screw on bands until fingertip-tight.

6. Place jars in canner, making sure they are covered by at least 1 inch (2.5 cm) of water. Cover and bring to a gentle boil. Process 4-ounce (125 mL) jars and 8-ounce (250 mL) jars for 15 minutes.

7. Remove jars from canner and place on a wire rack or cloth towel. Let cool for 24 hours, then check seals. Wash and dry jars and store in the refrigerator for up to 3 months.

Lime Curd

✳

I love lime curd. It has a delightful, tangy flavor that is very refreshing.

Tips: Use ripe, juicy limes that have a strong, luscious lime flavor.

As an alternative to water bath processing, curds may be stored in the refrigerator in a tightly covered container. Gently press a piece of plastic wrap on the surface of the curd to prevent a skin from forming. The curd will maintain its flavor and texture in the refrigerator for up to 1 month.

3	large eggs	3
3	large egg yolks	3
1 1/2 cups	superfine sugar	375 mL
2 tbsp	very thinly sliced lime zest	30 mL
1/2 cup	strained freshly squeezed lime juice	125 mL
1/3 cup	cold unsalted butter, cut into pieces	75 mL

1. Prepare canning jars and lids and bring water in water bath canner to a boil.

2. In the top pan of a stainless steel double boiler, using a wire whisk, lightly beat together eggs and egg yolks. Add sugar and beat until well blended. Gradually whisk in lime juice. Add lime zest and butter.

3. Place pan over boiling water. Make sure the water does not touch the bottom of the pan; otherwise, the curd may cook too quickly and cause the eggs to curdle. Stirring constantly to prevent scorching, cook until the mixture will thickly coat the back of a metal spoon or heatproof spatula, about 7 minutes. Do not let boil.

4. Place a fine-mesh strainer over a heatproof bowl or pan and pour hot curd through the strainer to remove the zest and any lumps.

5. Ladle hot curd into hot jars, leaving 1/4 inch (0.5 cm) headspace. Remove any air bubbles. Wipe jar rims and threads with a clean, damp paper towel. Center hot lids on jars and screw on bands until fingertip-tight.

6. Place jars in canner, making sure they are covered by at least 1 inch (2.5 cm) of water. Cover and bring to a gentle boil. Process 4-ounce (125 mL) jars and 8-ounce (250 mL) jars for 15 minutes.

7. Remove jars from canner and place on a wire rack or cloth towel. Let cool for 24 hours, then check seals. Wash and dry jars and store in the refrigerator for up to 3 months.

Orange Curd

✳

*Made with fresh
orange juice, this curd
has a delicate orange
flavor and a smooth
texture.*

Tips: Valencia oranges
or juice oranges should
be used for making
curd. Navel oranges
may have a stronger
flavor, but they also
contain an enzyme that
turns the orange juice
bitter during storage.

As an alternative to
water bath processing,
curds may be stored
in the refrigerator in
a tightly covered
container. Gently press
a piece of plastic wrap
on the surface of the
curd to prevent a skin
from forming. The curd
will maintain its flavor
and texture in the
refrigerator for up
to 1 month.

3	large eggs	3
4	large egg yolks	4
1 cup	superfine sugar	250 mL
2 tbsp	very thinly sliced orange zest	30 mL
1/2 cup	strained freshly squeezed orange juice	125 mL
1/3 cup	cold unsalted butter, cut into pieces	75 mL

1. Prepare canning jars and lids and bring water in water bath canner to a boil.

2. In the top pan of a stainless steel double boiler, using a wire whisk, lightly beat together eggs and egg yolks. Add sugar and beat until well blended. Gradually whisk in orange juice. Add orange zest and butter.

3. Place pan over boiling water. Make sure the water does not touch the bottom of the pan; otherwise, the curd may cook too quickly and cause the eggs to curdle. Stirring constantly to prevent scorching, cook until the mixture will thickly coat the back of a metal spoon or heatproof spatula, about 7 minutes. Do not let boil.

4. Place a fine-mesh strainer over a heatproof bowl or pan and pour hot curd through the strainer to remove the zest and any lumps.

5. Ladle hot curd into hot jars, leaving 1/4 inch (0.5 cm) headspace. Remove any air bubbles. Wipe jar rims and threads with a clean, damp paper towel. Center hot lids on jars and screw on bands until fingertip-tight.

6. Place jars in canner, making sure they are covered by at least 1 inch (2.5 cm) of water. Cover and bring to a gentle boil. Process 4-ounce (125 mL) jars and 8-ounce (250 mL) jars for 15 minutes.

7. Remove jars from canner and place on a wire rack or cloth towel. Let cool for 24 hours, then check seals. Wash and dry jars and store in the refrigerator for up to 3 months.

Orange Juice Curd

✳

Orange juice concentrate gives this curd a vibrant orange flavor and a lovely color.

Tips: Choose a frozen orange juice concentrate that has a strong orange flavor and a deep orange color. For the best texture, do not use an orange juice concentrate that has lots of pulp.

As an alternative to water bath processing, curds may be stored in the refrigerator in a tightly covered container. Gently press a piece of plastic wrap on the surface of the curd to prevent a skin from forming. The curd will maintain its flavor and texture in the refrigerator for up to 1 month.

3	large eggs	3
3	large egg yolks	3
1 cup	superfine sugar	250 mL
1/3 cup	frozen orange juice concentrate, thawed	75 mL
2 tbsp	very thinly sliced orange zest	30 mL
1/3 cup	cold unsalted butter, cut into pieces	75 mL

1. Prepare canning jars and lids and bring water in water bath canner to a boil.

2. In the top pan of a stainless steel double boiler, using a wire whisk, lightly beat together eggs and egg yolks. Add sugar and beat until well blended. Gradually whisk in orange juice concentrate. Add orange zest and butter.

3. Place pan over boiling water. Make sure the water does not touch the bottom of the pan; otherwise, the curd may cook too quickly and cause the eggs to curdle. Stirring constantly to prevent scorching, cook until the mixture will thickly coat the back of a metal spoon or heatproof spatula, about 7 minutes. Do not let boil.

4. Place a fine-mesh strainer over a heatproof bowl or pan and pour hot curd through the strainer to remove the zest and any lumps.

5. Ladle hot curd into hot jars, leaving 1/4 inch (0.5 cm) headspace. Remove any air bubbles. Wipe jar rims and threads with a clean, damp paper towel. Center hot lids on jars and screw on bands until fingertip-tight.

6. Place jars in canner, making sure they are covered by at least 1 inch (2.5 cm) of water. Cover and bring to a gentle boil. Process 4-ounce (125 mL) jars and 8-ounce (250 mL) jars for 15 minutes.

7. Remove jars from canner and place on a wire rack or cloth towel. Let cool for 24 hours, then check seals. Wash and dry jars and store in the refrigerator for up to 3 months.

Orange Tangerine Curd

✳

Makes about two 8-ounce (250 mL) jars or five 4-ounce (125 mL) jars

The wonderful flavors of summer shine through in this special curd.

Tips: Straining the orange and tangerine juices removes the pulp so the finished curd will be silky smooth.

As an alternative to water bath processing, curds may be stored in the refrigerator in a tightly covered container. Gently press a piece of plastic wrap on the surface of the curd to prevent a skin from forming. The curd will maintain its flavor and texture in the refrigerator for up to 1 month.

3	large eggs	3
4	large egg yolks	4
1 cup	superfine sugar	250 mL
1 tbsp	very thinly sliced orange zest	15 mL
1/4 cup	strained freshly squeezed orange juice	50 mL
1 tbsp	very thinly sliced tangerine zest	15 mL
1/4 cup	strained freshly squeezed tangerine juice	50 mL
1/3 cup	cold unsalted butter, cut into pieces	75 mL

1. Prepare canning jars and lids and bring water in water bath canner to a boil.

2. In the top pan of a stainless steel double boiler, using a wire whisk, lightly beat together eggs and egg yolks. Add sugar and beat until well blended. Gradually whisk in orange juice and tangerine juice. Add orange zest, tangerine zest and butter.

3. Place pan over boiling water. Make sure the water does not touch the bottom of the pan; otherwise, the curd may cook too quickly and cause the eggs to curdle. Stirring constantly to prevent scorching, cook until the mixture will thickly coat the back of a metal spoon or heatproof spatula, about 7 minutes. Do not let boil.

4. Place a fine-mesh strainer over a heatproof bowl or pan and pour the curd through the strainer to remove the zest and any lumps.

5. Ladle hot curd into hot jars, leaving 1/4 inch (0.5 cm) headspace. Remove any air bubbles. Wipe jar rims and threads with a clean, damp paper towel. Center hot lids on jars and screw on bands until fingertip-tight.

6. Place jars in canner, making sure they are covered by at least 1 inch (2.5 cm) of water. Cover and bring to a gentle boil. Process 4-ounce (125 mL) jars and 8-ounce (250 mL) jars for 15 minutes.

7. Remove jars from canner and place on a wire rack or cloth towel. Let cool for 24 hours, then check seals. Wash and dry jars and store in the refrigerator for up to 3 months.

Sunrise Curd

✳

Makes about two 8-ounce (250 mL) jars or five 4-ounce (125 mL) jars

Blending the flavors of orange and lemon gives this curd a great citrus flavor with a subtle tang.

Tips: A stainless steel pan or bowl is recommended for making curds, because aluminum and copper pans can react adversely with the eggs and citrus juice.

As an alternative to water bath processing, curds may be stored in the refrigerator in a tightly covered container. Gently press a piece of plastic wrap on the surface of the curd to prevent a skin from forming. The curd will maintain its flavor and texture in the refrigerator for up to 1 month.

3	large eggs	3
4	large egg yolks	4
1⅓ cups	superfine sugar	325 mL
1 tbsp	very thinly sliced orange zest	15 mL
⅓ cup	strained freshly squeezed orange juice	75 mL
1 tbsp	very thinly sliced lemon zest	15 mL
3 tbsp	strained freshly squeezed lemon juice	45 mL
⅓ cup	cold unsalted butter, cut into pieces	75 mL

1. Prepare canning jars and lids and bring water in water bath canner to a boil.

2. In the top pan of a stainless steel double boiler, using a wire whisk, lightly beat together eggs and egg yolks. Add sugar and beat until well blended. Gradually whisk in orange juice and lemon juice. Add orange zest, lemon zest and butter.

3. Place pan over boiling water. Make sure the water does not touch the bottom of the pan; otherwise, the curd may cook too quickly and cause the eggs to curdle. Stirring constantly to prevent scorching, cook until the mixture will thickly coat the back of a metal spoon or heatproof spatula, about 7 minutes. Do not let boil.

4. Place a fine-mesh strainer over a heatproof bowl or pan and pour hot curd through the strainer to remove the zest and any lumps.

5. Ladle hot curd into hot jars, leaving ¼ inch (0.5 cm) headspace. Remove any air bubbles. Wipe jar rims and threads with a clean, damp paper towel. Center hot lids on jars and screw on bands until fingertip-tight.

6. Place jars in canner, making sure they are covered by at least 1 inch (2.5 cm) of water. Cover and bring to a gentle boil. Process 4-ounce (125 mL) jars and 8-ounce (250 mL) jars for 15 minutes.

7. Remove jars from canner and place on a wire rack or cloth towel. Let cool for 24 hours, then check seals. Wash and dry jars and store in the refrigerator for up to 3 months.

Tangelo Curd

Tangelo juice creates a curd with wonderful citrus flavor.

Tips: Minneola tangelos work well in this recipe. If you prefer, Clementine tangerines or another strong-flavored tangerine may be used instead.

As an alternative to water bath processing, curds may be stored in the refrigerator in a tightly covered container. Gently press a piece of plastic wrap on the surface of the curd to prevent a skin from forming. The curd will maintain its flavor and texture in the refrigerator for up to 1 month.

3	large eggs	3
4	large egg yolks	4
1 cup	superfine sugar	250 mL
2 tbsp	very thinly sliced tangelo zest	30 mL
1/2 cup	strained freshly squeezed tangelo juice	125 mL
1/3 cup	cold unsalted butter, cut into pieces	75 mL

1. Prepare canning jars and lids and bring water in water bath canner to a boil.

2. In the top pan of a stainless steel double boiler, using a wire whisk, lightly beat together eggs and egg yolks. Add sugar and beat until well blended. Gradually whisk in tangelo juice. Add tangelo zest and butter.

3. Place pan over boiling water. Make sure the water does not touch the bottom of the pan; otherwise, the curd may cook too quickly and cause the eggs to curdle. Stirring constantly to prevent scorching, cook until the mixture will thickly coat the back of a metal spoon or heatproof spatula, about 7 minutes. Do not let boil.

4. Place a fine-mesh strainer over a heatproof bowl or pan and pour hot curd through the strainer to remove the zest and any lumps.

5. Ladle hot curd into hot jars, leaving 1/4 inch (0.5 cm) headspace. Remove any air bubbles. Wipe jar rims and threads with a clean, damp paper towel. Center hot lids on jars and screw on bands until fingertip-tight.

6. Place jars in canner, making sure they are covered by at least 1 inch (2.5 cm) of water. Cover and bring to a gentle boil. Process 4-ounce (125 mL) jars and 8-ounce (250 mL) jars for 15 minutes.

7. Remove jars from canner and place on a wire rack or cloth towel. Let cool for 24 hours, then check seals. Wash and dry jars and store in the refrigerator for up to 3 months.

Savory Spreads

✳

About Savory Spreads

ONE OF THE LATEST TRENDS in home canning is to combine fruit with herbs or hot peppers to create all manner of savory spreads. Other savories, such as garlic and onions, are being transformed into delicious and tantalizing spreads to delight the senses. These spreads are no longer just for the adventuresome, but have become a part of mainstream home canning and are accessible to everyone.

In addition to established varieties of savory spreads, such as Mint Jelly and Jalapeño Jelly, this chapter contains new and exciting spreads such as Apricot Habanero Jam, Tomato Basil Jam, Cranberry Jalapeño Jelly, Southwest Jelly, Lemon Dill Marmalade and Three Onion Marmalade. Creating these spreads was a fun adventure, and I am delighted to share them with you.

Balancing the savory flavors is extremely important. The heat of the peppers or the intensity of the herbs should not overpower the fruit. Add too many peppers, for instance, and all you will taste is heat. The wonderful fruit flavor will be lost. The key to a great savory spread is a blend of flavors that complement and enhance each other.

While savory spreads are often spread on bread or crackers or paired with a variety of cheeses to make enticing appetizers, they can also be served alongside meat, poultry, fish and egg dishes, added to sauces or used as a primary ingredient to create flavorful entrées or side dishes.

If you are looking to add a little extra zing to your jams and jellies, the recipes in this chapter should fit the bill. Salsa Jam and Tomato Basil Jam are favorites among my family and friends, and I love Orange Zing Marmalade as a dip for coconut shrimp. Have fun!

Tomatoes

Roma or other plum-type tomatoes are the best choice for spreads. Plum tomatoes are less juicy and have a firmer flesh than salad or slicing tomatoes. Juicy tomatoes will yield a soft or runny jam. Use tomatoes that are fully ripe but still firm and that have a deep red color. Tomatoes have a lower acidity than most other fruits. Lemon juice, lime juice or vinegar is added to tomato recipes to raise the acid level for safe canning.

To make short work of peeling ripe tomatoes, gently drop them, a few at a time, into a pan of boiling water. Let them soak in the water for 30 to 60 seconds, or until the skins just start to split. Using a slotted spoon, quickly remove the tomatoes from the boiling water and immediately plunge them into a bowl or pan of ice water. Let them sit in the ice water for 1 to 2 minutes to stop the cooking process. Remove the tomatoes from the water and drain well. Use a small, sharp paring knife to remove the peel from the tomatoes.

The seeds and juice should be removed from the center of the tomatoes before chopping. The seeds can become tough when cooked and detract from the texture of the finished spread, and the juice may make the spread too thin and keep it from setting. To seed tomatoes, cut peeled tomatoes in quarters. Remove the cores with a small paring knife and scrape the tomatoes with a spoon to remove the seeds and juice.

Chile Peppers

Handle chile peppers with caution when making spreads. Chile peppers will not just burn your tongue; they contain strong oils that can cause serious chemical burns on your skin. When seeding and chopping chile peppers, I strongly advise you to wear latex, plastic or rubber gloves to avoid direct contact between your skin and the peppers. Be careful not to rub your eyes when working with chile peppers, as the oils can also cause chemical burns in your eyes.

The hottest part of a chile pepper is the ribs that attach the seeds to the inside of the pepper. While the seeds can be a nice addition to fresh hot salsas, it is best to remove the seeds and ribs when making jams and jellies, as the heat can overpower the flavor of the other ingredients. The seeds can also become tough and chewy when cooked.

Fresh Herbs

Fresh herbs are delicate and bruise easily, so they should be handled with a gentle touch. Herbs should be rinsed and dried before use, as they may contain sand or dirt. Rinse fresh herbs well under cool, clean running water. Shake off as much water as possible, then spread the herbs out on paper towels and gently blot them dry.

To get the best flavor from fresh herbs, use only the tender, flavorful leaves and discard the stems. Some herbs can quickly start to turn brown around the edges after being cut. To maintain freshness and flavor, chop fresh herbs just before starting to make the spread.

Apricot Habanero Jam

✳

*The heat and color of
the habanero peppers
blends with the sweet
and tangy flavor of the
apricots in this lively
jam. Green, yellow or
red habanero peppers
may be used in place
of orange habanero
peppers, if you prefer.*

Tips: Habanero chile
peppers are extremely
hot and range in color
from immature green
peppers to fully ripe red
and orange peppers.
There are also white,
pink, yellow and brown
varieties. Adjust the
quantity of peppers
to suit your taste.

Habanero peppers are
often confused with
Scotch bonnet peppers.
They have a similar
appearance and are
both extremely hot,
but are not the same
pepper. Orange-colored
Scotch bonnets make
a good substitution for
habanero peppers in
this recipe.

For 4⅓ cups (1.075 L)
crushed apricots, you'll
need about 4 lbs (2 kg)
medium apricots.

4⅓ cups	crushed pitted peeled apricots	1.075 L
¼ cup	freshly squeezed lemon juice	50 mL
1 to 2	orange habanero peppers, deribbed, seeded and finely minced	1 to 2
1	package (1.75 oz/49 to 57 g) regular powdered fruit pectin	1
6⅓ cups	granulated sugar, divided	1.575 L
½ tsp	unsalted butter (optional)	2 mL

1. Prepare canning jars and lids and bring water in water bath canner to a boil.

2. In an 8-quart (8 L) stainless steel stockpot, combine apricots, lemon juice and habanero peppers.

3. In a small bowl, combine pectin and ¼ cup (50 mL) of the sugar. Gradually stir into fruit. Add butter, if using.

4. Bring fruit mixture to a full rolling boil over medium-high heat, stirring constantly. Gradually stir in the remaining sugar. Return to a full rolling boil, stirring constantly, and boil for 1 minute.

5. Remove pot from heat and skim off any foam. Let jam cool in the pot for 5 minutes, stirring occasionally.

6. Ladle hot jam into hot jars, leaving ¼ inch (0.5 cm) headspace. Remove any air bubbles. Wipe jar rims and threads with a clean, damp paper towel. Center hot lids on jars and screw on bands until fingertip-tight.

7. Place jars in canner, making sure they are covered by at least 1 inch (2.5 cm) of water. Cover and bring to a gentle boil. Process 4-ounce (125 mL) jars and 8-ounce (250 mL) jars for 10 minutes; process 1-pint (500 mL) jars for 15 minutes.

8. Remove jars from canner and place on a wire rack or cloth towel. Let cool for 24 hours, then check seals. Wash and dry jars and store in a cool, dry, dark location.

Raspberry Jalapeño Jam

✳

Makes about nine 8-ounce (250 mL) jars

Sweet and hot, this lively jam is a real taste treat.

Tips: Handle chile peppers with care. Chiles contain oils that can cause chemical burns on your skin. When seeding and chopping chile peppers, wear latex, plastic or rubber gloves to avoid direct contact with the peppers.

For 4¾ cups (1.175 L) crushed raspberries, you'll need about 3 lbs (1.5 kg) or 12 cups (3 L) raspberries.

4¾ cups	crushed red raspberries	1.175 L
¼ cup	finely chopped deribbed seeded jalapeño peppers	50 mL
1 tbsp	freshly squeezed lemon juice	15 mL
1	package (1.75 oz/49 to 57 g) regular powdered fruit pectin	1
7 cups	granulated sugar, divided	1.75 L
½ tsp	unsalted butter (optional)	2 mL

1. Prepare canning jars and lids and bring water in water bath canner to a boil.

2. In an 8-quart (8 L) stainless steel stockpot, combine raspberries, jalapeño peppers and lemon juice.

3. In a small bowl, combine pectin and ¼ cup (50 mL) of the sugar. Gradually stir into fruit. Add butter, if using.

4. Bring fruit mixture to a full rolling boil over medium-high heat, stirring constantly. Gradually stir in the remaining sugar. Return to a full rolling boil, stirring constantly, and boil for 1 minute.

5. Remove pot from heat and skim off any foam. Let jam cool in the pot for 5 minutes, stirring occasionally.

6. Ladle hot jam into hot jars, leaving ¼ inch (0.5 cm) headspace. Remove any air bubbles. Wipe jar rims and threads with a clean, damp paper towel. Center hot lids on jars and screw on bands until fingertip-tight.

7. Place jars in canner, making sure they are covered by at least 1 inch (2.5 cm) of water. Cover and bring to a gentle boil. Process 4-ounce (125 mL) jars and 8-ounce (250 mL) jars for 10 minutes; process 1-pint (500 mL) jars for 15 minutes.

8. Remove jars from canner and place on a wire rack or cloth towel. Let cool for 24 hours, then check seals. Wash and dry jars and store in a cool, dry, dark location.

Roasted Garlic and Caramelized Onion Jam

*A savory spread loaded
with rich, complex
flavors, this special
jam is excellent served
with meat or cheese.*

Tips: When choosing
whole garlic bulbs,
the heavier the better.
Heavy heads mean the
garlic cloves are fresher,
contain more natural oils
and have more flavor.

Vidalia, Walla Walla
or Maui sweet onions
are all good choices
for this recipe.

For 5 cups (1.25 L)
chopped sweet onions,
you'll need about
2½ lbs (1.25 kg) or
about 7 medium onions.

4	whole garlic bulbs	4
4 tbsp	water, divided	60 mL
3 tbsp	unsalted butter	45 mL
5 cups	chopped peeled sweet onions	1.25 L
½ cup	balsamic vinegar	125 mL
1 cup	cider vinegar	250 mL
3 cups	granulated sugar	750 mL
1	pouch (3 oz/85 mL) liquid pectin	1
	Salt	
	Freshly ground black pepper	

1. Preheat oven to 400°F (200°C).

2. Slice ½ inch (1 cm) off the top of each garlic bulb to expose the tops of individual cloves. Do not peel or separate cloves from bulb. Place each whole garlic bulb on a separate square of foil. Sprinkle each bulb with 1 tbsp (15 mL) water. Loosely wrap garlic in the foil and pinch the edges together to seal. Place foil packets on a baking sheet and roast for 45 minutes. Remove from the oven and carefully unwrap the hot packets. Let cool for 15 minutes. Squeeze the softened garlic into a small bowl. Set aside.

3. Prepare canning jars and lids and bring water in water bath canner to a boil.

4. In an 8-quart (8 L) stainless steel stockpot, melt butter over medium heat. Add onion, reduce heat to medium-low and sauté until onion is tender and light golden, about 30 minutes. Do not let onion turn brown or burn. Stir in balsamic vinegar and cook, stirring frequently, for 5 minutes.

5. Add roasted garlic and cider vinegar. Gradually stir in sugar. Bring to a boil over medium heat, stirring constantly until sugar is completely dissolved.

6. Increase heat to medium-high and bring to a full rolling boil, stirring constantly. Stir in pectin. Return to a full rolling boil, stirring constantly, and boil for 1 minute.

Tip: For the best flavor and texture, use jars of this spread within 3 months of canning.

7. Remove pot from heat and season to taste with salt and pepper. Let jam cool in the pot for 5 minutes, stirring occasionally.

8. Ladle hot jam into hot jars, leaving ¼ inch (0.5 cm) headspace. Remove any air bubbles. Wipe jar rims and threads with a clean, damp paper towel. Center hot lids on jars and screw on bands until fingertip-tight.

9. Place jars in canner, making sure they are covered by at least 1 inch (2.5 cm) of water. Cover and bring to a gentle boil. Process 4-ounce (125 mL) jars and 8-ounce (250 mL) jars for 10 minutes; process 1-pint (500 mL) jars for 15 minutes.

10. Remove jars from canner and place on a wire rack or cloth towel. Let cool for 24 hours, then check seals. Wash and dry jars and store in the refrigerator for up to 3 months.

Red Onion Jam

Makes six or seven 8-ounce (250 mL) jars

This vivid onion jam is perfect paired with meat or poultry

Tips: To vary the flavor of this jam, try using sweet onions in place of the red onions.

For 4 cups (1 L) chopped red onions, you'll need about 2 lbs (1 kg) or about 6 medium onions.

4 cups	finely chopped peeled red onions	1 L
2/3 cup	red wine vinegar	150 mL
1/2 cup	red wine	125 mL
2 tbsp	balsamic vinegar	30 mL
4 cups	granulated sugar	1 L
3/4 cup	firmly packed light brown sugar	175 mL
1	pouch (3 oz/85 mL) liquid pectin	1

1. Prepare canning jars and lids and bring water in water bath canner to a boil.

2. In an 8-quart (8 L) stainless steel stockpot, combine red onions, red wine vinegar, red wine and balsamic vinegar. Bring to a boil over medium heat. Reduce heat and simmer for 5 minutes. Gradually stir in granulated sugar and brown sugar. Bring to a boil over medium heat, stirring constantly until sugars are completely dissolved.

3. Increase heat to medium-high and bring to a full rolling boil, stirring constantly. Stir in pectin. Return to a full rolling boil, stirring constantly, and boil for 1 minute.

4. Remove pot from heat and skim off any foam. Let jam cool in the pot for 5 minutes, stirring occasionally.

5. Ladle hot jam into hot jars, leaving 1/4 inch (0.5 cm) headspace. Remove any air bubbles. Wipe jar rims and threads with a clean, damp paper towel. Center hot lids on jars and screw on bands until fingertip-tight.

6. Place jars in canner, making sure they are covered by at least 1 inch (2.5 cm) of water. Cover and bring to a gentle boil. Process 4-ounce (125 mL) jars and 8-ounce (250 mL) jars for 10 minutes; process 1-pint (500 mL) jars for 15 minutes.

7. Remove jars from canner and place on a wire rack or cloth towel. Let cool for 24 hours, then check seals. Wash and dry jars and store in a cool, dry, dark location.

Red Pepper Jam

※

*Red Pepper Jam is a
delightful condiment to
serve with warm baked
Brie or goat cheese.*

Tips: Remove the
fibrous white ribs from
the inside of the bell
peppers and jalapeño
peppers before
chopping. The white
ribs can turn quite
tough when cooked.

If red jalapeño peppers
are not available in your
area, you may use green
jalapeños instead.

For 2½ cups (625 mL)
finely chopped bell
peppers, you'll need
about 5 medium
peppers.

2½ cups	finely chopped deribbed seeded red bell peppers	625 mL
½ cup	finely chopped deribbed seeded red jalapeño peppers	125 mL
1 cup	red wine vinegar	250 mL
5¼ cups	granulated sugar	1.3 L
½ tsp	unsalted butter (optional)	2 mL
1	pouch (3 oz/85 mL) liquid pectin	1

1. Prepare canning jars and lids and bring water in water bath canner to a boil.

2. In an 8-quart (8 L) stainless steel stockpot, combine bell peppers, jalapeño peppers and vinegar. Bring to a boil over medium-high heat. Reduce heat, cover and simmer gently for 5 minutes. Gradually stir in sugar and butter, if using. Bring to a boil over medium heat, stirring constantly until sugar is completely dissolved.

3. Increase heat to medium-high and bring to a full rolling boil, stirring constantly. Stir in pectin. Return to a full rolling boil, stirring constantly, and boil for 1 minute.

4. Remove pot from heat and skim off any foam. Let jam cool in the pot for 5 minutes, stirring occasionally.

5. Ladle hot jam into hot jars, leaving ¼ inch (0.5 cm) headspace. Remove any air bubbles. Wipe jar rims and threads with a clean, damp paper towel. Center hot lids on jars and screw on bands until fingertip-tight.

6. Place jars in canner, making sure they are covered by at least 1 inch (2.5 cm) of water. Cover and bring to a gentle boil. Process 4-ounce (125 mL) jars and 8-ounce (250 mL) jars for 10 minutes; process 1-pint (500 mL) jars for 15 minutes.

7. Remove jars from canner and place on a wire rack or cloth towel. Let cool for 24 hours, then check seals. Wash and dry jars and store in a cool, dry, dark location.

Salsa Jam

✳

<table>
<tr><td>2 cups</td><td>chopped cored seeded peeled plum (Roma) tomatoes</td><td>500 mL</td></tr>
<tr><td>⅔ cup</td><td>chopped red onion</td><td>150 mL</td></tr>
<tr><td>⅔ cup</td><td>plain tomato sauce</td><td>150 mL</td></tr>
<tr><td>3 tbsp</td><td>finely chopped deribbed seeded jalapeño peppers</td><td>45 mL</td></tr>
<tr><td>1½ tsp</td><td>grated lime zest</td><td>7 mL</td></tr>
<tr><td>3 tbsp</td><td>freshly squeezed lime juice</td><td>45 mL</td></tr>
<tr><td>¼ tsp</td><td>hot pepper sauce</td><td>1 mL</td></tr>
<tr><td>5 cups</td><td>granulated sugar</td><td>1.25 L</td></tr>
<tr><td>½ tsp</td><td>unsalted butter (optional)</td><td>2 mL</td></tr>
<tr><td>1</td><td>pouch (3 oz/85 mL) liquid pectin</td><td>1</td></tr>
</table>

Makes about five 8-ounce (250 mL) jars

This festive jam is a tantalizing treat for anyone who likes a spread with a little zip and zing. To liven up your next appetizer party, spoon this zesty jam over softened goat cheese or cream cheese spread on crackers.

Tips: Choose tomatoes that are fully ripe but still firm and that have a deep red color. Tomatoes have a lower acidity than most other fruits. Lemon juice, lime juice or vinegar is added to tomato recipes to raise the acid level for safe canning.

For 2 cups (500 mL) chopped plum tomatoes, you'll need about 1 lb (500 g) or about 5 medium plum tomatoes.

1. Prepare canning jars and lids and bring water in water bath canner to a boil.

2. In an 8-quart (8 L) stainless steel stockpot, combine tomatoes, red onion, tomato sauce and jalapeño peppers. Bring to a boil over medium heat, stirring constantly. Reduce heat and simmer gently for 5 minutes, stirring frequently to prevent sticking. Add lime zest, lime juice and hot pepper sauce. Gradually stir in sugar and butter, if using. Bring to a boil over medium heat, stirring constantly until sugar is completely dissolved.

3. Increase heat to medium-high and bring to a full rolling boil, stirring constantly. Stir in pectin. Return to a full rolling boil, stirring constantly, and boil for 1 minute.

4. Remove pot from heat and skim off any foam. Let jam cool in the pot for 5 minutes, stirring occasionally.

5. Ladle hot jam into hot jars, leaving ¼ inch (0.5 cm) headspace. Remove any air bubbles. Wipe jar rims and threads with a clean, damp paper towel. Center hot lids on jars and screw on bands until fingertip-tight.

6. Place jars in canner, making sure they are covered by at least 1 inch (2.5 cm) of water. Cover and bring to a gentle boil. Process 4-ounce (125 mL) jars and 8-ounce (250 mL) jars for 10 minutes; process 1-pint (500 mL) jars for 15 minutes.

7. Remove jars from canner and place on a wire rack or cloth towel. Let cool for 24 hours, then check seals. Wash and dry jars and store in a cool, dry, dark location.

Tomato Basil Jam

*Tomatoes and
basil make a perfect
pairing in this savory
combination. Serve
this pleasing jam on
toast, alongside meats
or with cheese and
crackers.*

Tips: To easily peel
tomatoes, gently drop
them, a few at a time,
into a pan of boiling water
for 30 to 60 seconds.
Using a slotted spoon,
remove the tomatoes
and immediately plunge
into a bowl or pan of ice
water for 1 to 2 minutes
to stop the cooking
process. Drain well and
use a small knife to
remove peels. To seed
tomatoes, cut peeled
tomatoes into quarters.
Remove cores and
scrape with a spoon
to remove the seeds
and liquid.

Less-sugar-needed
pectins are also called
"light" pectins.

For 3½ cups (875 mL)
finely chopped plum
tomatoes, you'll need
about 2 lbs (1 kg) or
about 9 medium
plum tomatoes.

3½ cups	finely chopped cored seeded peeled plum (Roma) tomatoes	875 mL
⅓ cup	freshly squeezed lemon juice	75 mL
¼ cup	finely chopped fresh basil leaves	50 mL
1	package (1.75 oz/49 to 57 g) powdered fruit pectin for less-sugar-needed recipes	1
3 cups	granulated sugar, divided	750 mL

1. Prepare canning jars and lids and bring water in water bath canner to a boil.

2. In an 8-quart (8 L) stainless steel stockpot, bring tomatoes to a boil over medium heat, stirring constantly. Reduce heat, cover and simmer gently for 10 minutes, stirring frequently to prevent sticking. Stir in lemon juice and basil.

3. In a small bowl, combine pectin and ¼ cup (50 mL) of the sugar. Gradually stir into tomato mixture.

4. Bring tomato mixture to a full rolling boil over medium-high heat, stirring constantly. Gradually stir in the remaining sugar. Return to a full rolling boil, stirring constantly, and boil for 1 minute.

5. Remove pot from heat and skim off any foam. Let jam cool in the pot for 5 minutes, stirring occasionally.

6. Ladle hot jam into hot jars, leaving ¼ inch (0.5 cm) headspace. Remove any air bubbles. Wipe jar rims and threads with a clean, damp paper towel. Center hot lids on jars and screw on bands until fingertip-tight.

7. Place jars in canner, making sure they are covered by at least 1 inch (2.5 cm) of water. Cover and bring to a gentle boil. Process 4-ounce (125 mL) jars and 8-ounce (250 mL) jars for 10 minutes; process 1-pint (500 mL) jars for 15 minutes.

8. Remove jars from canner and place on a wire rack or cloth towel. Let cool for 24 hours, then check seals. Wash and dry jars and store in a cool, dry, dark location.

Apple Sage Jelly

Apple cider or apple juice makes a perfect base for herb jellies and is particularly nice with roast chicken or pork.

Tip: Apple juice will give the jelly a milder apple flavor than apple cider.

4 cups	unsweetened apple cider or apple juice	1 L
⅓ cup	coarsely chopped fresh sage leaves	75 mL
6½ cups	granulated sugar	1.625 L
2	pouches (each 3 oz/85 mL) liquid pectin	2

1. Prepare canning jars and lids and bring water in water bath canner to a boil.

2. In an 8-quart (8 L) stainless steel stockpot, combine apple cider and sage. Bring to a simmer over medium-high heat. Remove from heat, cover and let stand for 10 minutes.

3. Place a fine-mesh sieve over a pan or bowl and line the sieve with a piece of damp folded cheesecloth. Ladle the apple cider mixture into the sieve and drain the cider from the sage. Discard sage. Rinse the cheesecloth and strain the cider through the cheesecloth again. (The cider may be strained through a jelly bag instead, if you prefer.)

4. In an 8-quart (8 L) stainless steel stockpot, combine strained cider and sugar. Bring to a boil over medium heat, stirring constantly until sugar is completely dissolved.

5. Increase heat to medium-high and bring to a full rolling boil, stirring constantly. Stir in pectin. Return to a full rolling boil, stirring constantly, and boil for 1 minute.

6. Remove pot from heat and quickly skim off any foam.

7. Immediately ladle hot jelly into hot jars, leaving ¼ inch (0.5 cm) headspace. Wipe jar rims and threads with a clean, damp paper towel. Center hot lids on jars and screw on bands until fingertip-tight.

8. Place jars in canner, making sure they are covered by at least 1 inch (2.5 cm) of water. Cover and bring to a gentle boil. Process 4-ounce (125 mL) jars and 8-ounce (250 mL) jars for 10 minutes; process 1-pint (500 mL) jars for 15 minutes.

9. Remove jars from canner and place on a wire rack or cloth towel. Let cool for 24 hours, then check seals. Wash and dry jars and store in a cool, dry, dark location.

Jalapeño Jelly

✳

Makes five or six 8-ounce (250 mL) jars

Both pretty and festive, Jalapeño Jelly will spice up your morning toast and is also a great accompaniment to crackers and cheese.

Tips: You can make this spread with a single color of jalapeño pepper or use a combination of different-colored peppers — green, red, yellow and orange — to create a festive jelly.

The hottest part of a chile pepper is the ribs that attach the seeds to the inside of the pepper. While the seeds can be a nice addition to hot salsas, it is best to remove the seeds and ribs when making jams and jellies, as the heat can overpower the flavor of the other ingredients and the seeds can become tough when boiled.

2 cups	cider vinegar or white wine vinegar	500 mL
¾ cup	finely chopped deribbed seeded jalapeño peppers	175 mL
6 cups	granulated sugar	1.5 L
2	pouches (each 3 oz/85 mL) liquid pectin	2

1. Prepare canning jars and lids and bring water in water bath canner to a boil.

2. In an 8-quart (8 L) stainless steel stockpot, combine vinegar, jalapeño peppers and sugar. Bring to a boil over medium heat, stirring constantly until sugar is completely dissolved.

3. Increase heat to medium-high and bring to a full rolling boil, stirring constantly. Stir in pectin. Return to a full rolling boil, stirring constantly, and boil for 1 minute.

4. Remove pot from heat and quickly skim off any foam.

5. Immediately ladle hot jelly into hot jars, leaving ¼ inch (0.5 cm) headspace. Wipe jar rims and threads with a clean, damp paper towel. Center hot lids on jars and screw on bands until fingertip-tight.

6. Place jars in canner, making sure they are covered by at least 1 inch (2.5 cm) of water. Cover and bring to a gentle boil. Process 4-ounce (125 mL) jars and 8-ounce (250 mL) jars for 10 minutes; process 1-pint (500 mL) jars for 15 minutes.

7. Remove jars from canner and place on a wire rack or cloth towel. Let cool for 24 hours, then check seals. Wash and dry jars and store in a cool, dry, dark location.

Basil Jelly

*

*Aromatic basil makes
an excellent herb jelly.*

Tips: Green food
coloring is usually
added to herb jellies
to improve their
appearance. For best
results, add the food
coloring to the strained
infusion before making
the jelly. The color will
lighten a bit when the
sugar is added.

For the best flavor, use
fresh herbs as soon
after harvest as possible.

4½ cups	water	1.125 L
3 cups	chopped fresh basil leaves	750 mL
5 to 8	drops green food coloring	5 to 8
¼ cup	strained freshly squeezed lemon juice	50 mL
6½ cups	granulated sugar	1.625 L
2	pouches (each 3 oz/85 mL) liquid pectin	2

1. In a 4-quart (4 L) stainless steel saucepan, combine water and basil. Bring to a boil over medium-high heat. Remove from heat, cover and let stand for 30 minutes.

2. Place a fine-mesh sieve over a pan or bowl and line the sieve with a piece of damp folded cheesecloth. Ladle the basil infusion into the sieve and strain out the basil. Discard basil. Rinse the cheesecloth and strain the infusion through the cheesecloth again. (The infusion may be strained through a jelly bag instead, if you prefer.) Cover infusion and refrigerate for several hours or overnight to allow any remaining sediment to settle to the bottom of the container.

3. Prepare canning jars and lids and bring water in water bath canner to a boil.

4. Place a sieve over a pan or bowl and line it with a piece of damp folded cheesecloth. Ladle or pour basil infusion into the lined sieve, being careful not to disturb any sediment in the bottom of the container. Measure 3¼ cups (800 mL) infusion. Stir in food coloring to desired color.

5. In an 8-quart (8 L) stainless steel stockpot, combine strained infusion, lemon juice and sugar. Bring to a boil over medium heat, stirring constantly until sugar is completely dissolved.

6. Increase heat to medium-high and bring to a full rolling boil, stirring constantly. Stir in pectin. Return to a full rolling boil, stirring constantly, and boil for 1 minute.

7. Remove pot from heat and quickly skim off any foam.

Tip: Rinse fresh herbs well under cool running water to wash off any dirt. Shake off as much water as possible and gently blot the herbs dry with paper towels.

8. Immediately ladle hot jelly into hot jars, leaving $\frac{1}{4}$ inch (0.5 cm) headspace. Wipe jar rims and threads with a clean, damp paper towel. Center hot lids on jars and screw on bands until fingertip-tight.

9. Place jars in canner, making sure they are covered by at least 1 inch (2.5 cm) of water. Cover and bring to a gentle boil. Process 4-ounce (125 mL) jars and 8-ounce (250 mL) jars for 10 minutes; process 1-pint (500 mL) jars for 15 minutes.

10. Remove jars from canner and place on a wire rack or cloth towel. Let cool for 24 hours, then check seals. Wash and dry jars and store in a cool, dry, dark location.

Cranberry Jalapeño Jelly

✳

**Makes about
five 8-ounce
(250 mL) jars**

*Infused with jalapeño
flavor, the tart cranberry
juice makes a great
foil for the heat of
the peppers.*

Tip: A "not from
concentrate" cranberry
juice, if available, is the
preferred choice for this
recipe, rather than a
reconstituted cranberry
juice. The not-from-
concentrate juice will
have a stronger flavor
and a higher natural
pectin content, which
will produce a better
set. Using reconstituted
juice in this recipe
may yield a jelly with a
softer set. Not-from-
concentrate juice can be
found in the juice aisle,
with the refrigerated
juices or in the organic
section of many major
grocery stores, specialty
food stores and health
food stores.

2½ cups	unsweetened cranberry juice	625 mL
½ cup	white wine vinegar	125 mL
2	jalapeño peppers, seeded, deribbed and chopped	2
5 cups	granulated sugar	1.25 L
1	pouch (3 oz/85 mL) liquid pectin	1

1. Prepare canning jars and lids and bring water in water bath canner to a boil.

2. If the juice contains sediment or pulp, strain it before measuring. To strain juice, place a sieve over a pan or bowl and line it with a piece of damp folded cheesecloth. Pour juice into the lined sieve, being careful not to disturb any sediment in the bottom of the container.

3. In an 8-quart (8 L) stainless steel stockpot, combine cranberry juice, vinegar and jalapeño peppers. Bring to a boil over medium-high heat. Reduce heat, cover and simmer gently for 5 minutes. Remove from heat.

4. Place a fine-mesh sieve over a pan or bowl and line it with a piece of damp folded cheesecloth. Ladle the cranberry juice mixture into the sieve and drain the juice from the peppers. Discard peppers. Rinse the cheesecloth and strain the juice through the cheesecloth again. (The juice may be strained through a jelly bag instead, if you prefer.)

5. In an 8-quart (8 L) stainless steel stockpot, combine strained juice and sugar. Bring to a boil over medium heat, stirring constantly until sugar is completely dissolved.

6. Increase heat to medium-high and bring to a full rolling boil, stirring constantly. Stir in pectin. Return to a full rolling boil, stirring constantly, and boil for 1 minute.

7. Remove pot from heat and quickly skim off any foam.

Tips: Do not use cranberry juice cocktail. That fruit blend is mostly water and contains a lot of sugar, both of which will keep the jelly from setting.

When working with chile peppers, do not rub your eyes. The oils from the peppers can cause chemical burns in your eyes.

8. Immediately ladle hot jelly into hot jars, leaving $\frac{1}{4}$ inch (0.5 cm) headspace. Wipe jar rims and threads with a clean, damp paper towel. Center hot lids on jars and screw on bands until fingertip-tight.

9. Place jars in canner, making sure they are covered by at least 1 inch (2.5 cm) of water. Cover and bring to a gentle boil. Process 4-ounce (125 mL) jars and 8-ounce (250 mL) jars for 10 minutes; process 1-pint (500 mL) jars for 15 minutes.

10. Remove jars from canner and place on a wire rack or cloth towel. Let cool for 24 hours, then check seals. Wash and dry jars and store in a cool, dry, dark location.

Garlic Thyme Jelly

*The distinctive flavor
of garlic accents this
fragrant herb jelly.*

Tips: English thyme and
lemon thyme both make
wonderfully flavored
jellies and are good
choices for this recipe.

For the best flavor, use
fresh herbs as soon
after harvest as possible.

2½ cups	water	625 mL
2 cups	fresh thyme leaves	500 mL
6	cloves garlic, peeled and chopped	6
1¼ cups	white wine	300 mL
6 cups	granulated sugar	1.5 L
2	pouches (each 3 oz/85 mL) liquid pectin	2

1. In a 4-quart (4 L) stainless steel saucepan, combine water, thyme and garlic. Bring to a boil over medium-high heat. Remove from heat, cover and let stand for 30 minutes.

2. Place a fine-mesh sieve over a pan or bowl and line the sieve with a piece of damp folded cheesecloth. Ladle the thyme infusion into the sieve and strain out the thyme and garlic. Discard thyme and garlic. Rinse the cheesecloth and strain the infusion through the cheesecloth again. (The infusion may be strained through a jelly bag instead, if you prefer.) Cover infusion and refrigerate for several hours or overnight to allow any remaining sediment to settle to the bottom of the container.

3. Prepare canning jars and lids and bring water in water bath canner to a boil.

4. Place a sieve over a pan or bowl and line it with a piece of damp folded cheesecloth. Ladle or pour thyme infusion into the lined sieve, being careful not to disturb any sediment in the bottom of the container. Measure 2 cups (500 mL) infusion.

5. In an 8-quart (8 L) stainless steel stockpot, combine strained infusion, white wine and sugar. Bring to a boil over medium heat, stirring constantly until sugar is completely dissolved.

6. Increase heat to medium-high and bring to a full rolling boil, stirring constantly. Stir in pectin. Return to a full rolling boil, stirring constantly, and boil for 1 minute.

7. Remove pot from heat and quickly skim off any foam.

8. Immediately ladle hot jelly into hot jars, leaving $\frac{1}{4}$ inch (0.5 cm) headspace. Wipe jar rims and threads with a clean, damp paper towel. Center hot lids on jars and screw on bands until fingertip-tight.

9. Place jars in canner, making sure they are covered by at least 1 inch (2.5 cm) of water. Cover and bring to a gentle boil. Process 4-ounce (125 mL) jars and 8-ounce (250 mL) jars for 10 minutes; process 1-pint (500 mL) jars for 15 minutes.

10. Remove jars from canner and place on a wire rack or cloth towel. Let cool for 24 hours, then check seals. Wash and dry jars and store in a cool, dry, dark location.

Lime Mint Jelly

✳

*Lime juice and grated
zest add a refreshing
tang to this flavorful
herb jelly.*

Tips: Rinse fresh herbs
well under cool running
water to wash off any
dirt. Shake off as much
water as possible and
gently blot the herbs dry
with paper towels.

Green food coloring is
usually added to herb
jellies to improve their
appearance. For best
results, add the food
coloring to the strained
juice infusion before
making the jelly. The
color will lighten a bit
when the sugar is added.

2¼ cups	water	550 mL
⅔ cup	chopped fresh mint leaves	150 mL
3 to 5	drops green food coloring	3 to 5
2 tbsp	finely grated lime zest	30 mL
¾ cup	strained freshly squeezed lime juice	175 mL
4 cups	granulated sugar	1 L
1	pouch (3 oz/85 mL) liquid pectin	1

1. In a 4-quart (4 L) stainless steel saucepan, combine water and mint. Bring to a boil over medium-high heat. Remove from heat, cover and let stand for 20 minutes.

2. Place a fine-mesh sieve over a pan or bowl and line the sieve with a piece of damp folded cheesecloth. Ladle the mint infusion into the sieve and strain out the mint. Discard mint. Rinse the cheesecloth and strain the infusion through the cheesecloth again. (The infusion may be strained through a jelly bag instead, if you prefer.) Cover infusion and refrigerate for several hours or overnight to allow any remaining sediment to settle to the bottom of the container.

3. Prepare canning jars and lids and bring water in water bath canner to a boil.

4. Place a sieve over a pan or bowl and line it with a piece of damp folded cheesecloth. Ladle or pour mint infusion into the lined sieve, being careful not to disturb any sediment in the bottom of the container. Measure 1¾ cups (425 mL) infusion. Stir in food coloring to desired color.

5. In an 8-quart (8 L) stainless steel stockpot, combine strained infusion, lime zest, lime juice and sugar. Bring to a boil over medium heat, stirring constantly until sugar is completely dissolved.

6. Increase heat to medium-high and bring to a full rolling boil, stirring constantly. Stir in pectin. Return to a full rolling boil, stirring constantly, and boil for 1 minute.

7. Remove pot from heat and quickly skim off any foam.

✳

8. Immediately ladle hot jelly into hot jars, leaving ¼ inch (0.5 cm) headspace. Wipe jar rims and threads with a clean, damp paper towel. Center hot lids on jars and screw on bands until fingertip-tight.

9. Place jars in canner, making sure they are covered by at least 1 inch (2.5 cm) of water. Cover and bring to a gentle boil. Process 4-ounce (125 mL) jars and 8-ounce (250 mL) jars for 10 minutes; process 1-pint (500 mL) jars for 15 minutes.

10. Remove jars from canner and place on a wire rack or cloth towel. Let cool for 24 hours, then check seals. Wash and dry jars and store in a cool, dry, dark location.

Mint Jelly

The crisp, refreshing flavor of mint has been the favored herb of jelly-makers for many years. Use Mint Jelly as a condiment or as a finishing glaze for roast lamb.

Tip: Mint infusion is a light yellow-brown in color. Adding green food coloring to the strained infusion gives the finished jelly a prettier, more appetizing appearance.

4½ cups	water	1.125 L
3 cups	chopped fresh mint leaves	750 mL
5 to 8	drops green food coloring	5 to 8
¼ cup	strained freshly squeezed lemon juice	50 mL
6½ cups	granulated sugar	1.625 L
2	pouches (each 3 oz/85 mL) liquid pectin	2

1. In a 4-quart (4 L) stainless steel saucepan, combine water and mint. Bring to a boil over medium-high heat. Remove from heat, cover and let stand for 30 minutes.

2. Place a fine-mesh sieve over a pan or bowl and line the sieve with a piece of damp folded cheesecloth. Ladle the mint infusion into the sieve and strain out the mint. Discard mint. Rinse the cheesecloth and strain the infusion through the cheesecloth again. (The infusion may be strained through a jelly bag instead, if you prefer.) Cover infusion and refrigerate for several hours or overnight to allow any remaining sediment to settle to the bottom of the container.

3. Prepare canning jars and lids and bring water in water bath canner to a boil.

4. Place a sieve over a pan or bowl and line it with a piece of damp folded cheesecloth. Ladle or pour mint infusion into the lined sieve, being careful not to disturb any sediment in the bottom of the container. Measure 3¼ cups (800 mL) infusion. Stir in food coloring to desired color.

5. In an 8-quart (8 L) stainless steel stockpot, combine strained infusion, lemon juice and sugar. Bring to a boil over medium heat, stirring constantly until sugar is completely dissolved.

6. Increase heat to medium-high and bring to a full rolling boil, stirring constantly. Stir in pectin. Return to a full rolling boil, stirring constantly, and boil for 1 minute.

7. Remove pot from heat and quickly skim off any foam.

Tip: To maintain freshness, store liquid pectin in the refrigerator. Bring the pectin to room temperature before using.

8. Immediately ladle hot jelly into hot jars, leaving ¼ inch (0.5 cm) headspace. Wipe jar rims and threads with a clean, damp paper towel. Center hot lids on jars and screw on bands until fingertip-tight.

9. Place jars in canner, making sure they are covered by at least 1 inch (2.5 cm) of water. Cover and bring to a gentle boil. Process 4-ounce (125 mL) jars and 8-ounce (250 mL) jars for 10 minutes; process 1-pint (500 mL) jars for 15 minutes.

10. Remove jars from canner and place on a wire rack or cloth towel. Let cool for 24 hours, then check seals. Wash and dry jars and store in a cool, dry, dark location.

Southwest Jelly

✳

Southwestern flavors blend beautifully to give this jelly its special zing.

Tips: Italian parsley, also called flat-leaf parsley, may be substituted for the cilantro, if you prefer.

You can use all red or all green jalapeño peppers in this recipe, depending on what is available in your area.

2 cups	water	500 mL
1 cup	chopped fresh cilantro leaves	250 mL
4 to 5	drops red food coloring	4 to 5
1 cup	white wine vinegar	250 mL
¾ cup	strained freshly squeezed lime juice	175 mL
1	small red jalapeño pepper, seeded, deribbed and finely chopped	1
1	small green jalapeño pepper, seeded, deribbed and finely chopped	1
6¼ cups	granulated sugar	1.55 L
2	pouches (each 3 oz/85 mL) liquid pectin	2

1. In a 4-quart (4 L) stainless steel saucepan, combine water and cilantro. Bring to a boil over medium-high heat. Remove from heat, cover and let stand for 20 minutes.

2. Place a fine-mesh sieve over a pan or bowl and line the sieve with a piece of damp folded cheesecloth. Ladle the cilantro infusion into the sieve and strain out the cilantro. Discard cilantro. Rinse the cheesecloth and strain the infusion through the cheesecloth again. (The infusion may be strained through a jelly bag instead, if you prefer.) Cover infusion and refrigerate for several hours or overnight to allow any remaining sediment to settle to the bottom of the container.

3. Prepare canning jars and lids and bring water in water bath canner to a boil.

4. Place a sieve over a pan or bowl and line it with a piece of damp folded cheesecloth. Ladle or pour cilantro infusion into the lined sieve, being careful not to disturb any sediment in the bottom of the container. Measure 1¾ cups (425 mL) infusion. Stir in food coloring to desired color.

5. In an 8-quart (8 L) stainless steel stockpot, combine strained infusion, vinegar, lime juice, red and green jalapeño peppers and sugar. Bring to a boil over medium heat, stirring constantly until sugar is completely dissolved.

6. Increase heat to medium-high and bring to a full rolling boil, stirring constantly. Stir in pectin. Return to a full rolling boil, stirring constantly, and boil for 1 minute.

7. Remove pot from heat and quickly skim off any foam.

8. Immediately ladle hot jelly into hot jars, leaving $\frac{1}{4}$ inch (0.5 cm) headspace. Wipe jar rims and threads with a clean, damp paper towel. Center hot lids on jars and screw on bands until fingertip-tight.

9. Place jars in canner, making sure they are covered by at least 1 inch (2.5 cm) of water. Cover and bring to a gentle boil. Process 4-ounce (125 mL) jars and 8-ounce (250 mL) jars for 10 minutes; process 1-pint (500 mL) jars for 15 minutes.

10. Remove jars from canner and place on a wire rack or cloth towel. Let cool for 24 hours, then check seals. Wash and dry jars and store in a cool, dry, dark location.

Lemon Dill Marmalade

✳

This tantalizing marmalade is refreshing on crackers or alongside fresh fish.

Tip: For the best flavor and texture, use fresh dill in this recipe. Dried dillweed will give the marmalade a gritty texture and will not have the same flavor as fresh dill. If you prefer a stronger dill flavor, increase the amount of fresh dill.

14 to 18	large lemons	14 to 18
1/8 tsp	baking soda	0.5 mL
5 cups	granulated sugar	1.25 L
1/2 tsp	unsalted butter (optional)	2 mL
1	pouch (3 oz/85 mL) liquid pectin	1
2 tsp	finely chopped fresh dill	10 mL

1. Prepare canning jars and lids and bring water in water bath canner to a boil.

2. Using a zester, remove only the outer colored portion of the peel in very thin strips from 6 of the lemons. Coarsely chop the zested peel. (The colored zest may also be removed from the fruit using a vegetable peeler, then cut into very thin strips with a sharp knife and coarsely chopped.) Peel all of the lemons, removing all of the outer white pith. Cut the fruit sections away from the membrane and remove any seeds. Discard the pith and membrane. Finely chop the fruit and measure 3 cups (750 mL).

3. In an 8-quart (8 L) stainless steel stockpot, combine chopped lemons, lemon zest and baking soda. Bring to a boil over medium-high heat. Reduce heat, cover and simmer gently for 3 minutes.

4. Gradually stir in sugar and butter, if using. Increase heat to medium-high and bring to a full rolling boil, stirring constantly. Stir in pectin. Return to a full rolling boil, stirring constantly, and boil for 1 minute.

5. Remove pot from heat and skim off any foam. Stir in dill. Let marmalade cool in the pot for 5 minutes, stirring occasionally.

6. Ladle hot marmalade into hot jars, leaving 1/4 inch (0.5 cm) headspace. Remove any air bubbles. Wipe jar rims and threads with a clean, damp paper towel. Center hot lids on jars and screw on bands until fingertip-tight.

Tip: For the best flavor, the lemons should be fully ripe and juicy and should have a peel with a good yellow color without any hint of green. Underripe lemons will make a very tart marmalade.

7. Place jars in canner, making sure they are covered by at least 1 inch (2.5 cm) of water. Cover and bring to a gentle boil. Process 4-ounce (125 mL) jars and 8-ounce (250 mL) jars for 10 minutes; process 1-pint (500 mL) jars for 15 minutes.

8. Remove jars from canner and place on a wire rack or cloth towel. Let cool for 24 hours, then check seals. Wash and dry jars and store in a cool, dry, dark location.

Orange Zing Marmalade

Makes about five 8-ounce (250 mL) jars

It may sound like an odd combination, but the hint of horseradish blended with the fresh orange in this unique and flavorful marmalade gives it a special zing.

Tip: Orange Zing Marmalade makes a fantastic dipping sauce for fried coconut shrimp. The combination of the coconut, orange and horseradish flavors is amazing!

12 to 14	medium Valencia oranges	12 to 14
3	medium lemons	3
1/8 tsp	baking soda	0.5 mL
5 cups	granulated sugar	1.25 L
1/2 tsp	unsalted butter (optional)	2 mL
1	pouch (3 oz/85 mL) liquid pectin	1
4 tsp	prepared horseradish	20 mL

1. Prepare canning jars and lids and bring water in water bath canner to a boil.

2. Using a zester, remove only the outer colored portion of the peel in very thin strips from 4 of the oranges and the 3 lemons. Coarsely chop the zested peel. (The colored zest may also be removed from the fruit using a vegetable peeler, then cut into very thin strips with a sharp knife and coarsely chopped.) Peel all of the oranges and lemons, removing all of the outer white pith. Cut the fruit sections away from the membrane and remove any seeds. Discard the pith and membrane. Finely chop the fruit, reserving the juice. Combine the fruit and enough of the juice to measure 2⅔ cups (650 mL).

3. In an 8-quart (8 L) stainless steel stockpot, combine chopped fruit and baking soda. Bring to a boil over medium-high heat. Reduce heat, cover and simmer gently for 8 minutes. Stir in orange zest and lemon zest until well distributed. Cover and simmer for 3 minutes.

4. Gradually stir in sugar and butter, if using. Increase heat to medium-high and bring to a full rolling boil, stirring constantly. Stir in pectin. Return to a full rolling boil, stirring constantly, and boil for 1 minute.

5. Remove pot from heat and skim off any foam. Stir in horseradish. Let marmalade cool in the pot for 5 minutes, stirring occasionally.

Tip: For the best flavor and texture, use bottled horseradish. Do not use a horseradish sauce, as it will make the marmalade cloudy and affect the set.

6. Ladle hot marmalade into hot jars, leaving ¼ inch (0.5 cm) headspace. Remove any air bubbles. Wipe jar rims and threads with a clean, damp paper towel. Center hot lids on jars and screw on bands until fingertip-tight.

7. Place jars in canner, making sure they are covered by at least 1 inch (2.5 cm) of water. Cover and bring to a gentle boil. Process 4-ounce (125 mL) jars and 8-ounce (250 mL) jars for 10 minutes; process 1-pint (500 mL) jars for 15 minutes.

8. Remove jars from canner and place on a wire rack or cloth towel. Let cool for 24 hours, then check seals. Wash and dry jars and store in a cool, dry, dark location.

Three Onion Marmalade

Makes about five 8-ounce (250 mL) jars

This wonderfully sweet and tangy marmalade is an excellent accompaniment for beef, pork, poultry, cheese or pâté.

Tips: Cooking the marmalade slowly allows the onions to absorb the flavors of the syrup and caramelize to a rich golden brown.

For 5 cups (1.25 L) thinly sliced sweet onions, you'll need about 2½ lbs (1.25 kg) or about 7 medium onions. For 3 cups (750 mL) thinly sliced red onions, you'll need about 1½ lbs (750 g) or about 4 medium onions. For 2 cups (500 mL) thinly sliced white onions, you'll need about 1 lb (500 g) or about 3 medium onions.

3 cups	granulated sugar	750 mL
1¾ cups	dry sherry	425 mL
1 cup	red wine vinegar or cider vinegar	250 mL
5 cups	thinly sliced peeled sweet onions (Vidalia, Walla Walla or Maui)	1.25 L
3 cups	thinly sliced peeled red onions	750 mL
2 cups	thinly sliced peeled white onions	500 mL
	Salt	
	Freshly ground black pepper	

1. Prepare canning jars and lids and bring water in water bath canner to a boil.

2. In an 8-quart (8 L) stainless steel stockpot, combine sugar, sherry and vinegar. Bring to a boil over medium-high heat, stirring constantly until sugar is completely dissolved.

3. Add sweet onions, red onions and white onions. Reduce heat to medium-low and simmer until onions are tender and translucent and most of the liquid has evaporated, about 90 minutes. As the liquid reduces, stir frequently to prevent sticking and scorching. Remove from heat and season to taste with salt and pepper.

4. Ladle hot marmalade into hot jars, leaving ¼ inch (0.5 cm) headspace. Remove any air bubbles. Wipe jar rims and threads with a clean, damp paper towel. Center hot lids on jars and screw on bands until fingertip-tight.

5. Place jars in canner, making sure they are covered by at least 1 inch (2.5 cm) of water. Cover and bring to a gentle boil. Process 4-ounce (125 mL) jars and 8-ounce (250 mL) jars for 10 minutes; process 1-pint (500 mL) jars for 15 minutes.

6. Remove jars from canner and place on a wire rack or cloth towel. Let cool for 24 hours, then check seals. Wash and dry jars and store in a cool, dry, dark location.

Salsa Jam (page 236)
Overleaf: Basil Jelly (page 240)

Drunken Spreads

Overleaf: Peacharita Jam (page 264)

Blush Wine Jelly (see variation, page 273) and
  Blackberry Cabernet Sauvignon Jam (page 261)

About Drunken Spreads

JAMS, JELLIES AND OTHER FRUIT spreads that contain flavored liqueurs and other spirits are rapidly gaining popularity. These tantalizing spreads offer unique combinations of flavors to please the senses and the palate. The secret to success is to balance the flavors so that the liqueurs enhance the flavor of the fruit without overpowering it. A delicate balance is required to achieve the perfect blend of flavors.

The recipes in this chapter do not scream alcohol; the flavor of the liqueurs is designed to be subtle. The purpose of adding liqueurs to the jams, jellies and marmalades is to heighten the flavor of the fruit while giving the spreads a warm, full-bodied flavor, not to have the alcohol flavor stand out and grab you.

A common mistake home canners make is adding too much of a liqueur to a spread. Some spreads are so strong on alcohol that the flavors of the fruit get lost and all you can taste is the overpowering flavor of the liqueur. Remember that some flavors intensify during storage.

When adding wine or a liqueur to the pan, make sure the pan is off the heat and away from any open flames. Wines and liqueurs are flammable, and the alcohol vapors can be ignited by open flames. In each recipe in this chapter, the alcohol is added to the pan before it is placed over the heat or after it has been moved off the heat.

Because additional liquid, particularly alcohol, can upset the ingredient balance and keep a spread from setting properly, the liqueurs in these recipes should not be increased by more than a tablespoon or two (15 or 25 mL). More than that and you run a serious risk of the spread failing to set.

Apple Calvados Jam

✳

**Makes about
six 8-ounce
(250 mL) jars**

*The crisp flavor of
apples is enhanced by
rich Calvados apple
brandy.*

Tips: Calvados, made in
the Normandy region of
France, is a full-flavored
apple brandy distilled
from apple cider.

For 6 cups (1.5 L) finely
chopped apples, you'll
need about 2½ lbs
(1.25 kg) or 7 medium
apples.

6 cups	finely chopped cored peeled apples	1.5 L
1¼ cups	unsweetened apple cider or apple juice	300 mL
1 tbsp	freshly squeezed lemon juice	15 mL
½ tsp	unsalted butter (optional)	2 mL
5 cups	granulated sugar	1.25 L
1	pouch (3 oz/85 mL) liquid pectin	1
⅓ cup	Calvados	75 mL

1. Prepare canning jars and lids and bring water in water bath canner to a boil.

2. In an 8-quart (8 L) stainless steel stockpot, combine apples, apple cider, lemon juice and butter, if using. Bring to a boil over medium heat. Reduce heat, cover and simmer for 5 minutes, stirring occasionally.

3. Uncover and gradually add sugar, stirring constantly until sugar is completely dissolved.

4. Increase heat to medium-high and bring to a full rolling boil, stirring constantly. Stir in pectin. Return to a full rolling boil, stirring constantly, and boil for 1 minute.

5. Remove pot from heat and skim off any foam. Stir in Calvados. Let jam cool in the pot for 5 minutes, stirring occasionally.

6. Ladle hot jam into hot jars, leaving ¼ inch (0.5 cm) headspace. Remove any air bubbles. Wipe jar rims and threads with a clean, damp paper towel. Center hot lids on jars and screw on bands until fingertip-tight.

7. Place jars in canner, making sure they are covered by at least 1 inch (2.5 cm) of water. Cover and bring to a gentle boil. Process 4-ounce (125 mL) jars and 8-ounce (250 mL) jars for 10 minutes; process 1-pint (500 mL) jars for 15 minutes.

8. Remove jars from canner and place on a wire rack or cloth towel. Let cool for 24 hours, then check seals. Wash and dry jars and store in a cool, dry, dark location.

Apricot Amaretto Jam

※

This amazing jam will vanish in a hurry.

Tips: Amaretto is an Italian liqueur with an almond flavor, although the base for the liqueur is primarily made from apricot pits.

For 4¼ cups (1.05 L) crushed apricots, you'll need about 4 lbs (2 kg) medium apricots.

4¼ cups	crushed pitted peeled apricots	1.05 L
¼ cup	freshly squeezed lemon juice	50 mL
1	package (1.75 oz/49 to 57 g) regular powdered fruit pectin	1
6⅓ cups	granulated sugar, divided	1.575 L
½ tsp	unsalted butter (optional)	2 mL
⅓ cup	amaretto	75 mL

1. Prepare canning jars and lids and bring water in water bath canner to a boil.

2. In an 8-quart (8 L) stainless steel stockpot, combine apricots and lemon juice.

3. In a small bowl, combine pectin and ¼ cup (50 mL) of the sugar. Gradually stir into fruit. Add butter, if using.

4. Bring fruit mixture to a full rolling boil over medium-high heat, stirring constantly. Gradually stir in the remaining sugar. Return to a full rolling boil, stirring constantly, and boil for 1 minute.

5. Remove pot from heat and skim off any foam. Stir in amaretto. Let jam cool in the pot for 5 minutes, stirring occasionally.

6. Ladle hot jam into hot jars, leaving ¼ inch (0.5 cm) headspace. Remove any air bubbles. Wipe jar rims and threads with a clean, damp paper towel. Center hot lids on jars and screw on bands until fingertip-tight.

7. Place jars in canner, making sure they are covered by at least 1 inch (2.5 cm) of water. Cover and bring to a gentle boil. Process 4-ounce (125 mL) jars and 8-ounce (250 mL) jars for 10 minutes; process 1-pint (500 mL) jars for 15 minutes.

8. Remove jars from canner and place on a wire rack or cloth towel. Let cool for 24 hours, then check seals. Wash and dry jars and store in a cool, dry, dark location.

Blackberry Cabernet Sauvignon Jam

✳

Makes seven or eight 8-ounce (250 mL) jars

The full-bodied flavor of Cabernet Sauvignon wine makes it a natural choice to pair with intense ripe blackberries.

Tips: Crush blackberries, one layer at a time, in a large pan using a vegetable masher or the back of a large spoon.

For 3¾ cups (925 mL) crushed blackberries, you'll need about 2½ lbs (1.25 kg) or about 6½ cups (1.625 L) blackberries.

3¾ cups	crushed blackberries	925 mL
1	package (1.75 oz/49 to 57 g) regular powdered fruit pectin	1
6⅓ cups	granulated sugar, divided	1.575 L
½ tsp	unsalted butter (optional)	2 mL
1 cup	Cabernet Sauvignon wine	250 mL

1. Prepare canning jars and lids and bring water in water bath canner to a boil.
2. Pour blackberries into an 8-quart (8 L) stainless steel stockpot.
3. In a small bowl, combine pectin and ¼ cup (50 mL) of the sugar. Gradually stir into fruit. Add butter, if using.
4. Bring fruit mixture to a full rolling boil over medium-high heat, stirring constantly. Gradually stir in the remaining sugar. Return to a full rolling boil, stirring constantly, and boil for 1 minute.
5. Remove pot from heat and skim off any foam. Stir in wine. Let jam cool in the pot for 5 minutes, stirring occasionally.
6. Ladle hot jam into hot jars, leaving ¼ inch (0.5 cm) headspace. Remove any air bubbles. Wipe jar rims and threads with a clean, damp paper towel. Center hot lids on jars and screw on bands until fingertip-tight.
7. Place jars in canner, making sure they are covered by at least 1 inch (2.5 cm) of water. Cover and bring to a gentle boil. Process 4-ounce (125 mL) jars and 8-ounce (250 mL) jars for 10 minutes; process 1-pint (500 mL) jars for 15 minutes.
8. Remove jars from canner and place on a wire rack or cloth towel. Let cool for 24 hours, then check seals. Wash and dry jars and store in a cool, dry, dark location.

Cherry Brandy Jam

✳

Makes about six 8-ounce (250 mL) jars

Fresh sweet cherries and brandy — an intoxicating combination!

Tips: Kirsch, also called kirschwasser, is a clear brandy distilled from black cherries that is made mostly in Germany and France.

For 3¾ cups (925 mL) finely chopped cherries, you'll need about 3 lbs (1.5 kg) cherries.

3¾ cups	finely chopped pitted fresh sweet cherries	925 mL
½ cup	freshly squeezed lemon juice	125 mL
5 cups	granulated sugar	1.25 L
½ tsp	unsalted butter (optional)	2 mL
1	pouch (3 oz/85 mL) liquid pectin	1
¼ cup	kirsch	50 mL

1. Prepare canning jars and lids and bring water in water bath canner to a boil.

2. In an 8-quart (8 L) stainless steel stockpot, combine cherries and lemon juice. Gradually stir in sugar and butter, if using. Bring to a boil over medium heat, stirring constantly until sugar is completely dissolved.

3. Increase heat to medium-high and bring to a full rolling boil, stirring constantly. Stir in pectin. Return to a full rolling boil, stirring constantly, and boil for 1 minute.

4. Remove pot from heat and skim off any foam. Stir in kirsch. Let jam cool in the pot for 5 minutes, stirring occasionally.

5. Ladle hot jam into hot jars, leaving ¼ inch (0.5 cm) headspace. Remove any air bubbles. Wipe jar rims and threads with a clean, damp paper towel. Center hot lids on jars and screw on bands until fingertip-tight.

6. Place jars in canner, making sure they are covered by at least 1 inch (2.5 cm) of water. Cover and bring to a gentle boil. Process 4-ounce (125 mL) jars and 8-ounce (250 mL) jars for 10 minutes; process 1-pint (500 mL) jars for 15 minutes.

7. Remove jars from canner and place on a wire rack or cloth towel. Let cool for 24 hours, then check seals. Wash and dry jars and store in a cool, dry, dark location.

Orange Grand Marnier Jam

✳

**Makes about
five 8-ounce
(250 mL) jars**

*The blending of
orange flavors gives
this gleaming jam a
vibrant finish.*

Tips: Grand Marnier is a
sweet, orange-flavored,
cognac-based French
liqueur made from the
skins of oranges.

For 2¼ cups (550 mL)
finely chopped Valencia
oranges, you'll need
about 14 to 17 medium
oranges.

2¼ cups	finely chopped sectioned peeled Valencia oranges	550 mL
3 tbsp	freshly squeezed lemon juice	45 mL
4¾ cups	granulated sugar	1.175 L
½ tsp	unsalted butter (optional)	2 mL
1	pouch (3 oz/85 mL) liquid pectin	1
⅓ cup	Grand Marnier	75 mL

1. Prepare canning jars and lids and bring water in water bath canner to a boil.

2. In an 8-quart (8 L) stainless steel stockpot, combine oranges and lemon juice. Gradually stir in sugar and butter, if using. Bring to a boil over medium heat, stirring constantly until sugar is completely dissolved.

3. Increase heat to medium-high and bring to a full rolling boil, stirring constantly. Stir in pectin. Return to a full rolling boil, stirring constantly, and boil for 1 minute.

4. Remove pot from heat and skim off any foam. Stir in Grand Marnier. Let jam cool in the pot for 5 minutes, stirring occasionally.

5. Ladle hot jam into hot jars, leaving ¼ inch (0.5 cm) headspace. Remove any air bubbles. Wipe jar rims and threads with a clean, damp paper towel. Center hot lids on jars and screw on bands until fingertip-tight.

6. Place jars in canner, making sure they are covered by at least 1 inch (2.5 cm) of water. Cover and bring to a gentle boil. Process 4-ounce (125 mL) jars and 8-ounce (250 mL) jars for 10 minutes; process 1-pint (500 mL) jars for 15 minutes.

7. Remove jars from canner and place on a wire rack or cloth towel. Let cool for 24 hours, then check seals. Wash and dry jars and store in a cool, dry, dark location.

Peacharita Jam

✳

*A peachy twist on a
classic cocktail creates
a fun and fanciful jam.*

Tips: Triple Sec is
a colorless, sweet,
orange-flavored liqueur.

For 3 cups (750 mL)
crushed peaches, you'll
need about 3 lbs (1.5 kg)
or 9 medium peaches.

3 cups	crushed pitted peeled peaches	750 mL
⅔ cup	freshly squeezed lime juice	150 mL
½ cup	tequila	125 mL
¼ cup	Triple Sec	50 mL
6 cups	granulated sugar	1.5 L
½ tsp	unsalted butter (optional)	2 mL
1	pouch (3 oz/85 mL) liquid pectin	1

1. Prepare canning jars and lids and bring water in water bath canner to a boil.

2. In an 8-quart (8 L) stainless steel stockpot, combine peaches, lime juice, tequila and Triple Sec. Gradually stir in sugar and butter, if using. Bring to a boil over medium heat, stirring constantly until sugar is completely dissolved.

3. Increase heat to medium-high and bring to a full rolling boil, stirring constantly. Stir in pectin. Return to a full rolling boil, stirring constantly, and boil for 1 minute.

4. Remove pot from heat and skim off any foam. Let jam cool in the pot for 5 minutes, stirring occasionally.

5. Ladle hot jam into hot jars, leaving ¼ inch (0.5 cm) headspace. Remove any air bubbles. Wipe jar rims and threads with a clean, damp paper towel. Center hot lids on jars and screw on bands until fingertip-tight.

6. Place jars in canner, making sure they are covered by at least 1 inch (2.5 cm) of water. Cover and bring to a gentle boil. Process 4-ounce (125 mL) jars and 8-ounce (250 mL) jars for 10 minutes; process 1-pint (500 mL) jars for 15 minutes.

7. Remove jars from canner and place on a wire rack or cloth towel. Let cool for 24 hours, then check seals. Wash and dry jars and store in a cool, dry, dark location.

Pineapple Rum Jam

3	cans (each 20 oz/567 mL) juice-packed crushed pineapple, very well drained	3
1/3 cup	freshly squeezed lemon juice	75 mL
1	package (1.75 oz/49 to 57 g) regular powdered fruit pectin	1
5 cups	granulated sugar, divided	1.25 L
1/2 tsp	unsalted butter (optional)	2 mL
1/3 cup	rum	75 mL

Makes about six 8-ounce (250 mL) jars

Spoon this tantalizing jam over vanilla ice cream for a heavenly tropical dessert.

Tips: Rum is distilled from the fermented juice of sugar cane or molasses.

A 20-oz can (567 mL) of crushed pineapple will yield about 1 1/8 cups (280 mL) drained pineapple. If using a can size other than 20 oz (567 mL), you will need 3 3/8 cups (840 mL) drained crushed pineapple for this recipe.

1. Prepare canning jars and lids and bring water in water bath canner to a boil.

2. In an 8-quart (8 L) stainless steel stockpot, combine pineapple and lemon juice.

3. In a small bowl, combine pectin and 1/4 cup (50 mL) of the sugar. Gradually stir into fruit. Add butter, if using.

4. Bring fruit mixture to a full rolling boil over medium-high heat, stirring constantly. Gradually stir in the remaining sugar. Return to a full rolling boil, stirring constantly, and boil for 1 minute.

5. Remove pot from heat and skim off any foam. Stir in rum. Let jam cool in the pot for 5 minutes, stirring occasionally.

6. Ladle hot jam into hot jars, leaving 1/4 inch (0.5 cm) headspace. Remove any air bubbles. Wipe jar rims and threads with a clean, damp paper towel. Center hot lids on jars and screw on bands until fingertip-tight.

7. Place jars in canner, making sure they are covered by at least 1 inch (2.5 cm) of water. Cover and bring to a gentle boil. Process 4-ounce (125 mL) jars and 8-ounce (250 mL) jars for 10 minutes; process 1-pint (500 mL) jars for 15 minutes.

8. Remove jars from canner and place on a wire rack or cloth towel. Let cool for 24 hours, then check seals. Wash and dry jars and store in a cool, dry, dark location.

Plum Rum Jam

✳

Plums and rum — a perfect pairing!

Tips: Red or purple plums are both good choices for this flavorful jam.

Rum comes in both light and dark varieties. Dark rum gets its color from aging in oak casks or from the addition of caramel color. Either dark or light rum may be used in jams, depending on your preference.

For 3¾ cups (925 mL) crushed plums, you'll need about 3½ lbs (1.75 kg) medium plums.

3¾ cups	crushed pitted peeled plums	925 mL
6½ cups	granulated sugar	1.625 L
½ tsp	unsalted butter (optional)	2 mL
1	pouch (3 oz/85 mL) liquid pectin	1
⅓ cup	rum	75 mL

1. Prepare canning jars and lids and bring water in water bath canner to a boil.

2. In an 8-quart (8 L) stainless steel stockpot, combine plums, sugar and butter, if using. Bring to a boil over medium heat, stirring constantly until sugar is completely dissolved.

3. Increase heat to medium-high and bring to a full rolling boil, stirring constantly. Stir in pectin. Return to a full rolling boil, stirring constantly, and boil for 1 minute.

4. Remove pot from heat and skim off any foam. Stir in rum. Let jam cool in the pot for 5 minutes, stirring occasionally.

5. Ladle hot jam into hot jars, leaving ¼ inch (0.5 cm) headspace. Remove any air bubbles. Wipe jar rims and threads with a clean, damp paper towel. Center hot lids on jars and screw on bands until fingertip-tight.

6. Place jars in canner, making sure they are covered by at least 1 inch (2.5 cm) of water. Cover and bring to a gentle boil. Process 4-ounce (125 mL) jars and 8-ounce (250 mL) jars for 10 minutes; process 1-pint (500 mL) jars for 15 minutes.

7. Remove jars from canner and place on a wire rack or cloth towel. Let cool for 24 hours, then check seals. Wash and dry jars and store in a cool, dry, dark location.

Raspberry Chambord Jam

✳

Makes about nine 8-ounce (250 mL) jars

Try spreading Raspberry Chambord Jam between layers of a chocolate cake for an elegant dessert.

Tips: To reduce the amount of seeds in the finished jam, press about three-quarters of the raspberry pulp through a fine-mesh sieve to remove the seeds before measuring, if desired.

Chambord is a velvety, rich raspberry liqueur from the Loire Valley in France. If you prefer, framboise, another raspberry-flavored liqueur, may be substituted for Chambord; however, the jam will have a mild flavor. Do not use a Belgian lambic beer also named Framboise, as the spread may not set properly.

For 4¾ cups (1.175 L) crushed raspberries, you'll need about 3 lbs (1.5 kg) or 12 cups (3 L) raspberries.

4¾ cups	crushed red raspberries	1.175 L
1 tbsp	freshly squeezed lemon juice	15 mL
1	package (1.75 oz/49 to 57 g) regular powdered fruit pectin	1
6¾ cups	granulated sugar, divided	1.675 L
½ tsp	unsalted butter (optional)	2 mL
⅓ cup	Chambord	75 mL

1. Prepare canning jars and lids and bring water in water bath canner to a boil.

2. In an 8-quart (8 L) stainless steel stockpot, combine raspberries and lemon juice.

3. In a small bowl, combine pectin and ¼ cup (50 mL) of the sugar. Gradually stir into fruit. Add butter, if using.

4. Bring fruit mixture to a full rolling boil over medium-high heat, stirring constantly. Gradually stir in the remaining sugar. Return to a full rolling boil, stirring constantly, and boil for 1 minute.

5. Remove pot from heat and skim off any foam. Stir in Chambord. Let jam cool in the pot for 5 minutes, stirring occasionally.

6. Ladle hot jam into hot jars, leaving ¼ inch (0.5 cm) headspace. Remove any air bubbles. Wipe jar rims and threads with a clean, damp paper towel. Center hot lids on jars and screw on bands until fingertip-tight.

7. Place jars in canner, making sure they are covered by at least 1 inch (2.5 cm) of water. Cover and bring to a gentle boil. Process 4-ounce (125 mL) jars and 8-ounce (250 mL) jars for 10 minutes; process 1-pint (500 mL) jars for 15 minutes.

8. Remove jars from canner and place on a wire rack or cloth towel. Let cool for 24 hours, then check seals. Wash and dry jars and store in a cool, dry, dark location.

Sherried Strawberry Jam

✳

A sophisticated and elegant jam. The sherry pairs quite nicely with the succulent strawberries.

Tips: Sherry is a fortified Spanish wine that has a higher alcohol content because of the addition of brandy. The flavor of sherry ranges from very sweet to very dry. For making spreads, choose a moderately dry sherry.

For 4¾ cups (1.175 L) crushed strawberries, you'll need about 3½ lbs (1.75 kg) or 10 cups (2.5 L) strawberries.

4¾ cups	crushed strawberries	1.175 L
2 tbsp	freshly squeezed lemon juice	30 mL
1	package (1.75 oz/49 to 57 g) regular powdered fruit pectin	1
6¾ cups	granulated sugar, divided	1.675 L
½ tsp	unsalted butter (optional)	2 mL
⅓ cup	dry sherry	75 mL

1. Prepare canning jars and lids and bring water in water bath canner to a boil.

2. In an 8-quart (8 L) stainless steel stockpot, combine strawberries and lemon juice.

3. In a small bowl, combine pectin and ¼ cup (50 mL) of the sugar. Gradually stir into fruit. Add butter, if using.

4. Bring fruit mixture to a full rolling boil over medium-high heat, stirring constantly. Gradually stir in the remaining sugar. Return to a full rolling boil, stirring constantly, and boil for 1 minute.

5. Remove pot from heat and skim off any foam. Stir in sherry. Let jam cool in the pot for 5 minutes, stirring occasionally.

6. Ladle hot jam into hot jars, leaving ¼ inch (0.5 cm) headspace. Remove any air bubbles. Wipe jar rims and threads with a clean, damp paper towel. Center hot lids on jars and screw on bands until fingertip-tight.

7. Place jars in canner, making sure they are covered by at least 1 inch (2.5 cm) of water. Cover and bring to a gentle boil. Process 4-ounce (125 mL) jars and 8-ounce (250 mL) jars for 10 minutes; process 1-pint (500 mL) jars for 15 minutes.

8. Remove jars from canner and place on a wire rack or cloth towel. Let cool for 24 hours, then check seals. Wash and dry jars and store in a cool, dry, dark location.

Strawberry Daiquiri Jam

**Makes about
seven 8-ounce
(250 mL) jars**

*With one of my favorite
drinks for inspiration,
this glorious jam
conjures up images of
tropical sunsets.*

Tips: For a uniform
texture, cut strawberries
into pieces before gently
crushing them with a
potato or vegetable
masher.

For 2¼ cups (550 mL)
crushed strawberries,
you'll need about 2 lbs
(1 kg) or 5 cups (1.25 L)
strawberries.

2¼ cups	crushed strawberries	550 mL
¾ cup	drained juice-packed crushed pineapple	175 mL
⅔ cup	freshly squeezed lime juice	150 mL
½ cup	rum	125 mL
6 cups	granulated sugar	1.5 L
½ tsp	unsalted butter (optional)	2 mL
1	pouch (3 oz/85 mL) liquid pectin	1

1. Prepare canning jars and lids and bring water in water bath canner to a boil.

2. In an 8-quart (8 L) stainless steel stockpot, combine strawberries, pineapple, lime juice and rum. Gradually stir in sugar and butter, if using. Bring to a boil over medium heat, stirring constantly until sugar is completely dissolved.

3. Increase heat to medium-high and bring to a full rolling boil, stirring constantly. Stir in pectin. Return to a full rolling boil, stirring constantly, and boil for 1 minute.

4. Remove pot from heat and skim off any foam. Let jam cool in the pot for 5 minutes, stirring occasionally.

5. Ladle hot jam into hot jars, leaving ¼ inch (0.5 cm) headspace. Remove any air bubbles. Wipe jar rims and threads with a clean, damp paper towel. Center hot lids on jars and screw on bands until fingertip-tight.

6. Place jars in canner, making sure they are covered by at least 1 inch (2.5 cm) of water. Cover and bring to a gentle boil. Process 4-ounce (125 mL) jars and 8-ounce (250 mL) jars for 10 minutes; process 1-pint (500 mL) jars for 15 minutes.

7. Remove jars from canner and place on a wire rack or cloth towel. Let cool for 24 hours, then check seals. Wash and dry jars and store in a cool, dry, dark location.

Strawberry Margarita Jam

✳

**Makes about
seven 8-ounce
(250 mL) jars**

*Based on the classic
drink, this jam is
loaded with flavor and
packs a nice kick.*

Tips: While the term
"triple sec" normally
translates as "triple
dry," in the case of
Triple Sec liqueur it
means "triple distilled."

For 3 cups (750 mL)
crushed strawberries,
you'll need about 2½ lbs
(1.25 kg) or 6 cups (1.5 L)
strawberries.

3 cups	crushed strawberries	750 mL
⅔ cup	freshly squeezed lime juice	150 mL
½ cup	tequila	125 mL
¼ cup	Triple Sec	50 mL
6 cups	granulated sugar	1.5 L
½ tsp	unsalted butter (optional)	2 mL
1	pouch (3 oz/85 mL) liquid pectin	1

1. Prepare canning jars and lids and bring water in water bath canner to a boil.

2. In an 8-quart (8 L) stainless steel stockpot, combine strawberries, lime juice, tequila and Triple Sec. Gradually stir in sugar and butter, if using. Bring to a boil over medium heat, stirring constantly until sugar is completely dissolved.

3. Increase heat to medium-high and bring to a full rolling boil, stirring constantly. Stir in pectin. Return to a full rolling boil, stirring constantly, and boil for 1 minute.

4. Remove pot from heat and skim off any foam. Let jam cool in the pot for 5 minutes, stirring occasionally.

5. Ladle hot jam into hot jars, leaving ¼ inch (0.5 cm) headspace. Remove any air bubbles. Wipe jar rims and threads with a clean, damp paper towel. Center hot lids on jars and screw on bands until fingertip-tight.

6. Place jars in canner, making sure they are covered by at least 1 inch (2.5 cm) of water. Cover and bring to a gentle boil. Process 4-ounce (125 mL) jars and 8-ounce (250 mL) jars for 10 minutes; process 1-pint (500 mL) jars for 15 minutes.

7. Remove jars from canner and place on a wire rack or cloth towel. Let cool for 24 hours, then check seals. Wash and dry jars and store in a cool, dry, dark location.

Strawberry Peach Grand Marnier Jam

*The orange flavor of
the Grand Marnier
blends beautifully with
the strawberries and
peaches in this
delectable jam.*

Tips: For the best flavor
and texture, use fully
ripe strawberries and
yellow-fleshed peaches
that are fully ripe and
slightly soft to the touch
when gently pressed.

For 2¼ cups (550 mL)
crushed strawberries,
you'll need about 2 lbs
(1 kg) or 5 cups (1.25 L)
strawberries. For 2 cups
(500 mL) crushed
peaches, you'll need
about 2 lbs (1 kg) or
about 6 medium
peaches.

2¼ cups	crushed strawberries	550 mL
2 cups	crushed pitted peeled peaches	500 mL
2 tbsp	freshly squeezed lemon juice	30 mL
1	package (1.75 oz/49 to 57 g) regular powdered fruit pectin	1
6¾ cups	granulated sugar, divided	1.675 L
½ tsp	unsalted butter (optional)	2 mL
⅓ cup	Grand Marnier	75 mL

1. Prepare canning jars and lids and bring water in water bath canner to a boil.

2. In an 8-quart (8 L) stainless steel stockpot, combine strawberries, peaches and lemon juice.

3. In a small bowl, combine pectin and ¼ cup (50 mL) of the sugar. Gradually stir into fruit. Add butter, if using.

4. Bring fruit mixture to a full rolling boil over medium-high heat, stirring constantly. Gradually stir in the remaining sugar. Return to a full rolling boil, stirring constantly, and boil for 1 minute.

5. Remove pot from heat and skim off any foam. Stir in Grand Marnier. Let jam cool in the pot for 5 minutes, stirring occasionally.

6. Ladle hot jam into hot jars, leaving ¼ inch (0.5 cm) headspace. Remove any air bubbles. Wipe jar rims and threads with a clean, damp paper towel. Center hot lids on jars and screw on bands until fingertip-tight.

7. Place jars in canner, making sure they are covered by at least 1 inch (2.5 cm) of water. Cover and bring to a gentle boil. Process 4-ounce (125 mL) jars and 8-ounce (250 mL) jars for 10 minutes; process 1-pint (500 mL) jars for 15 minutes.

8. Remove jars from canner and place on a wire rack or cloth towel. Let cool for 24 hours, then check seals. Wash and dry jars and store in a cool, dry, dark location.

Apple Cider Calvados Jelly

✳

Makes about seven 8-ounce (250 mL) jars

The addition of Calvados takes apple jelly to a whole new level. Try brushing this delicious jelly on a pork roast or pork chops as they cook.

Tip: Unsweetened apple juice may be substituted for the apple cider.

3½ cups	unsweetened apple cider	875 mL
6½ cups	granulated sugar	1.625 L
2	pouches (each 3 oz/85 mL) liquid pectin	2
⅓ cup	Calvados	75 mL

1. Prepare canning jars and lids and bring water in water bath canner to a boil.

2. If the cider contains sediment or pulp, strain it before measuring. To strain cider, place a sieve over a pan or bowl and line it with a piece of damp folded cheesecloth. Pour cider into the lined sieve, being careful not to disturb any sediment in the bottom of the container.

3. In an 8-quart (8 L) stainless steel stockpot, combine apple cider and sugar. Bring to a boil over medium heat, stirring constantly until sugar is completely dissolved.

4. Increase heat to medium-high and bring to a full rolling boil, stirring constantly. Stir in pectin. Return to a full rolling boil, stirring constantly, and boil for 1 minute.

5. Remove pot from heat and stir in Calvados. Quickly skim off any foam.

6. Immediately ladle hot jelly into hot jars, leaving ¼ inch (0.5 cm) headspace. Wipe jar rims and threads with a clean, damp paper towel. Center hot lids on jars and screw on bands until fingertip-tight.

7. Place jars in canner, making sure they are covered by at least 1 inch (2.5 cm) of water. Cover and bring to a gentle boil. Process 4-ounce (125 mL) jars and 8-ounce (250 mL) jars for 10 minutes; process 1-pint (500 mL) jars for 15 minutes.

8. Remove jars from canner and place on a wire rack or cloth towel. Let cool for 24 hours, then check seals. Wash and dry jars and store in a cool, dry, dark location.

Cabernet Sauvignon Wine Jelly

✳

Makes six or seven 8-ounce (250 mL) jars

Choose a full-bodied Cabernet Sauvignon for this lovely jelly. It is outstanding spread on crackers with softened cream cheese or warmed goat cheese.

Tip: You will need two 750-mL bottles of wine or a 1.5-L double bottle of wine to make this recipe.

Variations

Chardonnay Wine Jelly: Substitute Chardonnay wine for the Cabernet. Choose a dry Chardonnay wine that is not too sweet.

Blush Wine Jelly: Substitute blush wine for the Cabernet. Choose a blush or rosé wine with deep color and lots of flavor. White Zinfandel, white Cabernet and white Merlot all make wonderful blush jellies.

3¾ cups	Cabernet Sauvignon wine	925 mL
6 cups	granulated sugar	1.5 L
2	pouches (each 3 oz/85 mL) liquid pectin	2

1. Prepare canning jars and lids and bring water in water bath canner to a boil.

2. In a 4-quart (4 L) stainless steel saucepan, combine wine and sugar. Heat over medium heat, stirring constantly, until sugar is completely dissolved. Continue heating until tiny bubbles form on the bottom of the pan. Do not let wine boil.

3. Remove pan from heat and quickly stir in pectin. Stir constantly until pectin is completely dissolved and distributed through the jelly, about 1 minute. Quickly skim off any foam.

4. Immediately ladle hot jelly into hot jars, leaving ¼ inch (0.5 cm) headspace. Wipe jar rims and threads with a clean, damp paper towel. Center hot lids on jars and screw on bands until fingertip-tight.

5. Place jars in canner, making sure they are covered by at least 1 inch (2.5 cm) of water. Cover and bring to a gentle boil. Process 4-ounce (125 mL) jars and 8-ounce (250 mL) jars for 10 minutes; process 1-pint (500 mL) jars for 15 minutes.

6. Remove jars from canner and place on a wire rack or cloth towel. Let cool for 24 hours, then check seals. Wash and dry jars and store in a cool, dry, dark location.

Cherry Amaretto Jelly

✳

5½ lbs	sweet cherries, pitted and chopped	2.75 kg
1 cup	water	250 mL
¼ cup	freshly squeezed lemon juice	50 mL
6½ cups	granulated sugar	1.625 L
2	pouches (each 3 oz/85 mL) liquid pectin	2
⅓ cup	amaretto	75 mL

Makes about seven 8-ounce (250 mL) jars

Amaretto enhances the intense flavor of the cherries in this spectacular jelly.

Tips: If using sour cherries, reduce the lemon juice to 1 tbsp (15 mL).

A cherry pitter makes quick work of removing pits from cherries. Handheld cherry pitters are available in most kitchen supply stores and some grocery stores. Many stores also carry more elaborate cherry pitters, which can really come in handy when you're pitting large quantities of cherries.

1. In an 8-quart (8 L) stainless steel stockpot, combine cherries and water. Bring to a boil over medium-high heat. Reduce heat, cover and simmer gently for 10 minutes. Remove from heat and let stand for 20 minutes.

2. Place a fine-mesh sieve over a pan or bowl. Ladle the cooked cherries into the sieve and drain the juice from the fruit pulp. Discard the pulp. Rinse the sieve and line it with a piece of damp folded cheesecloth. Strain juice through the cheesecloth twice, rinsing cheesecloth as necessary to remove any sediment that blocks the juice flow. (The juice may be strained through a jelly bag instead, if you prefer.) Cover juice and refrigerate for several hours or overnight to allow any remaining sediment to settle to the bottom of the container.

3. Prepare canning jars and lids and bring water in water bath canner to a boil.

4. Place a sieve over a pan or bowl and line it with a piece of damp folded cheesecloth. Ladle or pour juice into the lined sieve, being careful not to disturb any sediment in the bottom of the container. Measure 3½ cups (875 mL) juice.

5. In an 8-quart (8 L) stainless steel stockpot, combine cherry juice, lemon juice and sugar. Bring to a boil over medium heat, stirring constantly until sugar is completely dissolved.

6. Increase heat to medium-high and bring to a full rolling boil, stirring constantly. Stir in pectin. Return to a full rolling boil, stirring constantly, and boil for 1 minute.

7. Remove pot from heat and stir in amaretto. Quickly skim off any foam.

8. Immediately ladle hot jelly into hot jars, leaving $1/4$ inch (0.5 cm) headspace. Wipe jar rims and threads with a clean, damp paper towel. Center hot lids on jars and screw on bands until fingertip-tight.

9. Place jars in canner, making sure they are covered by at least 1 inch (2.5 cm) of water. Cover and bring to a gentle boil. Process 4-ounce (125 mL) jars and 8-ounce (250 mL) jars for 10 minutes; process 1-pint (500 mL) jars for 15 minutes.

10. Remove jars from canner and place on a wire rack or cloth towel. Let cool for 24 hours, then check seals. Wash and dry jars and store in a cool, dry, dark location.

Champagne Jelly

Makes six or seven 8-ounce (250 mL) jars

The delicate Champagne flavor of this jelly is delightful. Serve it for brunch or other special occasions.

Tip: Because of the added sugar, choose a Champagne or sparkling wine that is not too sweet.

3¾ cups	Champagne or sparkling wine	925 mL
6 cups	granulated sugar	1.5 L
2	pouches (each 3 oz/85 mL) liquid pectin	2

1. Prepare canning jars and lids and bring water in water bath canner to a boil.

2. In a 4-quart (4 L) stainless steel saucepan, combine Champagne and sugar. Heat over medium heat, stirring constantly, until sugar is completely dissolved. Continue heating until tiny bubbles form on the bottom of the pan. Do not let Champagne boil.

3. Remove pan from heat and quickly stir in pectin. Stir constantly until pectin is completely dissolved and distributed through the jelly, about 1 minute. Quickly skim off any foam.

4. Immediately ladle hot jelly into hot jars, leaving ¼ inch (0.5 cm) headspace. Wipe jar rims and threads with a clean, damp paper towel. Center hot lids on jars and screw on bands until fingertip-tight.

5. Place jars in canner, making sure they are covered by at least 1 inch (2.5 cm) of water. Cover and bring to a gentle boil. Process 4-ounce (125 mL) jars and 8-ounce (250 mL) jars for 10 minutes; process 1-pint (500 mL) jars for 15 minutes.

6. Remove jars from canner and place on a wire rack or cloth towel. Let cool for 24 hours, then check seals. Wash and dry jars and store in a cool, dry, dark location.

Margarita Jelly

*Margarita Jelly is
fantastic served with
crackers and softened
cream cheese.*

Tip: The classic
margarita cocktail is
made with lime juice,
tequila and an orange-
flavored liqueur (such
as Triple Sec), and is
served either blended
or on the rocks.

1½ cups	water	375 mL
1 cup	strained freshly squeezed lime juice	250 mL
½ cup	tequila	125 mL
¼ cup	Triple Sec	50 mL
4½ cups	granulated sugar	1.125 L
1	pouch (3 oz/85 mL) liquid pectin	1

1. Prepare canning jars and lids and bring water in water bath canner to a boil.

2. In an 8-quart (8 L) stainless steel stockpot, combine water, lime juice, tequila, Triple Sec and sugar. Bring to a boil over medium heat, stirring constantly until sugar is completely dissolved.

3. Increase heat to medium-high and bring to a full rolling boil, stirring constantly. Stir in pectin. Return to a full rolling boil, stirring constantly, and boil for 1 minute.

4. Remove pot from heat and quickly skim off any foam.

5. Immediately ladle hot jelly into hot jars, leaving ¼ inch (0.5 cm) headspace. Wipe jar rims and threads with a clean, damp paper towel. Center hot lids on jars and screw on bands until fingertip-tight.

6. Place jars in canner, making sure they are covered by at least 1 inch (2.5 cm) of water. Cover and bring to a gentle boil. Process 4-ounce (125 mL) jars and 8-ounce (250 mL) jars for 10 minutes; process 1-pint (500 mL) jars for 15 minutes.

7. Remove jars from canner and place on a wire rack or cloth towel. Let cool for 24 hours, then check seals. Wash and dry jars and store in a cool, dry, dark location.

Mimosa Jelly

✳

The classic blending of Champagne and orange juice makes a jelly worthy of celebration.

Tip: For best flavor, use a good-quality Champagne or sparkling wine that is not too sweet.

2½ cups	Champagne or sparkling wine	625 mL
1½ cups	strained freshly squeezed orange juice	375 mL
4¾ cups	granulated sugar	1.175 L
2	pouches (each 3 oz/85 mL) liquid pectin	2

1. Prepare canning jars and lids and bring water in water bath canner to a boil.

2. In an 8-quart (8 L) stainless steel stockpot, combine Champagne, orange juice and sugar. Bring to a boil over medium heat, stirring constantly until sugar is completely dissolved.

3. Increase heat to medium-high and bring to a full rolling boil, stirring constantly. Stir in pectin. Return to a full rolling boil, stirring constantly, and boil for 1 minute.

4. Remove pot from heat and quickly skim off any foam.

5. Immediately ladle hot jelly into hot jars, leaving ¼ inch (0.5 cm) headspace. Wipe jar rims and threads with a clean, damp paper towel. Center hot lids on jars and screw on bands until fingertip-tight.

6. Place jars in canner, making sure they are covered by at least 1 inch (2.5 cm) of water. Cover and bring to a gentle boil. Process 4-ounce (125 mL) jars and 8-ounce (250 mL) jars for 10 minutes; process 1-pint (500 mL) jars for 15 minutes.

7. Remove jars from canner and place on a wire rack or cloth towel. Let cool for 24 hours, then check seals. Wash and dry jars and store in a cool, dry, dark location.

Piña Colada Jelly

*Pineapple, coconut
and rum blend for a
heavenly treat in this
tropical jelly.*

Tip: Straining the
pineapple juice makes
the jelly clearer and
gives it a smoother
texture.

1½ cups	unsweetened pineapple juice	375 mL
⅔ cup	rum	150 mL
½ cup	water	125 mL
4¼ cups	granulated sugar	1.05 L
1	pouch (3 oz/85 mL) liquid pectin	1
1 tsp	coconut extract	5 mL

1. Prepare canning jars and lids and bring water in water bath canner to a boil.

2. If the juice contains sediment or pulp, strain it before measuring. To strain juice, place a sieve over a pan or bowl and line it with a piece of damp folded cheesecloth. Pour juice into the lined sieve, being careful not to disturb any sediment in the bottom of the container.

3. In an 8-quart (8 L) stainless steel stockpot, combine pineapple juice, rum, water and sugar. Bring to a boil over medium heat, stirring constantly until sugar is completely dissolved.

4. Increase heat to medium-high and bring to a full rolling boil, stirring constantly. Stir in pectin. Return to a full rolling boil, stirring constantly, and boil for 1 minute.

5. Remove pot from heat and stir in coconut extract. Quickly skim off any foam.

6. Immediately ladle hot jelly into hot jars, leaving ¼ inch (0.5 cm) headspace. Wipe jar rims and threads with a clean, damp paper towel. Center hot lids on jars and screw on bands until fingertip-tight.

7. Place jars in canner, making sure they are covered by at least 1 inch (2.5 cm) of water. Cover and bring to a gentle boil. Process 4-ounce (125 mL) jars and 8-ounce (250 mL) jars for 10 minutes; process 1-pint (500 mL) jars for 15 minutes.

8. Remove jars from canner and place on a wire rack or cloth towel. Let cool for 24 hours, then check seals. Wash and dry jars and store in a cool, dry, dark location.

Raspberry Chambord Jelly

✳

This elegant, jewel-toned jelly is bursting with stunning raspberry flavor.

Tips: Chambord is a velvety rich raspberry liqueur from the Loire Valley in France.

Frozen berries make great jellies. As they thaw, they start releasing their flavorful juice, making it easier to extract. If you have an abundance of fresh raspberries, they also make wonderful jelly. You will need about 16 cups (4 L) fresh raspberries to make this jelly.

4	bags (each 12 oz/340 g) frozen unsweetened red raspberries, thawed	4
1 cup	water	250 mL
7 cups	granulated sugar	1.75 L
2	pouches (each 3 oz/85 mL) liquid pectin	2
⅓ cup	Chambord	75 mL

1. In a flat-bottomed pan or bowl, crush raspberries in batches using a vegetable masher or the back of a large spoon.

2. In an 8-quart (8 L) stainless steel stockpot, combine crushed raspberries and water. Bring to a boil over medium-high heat. Reduce heat, cover and simmer gently for 5 minutes. Remove from heat and let stand for 20 minutes.

3. Place a fine-mesh sieve over a pan or bowl. Ladle the cooked raspberries into the sieve and drain the juice from the fruit pulp. Discard the pulp. Rinse the sieve and line it with a piece of damp folded cheesecloth. Strain juice through the cheesecloth twice, rinsing cheesecloth as necessary to remove any sediment that blocks the juice flow. (The juice may be strained through a jelly bag instead, if you prefer.) Cover juice and refrigerate for several hours or overnight to allow any remaining sediment to settle to the bottom of the container.

4. Prepare canning jars and lids and bring water in water bath canner to a boil.

5. Place a sieve over a pan or bowl and line it with a piece of damp folded cheesecloth. Ladle or pour juice into the lined sieve, being careful not to disturb any sediment in the bottom of the container. Measure 3¾ cups (925 mL) juice.

6. In an 8-quart (8 L) stainless steel stockpot, combine raspberry juice and sugar. Bring to a boil over medium heat, stirring constantly until sugar is completely dissolved.

7. Increase heat to medium-high and bring to a full rolling boil, stirring constantly. Stir in pectin. Return to a full rolling boil, stirring constantly, and boil for 1 minute.

8. Remove pot from heat and stir in Chambord. Quickly skim off any foam.

9. Immediately ladle hot jelly into hot jars, leaving ¼ inch (0.5 cm) headspace. Wipe jar rims and threads with a clean, damp paper towel. Center hot lids on jars and screw on bands until fingertip-tight.

10. Place jars in canner, making sure they are covered by at least 1 inch (2.5 cm) of water. Cover and bring to a gentle boil. Process 4-ounce (125 mL) jars and 8-ounce (250 mL) jars for 10 minutes; process 1-pint (500 mL) jars for 15 minutes.

11. Remove jars from canner and place on a wire rack or cloth towel. Let cool for 24 hours, then check seals. Wash and dry jars and store in a cool, dry, dark location.

Sangria Jelly

*This entrancing
jelly gets its flavor
inspiration from the
Spanish drink made of
wine and fruit juice.*

Tip: Cointreau, a high-
quality orange-flavored
liqueur, gives this jelly
a richer flavor, but you
may use Triple Sec,
if you prefer.

1	bottle (750 mL) red Burgundy wine	1
½ cup	strained freshly squeezed orange juice	125 mL
¼ cup	strained freshly squeezed lemon juice	50 mL
¼ cup	Cointreau or Triple Sec	50 mL
6 cups	granulated sugar	1.5 L
2	pouches (each 3 oz/85 mL) liquid pectin	2

1. Prepare canning jars and lids and bring water in water bath canner to a boil.

2. In an 8-quart (8 L) stainless steel stockpot, combine wine, orange juice, lemon juice, Cointreau and sugar. Bring to a boil over medium heat, stirring constantly until sugar is completely dissolved.

3. Increase heat to medium-high and bring to a full rolling boil, stirring constantly. Stir in pectin. Return to a full rolling boil, stirring constantly, and boil for 1 minute.

4. Remove pot from heat and quickly skim off any foam.

5. Immediately ladle hot jelly into hot jars, leaving ¼ inch (0.5 cm) headspace. Wipe jar rims and threads with a clean, damp paper towel. Center hot lids on jars and screw on bands until fingertip-tight.

6. Place jars in canner, making sure they are covered by at least 1 inch (2.5 cm) of water. Cover and bring to a gentle boil. Process 4-ounce (125 mL) jars and 8-ounce (250 mL) jars for 10 minutes; process 1-pint (500 mL) jars for 15 minutes.

7. Remove jars from canner and place on a wire rack or cloth towel. Let cool for 24 hours, then check seals. Wash and dry jars and store in a cool, dry, dark location.

Tarragon Wine Jelly

✳

Makes about four 8-ounce (250 mL) jars

Layers of tarragon flavors combined with the wine give this jelly its special flavor.

Tip: Tarragon-flavored vinegar can be found in most major supermarkets and in specialty wine stores.

2 cups	dry white wine	500 mL
2 tbsp	tarragon-flavored vinegar or white wine vinegar	30 mL
¼ cup	fresh tarragon leaves	50 mL
3 cups	granulated sugar	750 mL
1	pouch (3 oz/85 mL) liquid pectin	1

1. Prepare canning jars and lids and bring water in water bath canner to a boil.

2. In a 4-quart (4 L) stainless steel saucepan, combine wine, vinegar and tarragon. Heat over medium heat, stirring constantly, until hot. Do not bring to a boil. Remove from heat, cover and let stand for 10 minutes.

3. Place a fine-mesh sieve over a pan or bowl and line the sieve with a piece of damp folded cheesecloth. Ladle the wine mixture into the sieve and drain the wine from the tarragon. Discard tarragon.

4. In a 4-quart (4 L) stainless steel saucepan, combine strained wine and sugar. Heat over medium heat, stirring constantly, until sugar is completely dissolved. Continue heating until tiny bubbles form on the bottom of the pan. Do not let wine boil.

5. Remove pan from heat and quickly stir in pectin. Stir constantly until pectin is completely dissolved and distributed through the jelly, about 1 minute. Quickly skim off any foam.

6. Immediately ladle hot jelly into hot jars, leaving ¼ inch (0.5 cm) headspace. Wipe jar rims and threads with a clean, damp paper towel. Center hot lids on jars and screw on bands until fingertip-tight.

7. Place jars in canner, making sure they are covered by at least 1 inch (2.5 cm) of water. Cover and bring to a gentle boil. Process 4-ounce (125 mL) jars and 8-ounce (250 mL) jars for 10 minutes; process 1-pint (500 mL) jars for 15 minutes.

8. Remove jars from canner and place on a wire rack or cloth towel. Let cool for 24 hours, then check seals. Wash and dry jars and store in a cool, dry, dark location.

Orange Jack Marmalade

Makes about five 8-ounce (250 mL) jars

Jack Daniels whiskey gives orange marmalade a warm flavor and special kick in this luscious spread.

Tips: Jack Daniels is a smooth, oak-barrel-aged Tennessee whiskey. Brandy or bourbon may be substituted, if you prefer.

Do not use navel oranges for making marmalade. Navel oranges become tough when cooked, and they contain an enzyme that will cause the fruit to turn bitter during storage.

12 to 14	medium Valencia oranges	12 to 14
¼ cup	freshly squeezed lemon juice	50 mL
⅛ tsp	baking soda	0.5 mL
5 cups	granulated sugar	1.25 L
½ tsp	unsalted butter (optional)	2 mL
1	pouch (3 oz/85 mL) liquid pectin	1
¼ cup	Jack Daniels, or other Tennessee whiskey	50 mL

1. Prepare canning jars and lids and bring water in water bath canner to a boil.

2. Using a zester, remove only the outer colored portion of the peel in very thin strips from 6 of the oranges. Coarsely chop the zested peel. (The colored zest may also be removed from the fruit using a vegetable peeler, then cut into very thin strips with a sharp knife and coarsely chopped.) Peel all of the oranges, removing all of the outer white pith. Cut the fruit sections away from the membrane and remove any seeds. Discard the pith and membrane. Finely chop the fruit, reserving the juice. Combine the fruit and enough of the juice to measure 2½ cups (625 mL).

3. In an 8-quart (8 L) stainless steel stockpot, combine chopped oranges, lemon juice and baking soda. Bring to a boil over medium-high heat. Reduce heat, cover and simmer gently for 8 minutes. Stir in orange zest until well distributed. Cover and simmer for 3 minutes.

4. Gradually stir in sugar and butter, if using. Increase heat to medium-high and bring to a full rolling boil, stirring constantly. Stir in pectin. Return to a full rolling boil, stirring constantly, and boil for 1 minute.

5. Remove pot from heat and skim off any foam. Stir in whiskey. Let marmalade cool in the pot for 5 minutes, stirring occasionally.

6. Ladle hot marmalade into hot jars, leaving ¼ inch (0.5 cm) headspace. Remove any air bubbles. Wipe jar rims and threads with a clean, damp paper towel. Center hot lids on jars and screw on bands until fingertip-tight.

7. Place jars in canner, making sure they are covered by at least 1 inch (2.5 cm) of water. Cover and bring to a gentle boil. Process 4-ounce (125 mL) jars and 8-ounce (250 mL) jars for 10 minutes; process 1-pint (500 mL) jars for 15 minutes.

8. Remove jars from canner and place on a wire rack or cloth towel. Let cool for 24 hours, then check seals. Wash and dry jars and store in a cool, dry, dark location.

South Seas Marmalade

✳

Makes about six 8-ounce (250 mL) jars

The combination of pineapple, coconut, oranges and a splash of rum conjure up visions of relaxed tropical locales.

Tips: Coarsely chop the coconut before measuring to eliminate any long pieces. This will allow the coconut to distribute evenly throughout the marmalade and improve the texture.

If using a can size other than 20 oz (567 mL), you will need 1⅛ cups (280 mL) drained crushed pineapple for this recipe.

3	medium Valencia oranges	3
2	medium lemons	2
1	can (20 oz/567 mL) juice-packed crushed pineapple, drained (see tip, at left)	1
5 cups	granulated sugar	1.25 L
½ cup	coarsely chopped shredded or flaked sweetened coconut	125 mL
½ tsp	unsalted butter (optional)	2 mL
1	pouch (3 oz/85 mL) liquid pectin	1
⅓ cup	rum	75 mL

1. Prepare canning jars and lids and bring water in water bath canner to a boil.

2. Using a zester, remove only the outer colored portion of the peel from the oranges and lemons in very thin strips. Coarsely chop the zested peel. (The colored zest may also be removed from the fruit using a vegetable peeler, then cut into very thin strips with a sharp knife and coarsely chopped.) Peel the oranges and lemons, removing all of the white pith. Cut the fruit sections away from the membrane and remove any seeds. Discard the pith and membrane. Finely chop the fruit.

3. In an 8-quart (8 L) stainless steel stockpot, combine chopped oranges, chopped lemons and pineapple. Bring to a boil over medium-high heat. Reduce heat, cover and simmer gently for 5 minutes. Stir in orange zest and lemon zest until well distributed. Cover and simmer for 3 minutes.

4. Gradually stir in sugar, coconut and butter, if using. Increase heat to medium-high and bring to a full rolling boil, stirring constantly. Stir in pectin. Return to a full rolling boil, stirring constantly, and boil for 1 minute.

5. Remove pot from heat and skim off any foam. Stir in rum. Let marmalade cool in the pot for 5 minutes, stirring occasionally.

Tip: Fresh pineapples contain an enzyme that inhibits marmalades from setting. It is best to use canned pineapple in spread recipes to achieve a proper set.

6. Ladle hot marmalade into hot jars, leaving ¼ inch (0.5 cm) headspace. Remove any air bubbles. Wipe jar rims and threads with a clean, damp paper towel. Center hot lids on jars and screw on bands until fingertip-tight.

7. Place jars in canner, making sure they are covered by at least 1 inch (2.5 cm) of water. Cover and bring to a gentle boil. Process 4-ounce (125 mL) jars and 8-ounce (250 mL) jars for 10 minutes; process 1-pint (500 mL) jars for 15 minutes.

8. Remove jars from canner and place on a wire rack or cloth towel. Let cool for 24 hours, then check seals. Wash and dry jars and store in a cool, dry, dark location.

Tequila Lime Marmalade

*The strong tang of the
limes is complemented
by the flavor of tequila.*

Tips: Tequila is a strong
Mexican liquor made
by redistilling the
fermented juice of
the agave plant.

Bearss limes, a type of
Persian or Tahitian lime
and the most common
large green lime found
in grocery stores, have
an intense lime flavor
and are the best choice
for making marmalades
and other spreads.

22 to 28	medium limes	22 to 28
3 to 4	drops green food coloring (optional)	3 to 4
1/2 cup	water	125 mL
1/8 tsp	baking soda	0.5 mL
5 cups	granulated sugar	1.25 L
1/2 tsp	unsalted butter (optional)	2 mL
1	pouch (3 oz/85 mL) liquid pectin	1
1/3 cup	tequila	75 mL

1. Prepare canning jars and lids and bring water in water bath canner to a boil.

2. Using a zester, remove only the outer colored portion of the peel in very thin strips from 12 of the limes. Coarsely chop the zested peel. (The colored zest may also be removed from the fruit using a vegetable peeler, then cut into very thin strips with a sharp knife and coarsely chopped.) Peel all of the limes, removing all of the outer white pith. Cut the fruit sections away from the membrane and remove any seeds. Discard the pith and membrane. Finely chop the fruit and measure 2¾ cups (675 mL). Set aside.

3. If using green food coloring, add to the water and stir to combine.

4. In an 8-quart (8 L) stainless steel stockpot, combine chopped limes, water and baking soda. Bring to a boil over medium-high heat. Reduce heat, cover and simmer gently for 5 minutes. Stir in lime zest until well distributed. Cover and simmer for 3 minutes.

5. Gradually stir in sugar and butter, if using. Increase heat to medium-high and bring to a full rolling boil, stirring constantly. Stir in pectin. Return to a full rolling boil, stirring constantly, and boil for 1 minute.

6. Remove pot from heat and skim off any foam. Stir in tequila. Let marmalade cool in the pot for 5 minutes, stirring occasionally.

7. Ladle hot marmalade into hot jars, leaving $\frac{1}{4}$ inch (0.5 cm) headspace. Remove any air bubbles. Wipe jar rims and threads with a clean, damp paper towel. Center hot lids on jars and screw on bands until fingertip-tight.

8. Place jars in canner, making sure they are covered by at least 1 inch (2.5 cm) of water. Cover and bring to a gentle boil. Process 4-ounce (125 mL) jars and 8-ounce (250 mL) jars for 10 minutes; process 1-pint (500 mL) jars for 15 minutes.

9. Remove jars from canner and place on a wire rack or cloth towel. Let cool for 24 hours, then check seals. Wash and dry jars and store in a cool, dry, dark location.

Creative Gift-Giving

※

What a delight to receive a wonderful gift of jars of delicious homemade jams, jellies, marmalades or preserves! A homemade gift, given from the heart, is always a treasure. How excited the recipient of the gift will be when you present them with your special creations!

Designing the theme, labeling and wrapping the jars, and packaging the gift can be great fun. Think of all the special and everyday occasions when a gift of your homemade spreads would be warmly received. Holidays, birthdays, Mother's Day, Father's Day, Grandparents' Day, summer parties, housewarmings — any day is a reason to celebrate and share your homemade goodies. The possibilities are endless.

When it comes to packaging your delectable gifts, let your imagination and creativity flow. Let the occasion or event be your inspiration and guide the style and design of the packaging. Be inventive! Below are some ideas for how you can creatively label, wrap and present your jars.

Labels

Packaging a gift starts with choosing the jams, jellies or other spreads you think the recipient will enjoy. Then the jars need to be labeled. Use decorative labels to identify your special gifts and be sure to include the name of the spread and the date you made it on the label. Jar labels may be store-bought, handmade or even generated on your computer.

Self-adhesive labels attached directly to the jars arc always a good choice because there is no risk of the label accidentally being separated from the jar. Labels can also be hung from ribbons, string or raffia tied around the top of the jar, just below the screw threads. After applying the label, top off the jar with a shiny new screw band.

There is something special and gracious about a handwritten label that seems so appropriate for a homemade gift given from your heart. Customize and personalize your labels to reflect you as the giver and to suit the occasion for the gift and the lucky recipient of the gift.

Gift Basket Ideas

Use a container that fits the occasion. Baskets are always appropriate, but think about other decorative containers as well — a planter box or glazed plant pot for an avid gardener, a toolbox for a handyman, a lunchbox for a teacher, a heart-shaped gift box for Valentine's Day. For a festive presentation, line the container with a pretty cloth napkin or a fabric related to the occasion.

Here are just a few gift ideas to get you thinking. Have fun!

- **Welcome to the Neighborhood:** Pack two or three jars of your favorite spreads in a pretty basket and surround them with fresh-baked scones or breakfast biscuits.

- **Teacher Appreciation:** Line a basket or lunchbox with school-related fabric and fill with a few jars of spreads you and your child made together.

- **Good Morning Basket:** Place a jar or two of jam in a basket lined with a pretty napkin. Fill the basket with fresh-baked biscuits or bagels and a small bag of coffee.

- **Teatime Basket:** Fill a lined basket with a couple of jars of tantalizing marmalades or luscious curds and add some pretty china teacups, a package of Earl Grey or English Breakfast tea and some homemade scones. For a special touch, include a small glass or crystal serving bowl or a decorative jam jar and a serving spoon.

- **Taco Party or Mexican Fiesta:** Line a brightly colored bowl with a festive napkin or a piece of fabric covered with chile peppers and add a jar or two of Salsa Jam (page 236), Jalapeño Jelly (page 239), Cranberry Jalapeño Jelly (page 242) or Southwest Jelly (page 250). You can even add crackers or chips.

- **Country Kitchen:** Have a friend with a country kitchen? Wrap the tops of jars of jams and jellies with circles of gingham fabric and tie them on with pieces of raffia for a fun gift.

- **Garden Party:** Fill a pretty pot or planter box with fresh-from-the-garden spreads, such as Basil Jelly (page 240), Tomato Basil Jam (page 237), Plum Jam (page 65), Peach Apricot Preserves (page 191) and Nectarine Marmalade (page 164).

- **Valentine's Day:** Wrap a jar of ruby-colored jam, jelly or preserves in red cellophane or heart-covered tissue paper and tie with pink, red and white ribbons. Or place a jar of Red Raspberry Jam (page 66) or Red Raspberry Jelly (page 132) in a heart-shaped box or basket and surround it with homemade jam-filled heart-shaped cookies.

- **Spring Celebration:** Line a pretty handled basket with pastel napkins or a spring fabric. Fill the basket with jars of vibrant, jewel-toned spreads nestled in shredded plastic or paper grass. You could even add some homemade Easter egg–shaped cookies.

- **Picnic Basket:** Invited to a Memorial Day celebration or a Fourth of July picnic? Take a red, white and blue gift to your hosts. Line a basket with a patriotic napkin or fabric and pack it with a jar of jam or jelly in each color, such as Strawberry Jam (page 68), Pear Jam (page 63) and Blueberry Jam (page 55). In Canada, celebrate Canada Day with a basket lined with red and white napkins or fabric and packed with red and white spreads, such as Sunrise Jam (page 99) and Apple Pear Jam (page 71). Add a small Canadian flag for patriotic flair.

- **Thanksgiving or Fall Harvest:** Give a cornucopia of your favorite fall-themed spreads, such as Apple Pie Jam (page 49), Caramel Apple Jam (page 50), Cranberry Jelly (page 128), Peach Pie Preserves (page 190), Sweet Orange Marmalade (page 175) and Apple Butter (page 212).

- **Christmas/Holiday:** Fill a stocking with a variety of jars of different-flavored spreads. Give holiday-themed gift bags with jars nestled in red, green or white tissue paper. Wrap individual jars in vibrant red or green cellophane and tie with curling ribbon. Or select a container appropriate to the holiday of your choice, line with festive fabric, fill with colorful spreads and add embellishments to fit the theme.

Common Spread Problems

Problem	Cause	Solution
Spread fails to set	• Spread undercooked	• Cook spread at a full rolling boil.
	• Fruit was overripe or very juicy	• Do not use fruit that is overripe or very juicy.
	• Incorrect proportions of sugar, acid and fruit	• Use exact amount of ingredients stated in recipe. Measure accurately.
	• Not enough sugar in spread	• Do not reduce sugar quantity.
	• Fruit very low in pectin	• Use ripe fruit. Do not use overripe or damaged fruit.
	• Spread not brought to full rolling boil	• Bring spread mixture to full rolling boil as directed in recipe.
	• Spread cooked too long after adding pectin	• Cook spread for exact time indicated in recipe.
	• Cooking too large a batch at one time	• Do not double recipes.
	• Old or outdated pectin	• Buy fresh pectin each year.
Spread is too stiff	• Underripe fruit	• Use fruit that is fully ripe, not underripe or overripe.
	• Spread cooked too long	• Cook spread for time indicated in recipe.
	• Too much pectin	• Use size of pectin package listed in recipe.
Spread is tough or rubbery	• Spread overcooked or boiled too long	• Cook spread for time indicated in recipe.
	• Underripe fruit	• Use fruit that is fully ripe, not underripe or overripe.
	• Not enough sugar in spread	• Do not reduce sugar quantity.
Floating fruit in preserves Separation of fruit and jelly in jams	• Air trapped in fruit	• Let fruit stand in sugar before cooking.
	• Underripe fruit	• Use fruit that is fully ripe, not underripe or overripe.
	• Fruit chopped for jams, not crushed	• Crush fruit for jams and conserves rather than chopping.
	• Not enough sugar or acid	• Do not reduce sugar or acid in recipe.
	• Jam immediately ladled into jars	• Cool and stir spreads for 5 minutes before filling jars.
	• Honey substituted for part of the sugar	• Use granulated sugar in spread recipes.

Problem	Cause	Solution
Spread darkens in jar	• Fruit cooked too long	• Cook spread for time indicated in recipe.
	• Weak seal, or jar not heat processed in water bath canner	• Process all jars of soft spreads in water bath for time specified in recipe.
	• Too much headspace in jar — air not removed during processing	• Use ¼ inch (0.5 cm) headspace for all soft spreads.
	• Jar stored in a warm location or exposed to light during storage	• Store jars in a cool, dark location.
	• Spread kept longer than 1 year	• Use spreads within 1 year of canning.
Weeping in jellies	• Too much acid	• Use amount of acid specified in recipe.
	• Jelly cooked too long	• Cook jelly for time indicated in recipe.
	• Honey substituted for part of the sugar	• Use granulated sugar in spread recipes.
	• Jar stored in warm location	• Store jars in a cool location.
Formation of crystals in jellies	• Too much sugar in spread	• Measure sugar carefully.
	• Not enough acid in spread	• Do not reduce acid quantity.
	• Jelly not cooked long enough to dissolve sugar	• Make sure sugar is dissolved before boiling jelly.
	• Jelly cooked too long or too slowly	• Cook jelly for exact time indicated in recipe.
	• Pouring jelly directly from pan into jars	• Ladle jelly into jars to avoid picking up undissolved sugar from side of pan.
Cloudy jelly	• Starch from underripe fruit	• Use fruit that is fully ripe, not underripe or overripe.
	• Fruit for jelly was puréed before juicing	• Do not purée fruit for jellies.
	• Peels left on fruit during juicing	• Remove peels from fruit before making juice.
	• Fruit cooked too long before straining juice	• Cook fruit for time indicated in recipe.
	• Fruit particles not strained from juice	• Strain juice before making jelly.
	• Sediment in juice	• Let sediment settle before final straining.
	• Cheesecloth or jelly bag squeezed during juice extraction	• Do not squeeze cheesecloth or jelly bag; allow juice to drip.

(continued on next page...)

Problem	Cause	Solution
Cloudy jelly *(continued)*	• Butter added to jelly to reduce foaming	• Do not add butter to jellies.
	• Jelly was too cool when ladled into jars	• Immediately ladle hot jelly into jars.
	• Jelly ladled into jars too slowly, allowing it to cool	• Ladle hot jelly into jars quickly.
Air bubbles in spreads	• Spread ladled into jars too slowly	• Ladle spread into jars quickly to avoid trapping air bubbles.
	• Spread ladled into jars from too great a height	• Keep ladle close to funnel and jars when filling jars.
	• Spread too cool when ladled into jars	• Cool and stir spread only for the amount of time indicated in recipe.
	• Foam not skimmed from top of spread	• Skim foam from top of spread before filling jars.
Jar does not seal or fails to keep a seal	• Jar not heat processed in water bath canner or not processed for full recommended time	• Process all jars of soft spreads in water bath for time specified in recipe.
	• Jar not covered by water in water bath	• Make sure jars in water bath are covered by at least 1 inch (2.5 cm) of water.
	• Not enough headspace in jar — spread forced between lid and jar rim during processing	• Use $1/4$ inch (0.5 cm) headspace for all soft spreads.
	• Too much headspace in jar — vacuum fails to form during processing	• Use $1/4$ inch (0.5 cm) headspace for all soft spreads.
	• Lid compound old or damaged	• Buy new lids each year.
	• Lids heated in boiling water	• Heat lids in hot water; do not boil.
	• Jar inverted after water bath processing	• Do not invert jars after water bath processing.
	• Spread residue on jar rim	• Wipe jar rims before applying lids.
	• Processing time not adjusted for altitude	• Adjust processing time for altitude (see chart, page 38).
	• Chip or nick on jar rim	• Inspect all jars for damage before canning.
	• Over-tightening of screw band before processing	• Tighten screw bands only until fingertip-tight.
	• Retightening screw band after processing	• Do not tighten screw bands after water bath processing.
	• Using nonstandard jars not designed for home canning	• Use only standard canning jars manufactured for home canning.

Problem	Cause	Solution
Rust or corrosion on outside of lid	• Jars stored with screw bands in place	• Remove screw bands before storing jars.
	• Jars stored in a warm, moist location	• Store jars in a cool, dry, dark location.
Rust on underside of lid	• Coating on lid scratched or damaged	• Inspect lids before canning. Do not use any lid showing signs of damage.
Mold develops in jar during storage	• Jar not heat processed in water bath canner	• Process all jars of soft spreads in water bath for time specified in recipe.
	• Too much headspace in jar — air not removed during processing	• Use ¼ inch (0.5 cm) headspace for all soft spreads.
	• Spread residue on jar rim	• Wipe jar rims before applying lids.
	• Jar inverted after water bath processing	• Do not invert jars after water bath processing.
	• Seal on jar failed during storage	• Store jars in cool, dry, dark location.
Spread ferments in jar during storage	• Jar not heat processed in water bath canner	• Process all jars of soft spreads in water bath for time specified in recipe.
	• Not enough sugar in spread	• Do not reduce sugar quantity.
	• Seal on jar failed during storage	• Store jars in cool, dry, dark location.
Jars break during processing	• Using nonstandard jars not designed for home canning	• Use only standard canning jars manufactured for home canning.
	• Chipped or cracked jars	• Inspect all jars for damage before canning.
	• Empty canning jars heated in oven or microwave	• Do not heat empty jars in oven or microwave.
	• Unsafe processing method	• Do not process jars in oven or dishwasher.

Home Canning Resources

✳

National Center for Home Food Preservation
University of Georgia
www.uga.edu.nchfp
Home canning information and
USDA home canning publications

A Cook's Wares
211 37th Street
Beaver Falls, PA 15010-2103
(800) 915-9788
www.cookswares.com
Home canning tools and utensils

Ball
(Jarden Home Brands — USA)
P.O. Box 2729
Muncie, IN 47307-2729
www.freshpreserving.com
Ball and Kerr home canning jars,
lids and screw bands

Bernardin Ltd.
(Jarden Home Brands — Canada)
760 Pacific Road, Unit 7
Oakville, ON L6L 6M5
www.homecanning.ca
Bernardin mason jars, lids and
screw bands and utensils

Kitchen Krafts, Inc.
P.O. Box 442
Waukon, IA 52172-0442
(800) 776-0575
www.kitchenkrafts.com
Home canning equipment, utensils
and supplies

Kraft Canada
www.kraftcanada.com
Certo powdered and liquid pectin

Sure-Jell
(Kraft Foods, Inc.)
www.surejell.com
Sure-Jell powdered pectin and
Certo liquid pectin

Library and Archives Canada Cataloguing in Publication

Amendt, Linda J.
    175 best jams, jellies, marmalades & other soft spreads / Linda J. Amendt.

Includes index.
ISBN 978-0-7788-0183-2

    1. Jam. 2. Jelly. 3. Marmalade. 4. Canning and preserving. I. Title.
II. Title: One hundred seventy-five best jams, jellies, marmalades &
other soft spreads.

TX612.J3A44 2008   641.8'52   C2007-906971-1

Index